DATE DUE

MAR 2 1 2003	

BRODART

Cat. No. 23-221

RECOVERED MEMORIES: SEEKING THE MIDDLE GROUND

RECOVERED MEMORIES: SEEKING THE MIDDLE GROUND

Edited by

Graham M. Davies
University of Leicester, UK

and

Tim Dalgleish
MRC Cognition and Brain Sciences Unit, UK

JOHN WILEY & SONS, LTD

Chichester · New York · Weinheim · Brisbane · Singapore · Toronto

Copyright © 2001 by John Wiley & Sons Ltd,
Baffins Lane, Chichester,
West Sussex PO19 1UD, England

National   01243 779777
International   (+44) 1243 779777
e-mail (for orders and customer service enquiries):
cs-books@wiley.co.uk
Visit our Home Page on http://www.wiley.co.uk
or http://www.wiley.com

Other Wiley Editorial Offices

John Wiley & Sons, Inc., 605 Third Avenue,
New York, NY 10158-0012, USA

WILEY-VCH Verlag GmbH, Pappelallee 3,
D-69469 Weinheim, Germany

John Wiley Australia Ltd, 33 Park Road, Milton,
Queensland 4064, Australia

John Wiley & Sons (Asia) Pte Ltd, 2 Clementi Loop #02-01,
Jin Xing Distripark, Singapore 129809

John Wiley & Sons (Canada) Ltd, 22 Worcester Road,
Rexdale, Ontario M9W 1L1, Canada

Library of Congress Cataloging-in-Publication Data

Recovered memories: seeking the middle ground/edited by Graham M. Davies and Tim Dalgleish.

    p. cm.
    Includes bibliographical references and index.
    ISBN 0-471-49131-4 (cased) — ISBN 0-471-49132-2 (pbk.)
    1. Recovered memory. 2. False memory syndrome. 3. Adult child abuse victims — Psychology. 4. Child sexual abuse — Investigation. I. Davies, Graham, 1943- II. Dalgleish, Tim.

RC455.2.F35 R4285 2001
616.85′82239—de21
             2001033242

British Library Cataloguing in Publication Data

A catalogue record for this book is available from the British Library

ISBN 0-471-49131-4 (cased)
ISBN 0-471-49132-2 (paper)

Typeset in 10/12pt Palatino by Saxon Graphics Ltd, Derby
Printed and bound in Great Britain by Antony Rowe Ltd, Chippenham, Wilts
This book is printed on acid-free paper responsibly manufactured from sustainable forestry, in which at least two trees are planted for each one used for paper production.

CONTENTS

Part IV Concluding comments

ABOUT THE EDITORS

Graham Davies, DSc, is a Professor of Psychology at Leicester University, England. He is a Fellow of the British Psychological Society and a Chartered Forensic Psychologist. His major research interests lie in the eyewitness testimony of children and adults, on which he has published some 100 papers and five books. He was a co-author to the British Psychological Society's Report on Recovered Memories (1995) and of a commentary on the American Psychological Association's report on the same issue. He has acted as an adviser to the Home Office and to the police service on issues concerning adult and child testimony and is the lead author of *Achieving Best Evidence in Criminal Proceedings: Guidance for Vulnerable and Intimidated Witnesses, Including Children*, to be published by the Home Office in 2001.

He is the immediate past Chair of the Society of Applied Research in Memory and Cognition (SARMAC) and President-elect of the European Association of Psychology and Law.

Tim Dalgleish is a Research Scientist at the MRC Cognition and Brain Sciences Unit in Cambridge, UK and a practising Clinical Psychologist at Addenbrooke's Hospital, Cambridge. He carried out his doctoral thesis at the Institute of Psychiatry in London where he also completed his clinical training, before moving to Cambridge. His research interests include psychological reactions to trauma and cognition–emotion relations in emotional disorders in general. He has co-authored a book, *Cognition and Emotion: From Order to Disorder* with Mick Power with whom he also jointly edited the *Handbook of Cognition and Emotion*.

ABOUT THE CONTRIBUTORS

Dr. Bernice Andrews is Reader in Psychology at Royal Holloway University of London. She has researched and published extensively on childhood and adult abuse and was a member of the British Psychological Society's Working Party on Recovered Memories. She subsequently led an Economic and Social Research Council study on recovered memories in clinical practice.

Dr Debra A. Bekerian is the principal author of many papers on applied memory and forensic psychology. Her interests include eyewitness testimony, the development of personal memory in children, and the effects of trauma on personal memory. She is a Reader in Psychology at the University of East London.

Gisli Gudjonsson is a Professor of Forensic Psychology at the Institute of Psychiatry, London, and Head of the Forensic Psychology Services at the Maudsley. He has published extensively in the areas of psychological vulnerability and false confession and is the author of well over 200 scientific articles. He pioneered the empirical measurement of suggestibility and provided expert evidence in a number of high-profile cases. He is the author of *The Psychology of Interrogations, Confessions and Testimony* (Wiley, 1992).

Michael Kopelman is Professor of Neuropsychiatry within King's College London and the South London and Maudsley NHS Trust. He holds qualifications in both neuropsychiatry and neuropsychology, and has published widely on organic and psychogenic aspects of amnesia.

D. Stephen Lindsay is Professor of Psychology at the University of Victoria, British Columbia, Canada. He is a cognitive psychologist who earned his PhD from Princeton University. Much of his research has focused on memory source monitoring (e.g. studies of conditions under which people mistake memories of suggestions as memories of witnessed events) in adults and children.

Eilis Magner is Foundation Professor of Law at the University of New England. The university is located in Armidale, New South Wales (not in the north-eastern United States of America!). She took up the position in 1996 after spending 16 years as a member of faculty at the University of Sydney. She has written extensively in the areas of evidence law, therapeutic jurisprudence and company law.

Nicola Morant is a Senior Lecturer in Social Psychology at Anglia Polytechnic University (Cambridge, UK). Her research interests are broadly in the area of social processes related to mental health issues. This includes work on mental health service evaluation, service users' perspectives, social representations theory and therapeutic communities.

John Morton is a cognitive psychologist with a primary interest in modelling cognitive processes. He has been involved in lots of experimental work on memory with children as well as adults and was Chair of the Working Party of the British Psychological Society on Recovered Memories.

Max O'Neill is a post-graduate researcher in the department of psychology at the University of East London. He is currently working on research in the areas of memory and trauma and new projects involving the study of children's autobiographical memory acquisition. Max is also studying for an MSc in counselling psychology.

Patrick Parkinson is a Professor of Law and Pro-Dean at the Faculty of Law, University of Sydney. He is the author or editor of a number of books, including *Child Sexual Abuse and the Churches* (1997), and has written widely on family law and child protection. He was Chairperson of a major review of the state law concerning child welfare, which led to the enactment of the Children and Young Persons (Care and Protection) Act 1998 (NSW). He has also been involved in many other law reform issues concerning the protection of children.

Mick Power is currently Professor of Clinical Psychology at the University of Edinburgh, a practising clinical psychologist at the Royal Edinburgh Hospital, and a research adviser to the World Health Organisation. He has carried out extensive research in the area of cognition and emotion and written widely on related topics.

J. Don Read is Adjunct Professor of Psychology at the University of Victoria, British Columbia. He is a cognitive psychologist who earned his PhD from Kansas State University. He has published numerous studies on a variety of aspects of eyewitness memory (e.g. naturalistic studies of eyewitness suspect identification). Read and Lindsay organized a 1996 NATO Advanced Studies Institute on issues related to the recovered-memories controversy, and co-edited a book that grew out of that meeting, entitled, *Recollections of Trauma: Scientific Evidence and Clinical Practice* (Plenum, 1997).

Noelle Robertson is a chartered clinical psychologist in professional practice and heads the Medical Psychology Unit at Leicester General Hospital. She has written widely on changing professional practice and guideline development and implementation. She is a Visiting Fellow at the Clinical Governance Research and Development Unit, Department of General Practice and Primary Health Care, Leicester University, England.

Jonathan W. Schooler is an Associate Professor of Psychology at the University of Pittsburgh and a Research Scientist at the Learning Research and Development Center. He has published extensively on the mechanisms that lead to memory distortions in naturalistic settings, including examining the impact of post-event suggestion on event memories and assessing the disruptive consequences of verbalizing non-verbal memories. More recently he has applied this interest to evaluating the accuracies and inaccuracies of discovered memories of abuse.

Katharine Shobe, PhD, is a Research Psychologist at the Naval Submarine Medical Research Laboratory in Groton, CT. She received her doctoral degree in cognitive psychology from Yale University. Her current research involves applied issues of learning, memory, and attention as related to training and performance issues aboard submarines.

Adrian Skinner is Director of Clinical Psychology for Harrogate Health Care NHS Trust, North Yorkshire, England. He has published research in the areas of mental health, psychotherapy and neuropsychology. He is a former Chair of the Division of Clinical Psychology and presented a paper on recovered memories on the Division's behalf at the European Congress of Psychology in 1997.

INTRODUCTION

Graham M. Davies and Tim Dalgleish

Recovered memories refers to the recall of traumatic events, typically of sexual abuse in childhood, by adults who have exhibited little or no previous awareness of such experiences. The controversy over the reliability and veracity of such memories has not only split families, but also the psychological profession. The debate has continued, as much in the sober pages of scientific and professional journals, as in the public arenas of press, television and popular books. In the 1980s, this debate was characterised by proponents taking up extreme positions: either all such memories were, by definition, inevitably false or, alternatively, any move to question such memories was a cynical attempt to deny victims their belated right to confront their abusers. By the mid-1990s, the terms of the debate began to change. The controversy remained fierce and the issues for its victims just as real, but it was now more reasoned, assisted by the availability of more and better research evidence. This seemed an appropriate moment for a book which would draw together the researchers and professionals in an attempt to look at the evidence from a balanced perspective. *Recovered Memories: Seeking the Middle Ground* is the result.

If the terms of the debate have changed, recovered memories continue to be the cause of much stress and dissent for patients, families and their therapists. By 1996, the American-based False Memory Syndrome Foundation (FMSF), founded by a couple who believed themselves wrongly accused by their daughter of sexual abuse, had received over 7,000 enquiries and reported that there were some 700 repressed memory suits at trial level and a further 200 had reached the appeal stage (Johnston, 1997). FMSF has inspired similar organisations in the United Kingdom, Australia, New Zealand and elsewhere. The anguished parents and carers who contact such organisations complain that they are the victims of memories, which are not true fragments of the past, but rather fabrications, germinated by inappropriate suggestions implanted by over-zealous or incompetent therapists. These are then developed into full-blown allegations, through suspect therapeutic practices, such as hypnosis, role-play or free association. Their claims have derived support from recent research by experimental psychologists, which has demonstrated the malleability of human memory and its vulnerability to suggestion. According to these studies, normal adults can be led to believe with confidence, 'memories' that have no factual basis.

Conversely, there continue to be many adults who are convinced of the veracity of their recovered memories and who can on occasion point to direct or indirect corroboration of their accusations of abuse in childhood. They see the False Memory Societies and their supporters as providing no more than a cynical cover for abusers to escape their responsibilities. Allied to their position are many mainstream psychotherapists who, in surveys of clinical experience, report that partial or complete recovery of childhood experiences are almost a routine experience in the course of therapy.

Many national psychological associations including the British (British Psychological Society, 1995) and the American Societies (Alpert et al., 1998) instituted major inquiries into the phenomenon of recovered memories in an effort to provide guidance for their members and their clients. The British and American inquiries were surrounded by controversy, as proponents of both sides sought to accuse them of partiality or of ignoring vital evidence. When both societies published their reports, their conclusions were surprisingly similar. First, that it was possible, in some circumstances, for persons to recover memories of childhood events of which they had little or no previous awareness, even after long delays. Second, that memory was not fixed but malleable, and thus vulnerable to certain therapeutic techniques, which could in principle give rise to fictitious memories. Such conclusions gave little comfort to either wing of the debate, but did leave the great majority of conscientious therapists and clinical psychologists with considerable residual problems as to how to conduct themselves professionally in a way that was fair to the claims of their clients and at the same time did not encourage the manufacture of illusory experiences.

Recovered Memories: Seeking the Middle Ground is designed to provide a guide for such therapists as well as to provide the interested academic with an overview of the latest information on this ongoing debate. It deliberately eschews committed proponents of the views that all recovered memories are necessarily false or inherently true in an effort to explore the middle ground where many therapists and an increasing number of experimental psychologists situate themselves. There is an emphasis on seeking practical solutions and on providing solid information, both on the research findings for the interest of therapists and on the day-to-day realities of the consulting room for the interested experimentalist. In short, we seek light rather than heat, practical guidance rather than rhetorical positions.

The book is divided into three main sections. The first section deals with *social aspects* of the debate. In Chapter 1, Tim Dalgleish and Nicola Morant look at the controversy from a historical and sociological perspective and demonstrate that issues surrounding the legitimacy and reliability of victims' accounts have a long history. Gisli Gudjonsson then describes, in Chapter 2, the results of a survey conducted under the auspices of the British False Memory Society, which examined the impact on the family and the community of allegations based on recovered memories. The impact of recovering memories on the individual patient is considered in Chapter 3 by Adrian Skinner, using material taken from his extensive experience as a practising clinical psychologist. Finally, in Chapter 4, Eilis Magner and Patrick Parkinson survey the case law on recovered memories: how different legislatures have come to terms with the conflicting and fluctuating opinions on the value of such memories as evidence in civil and criminal trials.

The second section deals with the *evidential aspects* of the controversy. In Chapter 5, Stephen Lindsay and Don Read provide an up-to-date, dispassionate and comprehensive overview of the extensive experimental literature on techniques for implanting memories in adults, through suggestive questioning and related procedures. In Chapter 6, Katharine Shobe and Jonathan Schooler examine in detail a series of case studies which appear to support the reliability of at least some recovered memories and underline the value of a case study approach as an invaluable compliment to traditional experimental procedures. In Chapter 7 Graham Davies considers whether there are or could be objective procedures for distinguishing true from false recollections of abuse, based on the content of the allegations and the language used to express them.

A third section is concerned with *clinical aspects* of the problem. In Chapter 8 Debra Bekerian and Max O'Neill consider how the training, expectations and attitudes of client and therapist can influence what is reported in therapy and how errors of interpretation can be minimised. Bernice Andrews, in Chapter 9, describes the results of a survey of therapists on their beliefs and attitudes towards memories recovered in therapy and their preferred therapeutic techniques for aiding recall, when this appears necessary. In Chapter 10, Noelle Robertson examines how evidence-based clinical guidelines can be developed which will minimise the risks to therapist and patient of potentially misleading material emerging in the course of therapy, and finally, in Chapter 11, Michael Kopelman and John Morton consider the varieties of psychogenic amnesia and explore whether and how recovered memories might fit into the spectrum of functional memory loss, using a Headed Records framework.

In the concluding chapter (Chapter 12), Mick Power discusses the messages of the individual contributors within a framework in which true and false recovered memories are seen as an inevitable compliment of true and false continuous memories. He emphasises the need for therapists to have a view of memory function, which reflects contemporary research, and of experimental researchers to be aware the variety of memory experiences reported by patients which await systematic exploration and understanding. The editors hope that *Recovered Memories: Seeking the Middle Ground* will go some way towards providing that degree of mutual enlightenment.

ACKNOWLEDGEMENTS

We would like to acknowledge the patience and encouragement of our editors at John Wiley and to Rosemary Chapman who greatly assisted us in compiling the final text and did so much to ensure that the manuscript was submitted on time and in good shape.

REFERENCES

Alpert, J.L., Brown, L.S., Ceci, S.J., Courtois, C.A., Loftus, E.F. & Ornstein, P.A. (1998). Final report of the American Psychological Association Working Group on investigation of memories of childhood abuse. *Psychology, Public Policy and Law*, **4**, 931–1078.

British Psychological Society (1995). *Recovered Memories: The Report of the Working Party of the British Psychological Society*. Leicester: Author.

Johnston, M. (1997). *Spectral Evidence*. Boulder, CO: Westview Press.

PART I

THE SOCIAL ASPECTS

1

REPRESENTATIONS OF CHILD SEXUAL ABUSE: A BRIEF PSYCHOSOCIAL HISTORY AND COMMENTARY

Tim Dalgleish and Nicola Morant

INTRODUCTION

The closing decades of the twentieth century saw a proliferation of professional and academic interest in the subject of child sexual abuse (CSA). Careful research studies investigating the incidence and prevalence of CSA in the community, particularly in the United States (e.g. Finkelhor, Hotaling, Lewis & Smith, 1990), the psychological and psychiatric effects of having been abused (e.g. Herman, 1992), and the development of structured treatments and interventions for sexually abused individuals (e.g. Briere, 1989), have been paralleled by the development of specialist societies and the establishment of professional journals, for example *Child Abuse and Neglect* in 1977. The intensity of clinical and academic interest has been mirrored in the public domain. Printed word and broadcast media articles in their hundreds have appeared, including large-scale surveys such as that by the *Los Angeles*

Recovered Memories: Seeking the Middle Ground. Edited by Graham M. Davies and Tim Dalgleish. © 2001 John Wiley & Sons Ltd.

Times in 1985. The 1980s and 1990s also witnessed the establishment of numerous self-help groups, a proliferation of court cases brought on by the victims of CSA against their abusers, and, perhaps most importantly, a sharp rise in reports of suspected CSA cases with a consequent strain on professionals, resources and care systems All of these changes reflect the establishment and maintenance of a heightened social awareness of CSA and its consequences.

It may well be that the sheer extent of contemporary professional and public interest and awareness of CSA and its consequences represents a sea change in social and professional attitudes to the subject. Indeed, it is difficult to envisage a future in which CSA is almost never discussed in the public arena or where clinicians and academics have turned their backs on the issues, as was the case in the 1950s and 1960s. However, before we take too much heart from the picture we see in our crystal ball, it is worth reflecting on the circumstances that prevailed at the end of the nineteenth century and on the status of CSA and its consequences at that time. This proves to be a sobering exercise. The closing decades of the nineteenth century saw unprecedented professional interest in CSA and its putative consequences. Furthermore, this was mirrored by at least a degree of public debate and intrigue about the subject, and any writer at that time probably thought that CSA and its possible aetiological influence on the psychological problems of adulthood was an issue that had been firmly and permanently established in the professional arena. However, with the benefit of hindsight, we can see that shortly after the end of the nineteenth century the reality of CSA slipped readily from professional and public consciousness for some 50 or 60 years until its latter day resurgence. Why was this? What psychological and social factors were involved? Is it likely to happen again in the future? These are some of the questions that we shall try briefly to address in the present chapter.

We shall begin by reviewing the social history of CSA over the last 100 years or so. Later in the chapter we shall offer some thoughts and speculations on why the particular pattern of what Herman (1992) calls "intermittent amnesia" of CSA has occurred. In doing so, we shall consider not only societal factors but also the similarities and relationships between (a) mental processes, such as repression and suppression, that are traditionally considered at an intra-individual level, and (b) more global processes of socio-cultural denial. Finally, we shall return to a consideration of the future status of CSA in the professional and public domain. In particular, we shall consider whether we are justified in having any confidence that society has turned a corner in history where the intermittent amnesic episodes are firmly a thing of the past.

A PSYCHO-SOCIAL HISTORY OF THE STATUS OF CHILD SEXUAL ABUSE

Freud and the seduction hypothesis

Reading Freud's *The Aetiology of Hysteria* (Freud, 1896/1962) today can be a disconcerting experience. It is characterised by closely reasoned argument, with a compelling balance of theory and clinical description from 18 case studies. It is these case studies which are perhaps the most perturbing for the modern reader; not in terms of the detailed descriptions of the distress that the individuals are experiencing, but rather in the fact that these descriptions rival any contemporary case studies of the effects of CSA. Furthermore, this is the very interpretation that Freud himself makes of the cases he reviews. To quote famously:

> *I therefore put forward the thesis that at the bottom of every case of hysteria there are* one or more occurrences of premature sexual experience, *occurrences which belong to the earliest years of childhood, but which can be reproduced through the work of psycho-analysis in spite of the intervening decades. I believe that this is an important finding, the discovery of a* caput Nili [source of the Nile] *in neuropathology.* (Freud, 1896/1962, p. 203)

The Aetiology of Hysteria marks the culmination of some two decades of intense professional and public interest in the condition. The patriarch of what Herman (1992) has called "the heroic age of hysteria" was the French neurologist, Jean-Martin Charcot. Charcot was a leading physician at the Salpêtrière, a large asylum complex in Paris. As well as being a pioneering neurologist, Charcot was very much a showman and it was a combination of these two drives within him that put hysteria on the mental health map. Charcot ventured to study hysteria when previously it had achieved little serious currency. Prior to Charcot, sufferers of hysteria had been seen as malingerers, and hysteria had been "a dramatic medical metaphor for everything that men found mysterious or unmanageable in the opposite sex" (Micale, 1989, p. 319). Charcot approached hysteria in a somewhat obsessional, objective, scientific manner. He minutely documented the symptoms and presentations of his hysterical patients, drawing out similarities across cases and developing the idea that the symptoms were sometimes psychological in nature, despite their resemblance to neurological presentations.

Charcot called hysteria the "great neurosis" and captured the public imagination by characterising the study of hysteria as an adventure into the unknown. Famously, on a Tuesday, he would give a public lecture that invariably involved the presentation of patients to a mixed audience of professionals and men and women of letters. These visitors included Pierre Janet, William James and Sigmund Freud. Surprisingly, despite a commitment to the psychological basis of hysteria, Charcot showed little interest in the content of his patients' discourse. Reading an account of his case studies today (Goetz, 1987), it seems clear that the psychological inner worlds of his patients, as revealed by their words, provide clear indications of previous traumatic events, often sexual in nature.

Both Janet and Freud picked up the gauntlet thrown down by Charcot and pursued the study of hysteria, with the eventual goal of understanding its aetiology. Unlike Charcot, both Janet and Freud actually listened to what their patients had to say and both arrived at similar solutions to the problems: hysteria was a set of psychological reactions brought on by traumatic experiences earlier in the individual's life. Furthermore, lengthy 'therapy' sessions with hysterical patients could alleviate the symptoms by allowing them to articulate the traumatic experiences and the feelings that were associated with them. It was but a short step from these ideas concerning the traumatic basis of hysteria, to the idea that those traumas were predominantly sexual in nature and, hence, Freud's claim in The *Aetiology of Hysteria* that he had discovered the "source of the Nile" in neuropathology in 1896.

It was at this point that the first episode of Herman's "intermittent amnesia" in the study of CSA seemed to occur. The story of Freud's development of the seduction hypothesis, as outlined above, and his subsequent about turn, has been told many times (see Herman, 1981; Masson, 1984; Olafson, Corwin & Summit, 1993; Summit, 1988). It is clear from Freud's correspondence, particularly with Wilhelm Fliess (Bonaparte, Freud & Kries, 1954), that Freud was becoming increasingly distressed by the impact and the implications of his suggestion that every case of hysteria was a result of premature and unwanted sexual experience. In the intellectual arena, his stance had challenged long-held views that the utterances of hysterics were lies, by revealing that most hysterical patients recalled and talked about sexual abuse extremely reluctantly and with emotions such as shame and guilt (Masson, 1984). He had overturned the ideas of his mentor, Charcot, by suggesting that neurological degenerative problems alone, in the absence of sexual abuse, would not lead to hysterical difficulties. However, it was in the social arena that the implications of Freud's ideas came back to haunt him the most. He had implied that incest and CSA were far more common than had been suspected; moreover, he had argued that such practices were not restricted to the lower social classes but could also be found in individuals and families of the "greatest character and highest critical power" (Breuer & Freud, 1893–95/1955). The only conclusion that the seduction hypothesis would allow Freud was that sexual abuse of children was common, not only among the working classes of Paris, where he and Charcot had first investigated hysteria, but also within the respectable bourgeois society in Vienna, where he had a reputation and an established private practice to defend and maintain.

At a point soon after the publication of *The Aetiology of Hysteria*, it seems clear that Freud, at first privately and thereafter publicly, began to reject his earlier position as false. He began to refer to accounts of early childhood sexual experience as "fantasies" and "fictions", and his later case studies reveal a therapist reluctant to validate his patients' feelings of anger, shame and humiliation at their experiences, as in the famous case of Dora (Freud, 1963). Dora was to be Freud's last case study on hysteria. As Herman argues, "the breach of their alliance marked the bitter end of an era of collaboration between ambitious investigators and hysterical patients. For close to a century, these patients would again be scorned and silenced" (Herman, 1992, p. 14). Freud's recantation of the seduction hypothesis allowed him to replace his ground-breaking ideas with a more publicly acceptable account; that hysterical patients' descriptions of their experiences of CSA were untrue and, further, that they were fantasies which the patients had made up. In contrast to the closely documented and minutely researched case studies that led to the development of the seduction hypothesis, Freud's sexual fantasy account was conceived in the absence of any publicly declared clinical documentation that the CSA accounts were false. Within 10–15 years, the study of hysteria had ground to a halt; psychology, psychiatry and public interest had moved on.

Given the current emphasis on the ground-breaking nature of Freud's and Janet's work on CSA, one could be forgiven for thinking that, prior to the end of the nineteenth century, public awareness of CSA was virtually non-existent. However, in the centuries before Freud, there are abundant accounts, albeit mostly anecdotal, of CSA and some clear indications of its prevalence. What differed in the work of Freud and Janet was an emphasis on the *consequences* of such abuse and the suggestion that it was not limited to the lower social classes. In Britain, for example, some 25% of capital rape prosecutions at the Old Bailey in London in the middle part of the eighteenth century involved victims younger than 10 (see Simpson, 1988). Similarly, in France there are thousands of documented cases of CSA from this time (Olafson et al., 1993). Books by Tardieu, Fèrès and Bernard argued that sexual acts against children were frequent, that children's reports of these acts were largely truthful, that most of the acts were incestuous in nature, and, finally, that the acts were committed by families from all social classes (see Masson, 1984).

Similarly, early hints of the social pressures that were later to have a bearing on Freud's rejection of his own seduction hypothesis were evident in works by Brourardel, who proposed that 60–80% of sexual abuse complaints were false accusations, and by Fournier, who suggested that fathers of respectable families would be incapable of the sexual abuse of children (Masson, 1984). Freud would have been aware of these claims and counter-claims as he owned copies of books by Fèrès, Bernard, Tardieu and Brourardel (Olafson et al., 1993).

The consequences of Freud's change of heart regarding his seduction hypothesis were many and widespread. The work of Janet passed quickly out of fashion, even though he himself never reneged on his ideas. Indeed, it is only recently that Janet has enjoyed something of a renaissance as a pioneer of our understanding of the effects of early trauma (for example, see van der Kolk & van der Hart, 1989). Freud's silence on the issue of sexual trauma is surely a significant underlying factor in the absence of any real professional or public debate about the issue until the 1960s and 1970s. There is one notable exception to this (Olafson et al., 1993) in the work of Ferenczi; however, even here the pervasive influence of Freud was to lead to the suppression of ideas. Ferenczi (1955, p.161) argued that

> trauma, especially the sexual trauma, as the pathogenic factor cannot be valued highly enough. Even children of very respectable, sincerely puritanical families, fall victim to real violence or rape much more often than one had dared to suppose.

He was also eloquent about the putative consequences of such early sexual experience and presented descriptions very similar to contemporary understandings of the long-term sequelae of CSA. Ferenczi's publication of this work in 1932 clearly ran counter to Freud's own views, causing Freud to write in a letter to Ferenczi that he hoped he would come to see "the technical incorrectness" of his data but, regretfully noting, that "I no longer believe that you will correct yourself the way I corrected myself a generation ago" (Masson, 1984, p. 172). In other correspondence Freud implied that Ferenczi was being duped by his patients' fantasies into believing that real acts of CSA had occurred. On Ferenczi's death in 1933, followers of Freud successfully suppressed the distribution of his paper and the proofs of the English translation were destroyed (Olafson et al., 1993). With the exception of Ferenczi's work, there is almost no published work on the consequences of CSA in the first 60 years of the twentieth century.

THE RESURGENCE OF INTEREST IN CSA IN THE LATE 1960S AND 1970S

The late 1960s and 1970s witnessed a marked resurgence of the issue of CSA into the public consciousness. Since then, public, professional and media interest in CSA and its consequences has been sustained at unprecedented levels. Since 1970 there have been dozens of comparative research articles examining the prevalence of CSA in various populations. For example, Finkelhor et al. (1990) produced retrospective survey evidence suggesting that some 40 million adults in the USA had been sexually abused as children. Prevalence estimates in vulnerable groups were even higher. For example, Briere and Zaidi (1989) reported a CSA rate of 70% in their population of female psychiatric emergency room patients.

Research on the psychosocial sequelae of CSA has also burgeoned since the late 1960s and 1970s. Reported symptoms include low self-esteem, poor sleep, depression, anxiety, substance abuse, behavioural problems, sexual dysfunction and the abuse of others (e.g. Friedrich, 1990). The aetiological influence of CSA on a number of formal psychiatric conditions — such as traumatic stress disorders, personality disorders, eating disorders, affective disorders, dissociative disorders, and substance abuse disorders — is common. In 1985, delegates at the National Summit Conference on Diagnosing Child Sexual Abuse set out to draft a diagnostic category to be proposed for inclusion in the third, revised edition of the American Psychiatric Association's *Diagnostic and Statistical Manual* to be published in 1987 (DSM-III-R; American Psychiatric Association, 1987). Although they failed to reach a consensus diagnosis, the summit led to the founding of the American Professional Society on the Abuse of Children. This followed on from the founding of the International Society of Traumatic Stress Studies in the early 1980s with its in-house *Journal of Traumatic Stress,* and the International Society for the Prevention and Treatment of Child Abuse and Neglect in 1977 with its journal *Child Abuse and Neglect.* This proliferation of research, professional societies, diagnostic categories and specialist journals has involved mental health professionals from all persuasions and disciplines including social workers, trauma counsellors, psychologists, psychiatrists and physicians.

The resurgence of professional interest in CSA and its consequences since the late 1960s and 1970s has been mirrored by a rise in the public profile of these issues. Media attention to legal proceedings involving the prosecution of child molesters has been consistently high since the 1970s and stories about sexual abuse and incest appear with great frequency in international, national and local press, radio, television and films. There has been a widespread establishment of self-help organisations and survivor groups. These breakthroughs have been paralleled by formal changes in legislation, for example the Child Abuse and Treatment Act in 1973 in the USA.

THE 1980S BACKLASH AND THE RECOVERED MEMORY DEBATE

With a *fin de siècle* sense of *déjà vu*, the 1980s saw the emergence of a proactive counter-movement to the increasing prevalence of research and public interest into issues of CSA. There were suggestions that prevalence rates for CSA were over-reported (e.g. Bescherov, 1985a), especially in custody suits (e.g. Gardner, 1987). Arguments were made that children are highly suggestible and therefore likely to make false accusations (e.g. Coleman, 1986) and that this is exacerbated by over-enthusiastic investigators (Benedek & Schetky, 1987). These arguments inevitably aroused considerable public interest and have been echoed by a number of high-profile articles in the media (e.g. Cramer, 1991; Gelman, 1989; Rabinowitz, 1990).

Furthermore, and most pertinent to the present volume, there has been the lively and often polarised debate surrounding the issue of recovered memories. As reported in the other chapters in this volume, and echoing closely the concerns that Freud raised about his own seduction hypothesis, the debate centres on two questions:

1. Is it possible that someone who was abused as a child can have a period in later life when he or she has amnesia for that event and, if so, is it possible to then later recover a memory of the event for which he or she was previously amnesic?

2. Is it possible that there are instances when memory reports of CSA are substantial distortions of the original event or complete confabulations of events that never actually occurred?

This debate about the nature and reliability of recovered memories of CSA has been conducted in both the psychological laboratory and in the clinic (see Davies, this volume). On the one hand, studies have noted how fallible memory is and how confabulations of previous events are possible in certain contexts and circumstances (e.g. Loftus, 1993). In contrast, there is a growing number of studies of self-reported memory loss and subsequent memory recovery for traumatic events (e.g. Elliott & Briere, 1995). Furthermore, there are reports of experiences of memory loss of documented CSA, where there has been no subsequent memory recovery (e.g. Williams, 1994). Suprisingly, such polarisation of opinion in the professional arena has not attracted a degree of media attention. This is particularly focused around coverage of high-profile court cases involving allegations of abuse based on recovered memories (see Magner & Parkinson, this volume; and Underwager & Wakefield, 1998). Similarly, the flagship societies in Great Britain (the British Psychological Society) and in the United States (the American Psychological Association) both set up working parties to investigate recovered memories (e.g. see Andrews, this volume) and published guidelines concerning recovered memory research and therapy. The arguments and the passion these issues generate, as the publication of this volume suggests, continue unabated.

In summary, we have seen how the emergence of the beginnings of an understanding of CSA and its consequences, in the guise of Freud's seduction hypothesis, quickly gave way to a long period of silence on the issue in the public and professional domains. This started to change in the 1970s coinciding with the emergence of the women's movement and other social changes (see below), but now, with the recovered memory debate, there is some indication of a backlash against these more recent trends. In the next section we touch on the possible reasons for this historical pattern.

FACTORS INVOLVED IN THE INTERMITTENT AMNESIA OF CSA

What are the reasons for the pattern of "intermittent amnesia" of CSA in recent history? More specifically, what are the factors involved in the professional and social awareness of abuse and its consequences? These are difficult issues and in the present chapter we restrict our discussion to societal factors and social psychological factors, while acknowledging that, even together, these overlapping areas may not offer anything like a comprehensive answer to these questions.

SOCIAL PSYCHOLOGICAL FACTORS IN THE INTERMITTENT AMNESIA REGARDING CSA

Virginia Woolf in *Three Guineas* wrote "The public and private worlds are inseparably connected – the tyrannies and servilities of one are the tyrannies and servilities of the other" (1966, p. 147; quoted in Herman, 1992). One implication of this view for victims of trauma is that, not only are the episodes of intrusion and denial that characterise post-traumatic stress reactions in the individual mirrored by similar 'experiences' at the social level, but that, perhaps, the two spheres cannot be meaningfully distinguished or that the research and literature from each domain can potentially inform the other. Similar ideas can be found in the social science literature. In this section we examine the ideas from social psychology that bear on this issue of individual and collective denial, in an attempt to shed some light on the intermittent recurrence in social history of periods of understanding of abuse and its consequences.

Social processes that parallel psychodynamic defence mechanisms such as splitting, projection, depersonalisation and denial have been detected in collective responses to phenomena or situations which threaten the fabric and order of society (Gilman, 1988; Joffe, 1996) or the competence or identity of social groups (Jacques, 1955; Menzies-Lyth, 1960). These psychosocial coping mechanisms may come into play in response to phenomena which evoke collective threat and anxiety either through their novelty (for example, AIDS or biotechnology), or because they "pollute" the social group with inferences of badness, weakness, insanity or immorality. Such processes have been detected in relation to marginalised social groups such as Jews and gays, and phenomena such as illness and madness. In the threat it brings to social order and established morality, CSA could be reasonably added to this list. In order to illustrate this interrelationship between psychic and social processes, we will briefly discuss four proposed social psychological themes pertaining to CSA. First, the lack of social discourse about CSA in certain periods of recent history; secondly, the notion that memories of CSA are false and do not represent reality; thirdly, the way in which abuse and abusers have been socially represented as 'other'; and, finally, the evidence for a degree of cultural sanctioning of abuse and the minimising of its effects.

"The ordinary response to atrocities is to banish them from consciousness. Certain violations of the social compact are too terrible to utter aloud: this is the meaning of the word *unspeakable*" (Herman, 1992, p. 1). As we have seen, just as individuals who have experienced extreme traumas often go to great lengths to avoid the memories of those events, there have been long periods of 'silence' about CSA and its consequences in our recent history. The analysis of themes that are absent from public discourse, and the reasons for such "silences" is complex. Ideas may be unspoken for various reasons — because they are taboo, socially inadmissible, or taken-for-granted. On the other hand, ideas may *appear* — in research findings — to be absent from public consciousness because they are inexpressible in a verbal medium, because they are undetected by the research method utilised, or because of the self-censorship of research subjects (Gervais, Morant & Penn, 1999). Nevertheless, by using methodological triangulation and careful in-depth analytic techniques, social scientists have been able to draw some inferences about why certain topics are silenced in particular socio-historical contexts. For example, studies of how mental ill-health is socially represented have found that despite a lack of coherent representations in both verbal discourse and media narratives, social practices betray rejecting and fearful representations of those with mental health problems (Jodelet, 1991; Rose, 1998). Topics that engender profound psychosocial threat, such as mental illness or CSA may be denied in public discourse while at the same time communities obtain a sense of control over the threat by enacting powerful processes of marginalisation.

There is an intimate relationship, then, between the individual's own attempts to represent their abuse and society's representation of it. Societal suppression and denial reflect, and are reflected in, individual amnesia and repression of traumatic early sexual experiences. Social silence and individual silence about abuse are two sides of the same coin.

A more explicit social psychological theme in the representation of CSA is explicit denial of its reality. Most notable in Freud's recantation of his seduction hypothesis and recent arguments concerning 'false' memories, this theme was nevertheless constantly present throughout the twentieth century. No one denies that some accounts of abuse are false in the same way that some accounts are undoubtedly true; it is the credence placed on the majority of accounts that has proved to be a battleground of claims and counter-claims that look set to continue for the foreseeable future.

The third social psychological process associated with CSA is its social representation as something that is 'other' or beyond the limits of normality. Abuse, abusers and abused have been historically represented as 'other' in several ways. The common belief that CSA is more prevalent in marginalised social groups is part of a mythology surrounding the subject that serves to mask its prevalence across all sections of society (Busfield, 1996). Terms such as 'child molester' and 'paedophile' highlight the notion that abusers are represented as qualitatively different from other 'normal' people (Gordon, 1988; Olafson et al., 1993), again belying the prevalence statistics. In illustration, Freedman (1987) describes "sex crime panics" that occurred in the United States between 1920 and 1930. In these "panics" media portraits of homicidal child molesters roaming the streets led to police round-ups of so-called "sexual psychopaths", who in reality were generally minor offenders and male homosexuals. Victims, also, were not immune to this labelling process and were stigmatised as sexual delinquents (Schlossman & Wallach, 1978) or as willing participants in the incestual process (Olafson et al., 1993). This representation of the typical abuser as "other" — dangerous, different and marginalised from mainstream society — served to conceal the real prevalence of sexual assault within many families. It also prevented balanced social discourse on the psychological effects of CSA.

As we have already highlighted, projecting "bad" characteristics onto a minority social group who is then represented socially as "other" is a common strategy through which society is able to represent and tolerate behaviours or aspects of humanity that run counter to its dominant social value system and sense of social order. Creating scapegoated "others" allows society to locate and thus create a sense of control over primitive fears of collapse or loss of control (Gilman, 1988; Joffe, 1996). Thus gays, the diseased, the mentally ill, blacks and Jews have historically been represented as "other" (Gilman, 1985). In contemporary society, child abuse cases have become public spectacles of evil and scandal, while convicted child abusers are vilified as monsters and attract outpourings of hatred in the media.

The need to maintain a sharp delineation between mainstream society and its "normal" participants, and members of social groups represented as "other", onto whom feared, deviant and threatening characteristics are projected, is all the more important for phenomena which are in fact relatively common or map onto psychological processes found in all of us. In relation to mental health problems, Gilman (1988, p. 13) notes how

> (t)he banality of real mental illness comes into conflict with our need to
> have the mad be identifiable, different from ourselves. Our shock is that
> they are really just like us. This moment, when we say, "they are just
> like us" is most upsetting. Then we no longer know where lies the line
> that divides our normal, reliable world, a world that minimizes our fears,
> from that world in which lurks the fearful, the terrifying, and the aggres-
> sive. We want — no, we need — the "mad" to be different, so we create
> out of the stuff of their reality myths that make them different.

From an anthropological perspective, Douglas (1966) notes how ambiguous people or practices that transgress or challenge the boundaries between normality and abnormality are often represented as unclean or polluting to society's order and *status quo*. In the case of CSA it is obviously not appropriate to suggest that the potential for abuse exists in all of us. However, high prevalence rates of CSA, and the fact that in contemporary Western society boyish and young female forms are culturally valued and sexualised, may suggest that we no longer live in a society in which CSA can be so comfortably conceptualised as unambiguously "other". Again, the interrelationship between the individual and the social is clear. Societal representation of abuse, abusers and abused as "other", mirrors individuals' attempts to dissociate their experiences of abuse from the rest of their reality both at the time of the abuse and in subsequent recollection.

Perhaps it is these difficulties associated with efforts to represent CSA as beyond the bounds of mainstream society that has contributed to the fourth and final psychosocial process that we highlight, namely the normalising of CSA and associated attempts to minimise its effects.

In contrast to the representation of CSA and of abusers as 'other', the early and mid-parts of the twentieth century also witnessed a move towards normalising abuse in various ways. Three principal ways in which this occurred stand out: first, the idea that male sexual violence is normal and healthy; secondly, that the victims of such sexual violence may secretly solicit it and derive pleasure from it; and, thirdly, that CSA is harmless, with minimal or even positive long-term consequences.

Dijkstra (1986) eloquently describes the emergence in late nineteenth century European and American culture of justifications of male sexual violence and also of female masochism, including the idea that women enjoy being raped. This message was echoed by the influential work of Ellis (1905), who argued that normal women enjoy being ravished and physically abused and that normal men enjoy inflicting pain in this way. It survives today in culturally sanctioned rape myths in which women are thought to precipitate rape through their behaviour or appearance and the damaging effects of rape are minimalised (Brownmiller, 1975). Women are not seen as alone in soliciting such abusive advances from men. For example, the psychoanalytic writers Bender and Blau (1937) noted that "frequently we consider the possibility that the child might have been the actual seducer rather than the one innocently seduced" (p. 514). Similarly, Weiss et al. (1955) in a large-scale study of CSA victims at San Francisco's Langley Porter Clinic, characterised the majority of these victims as seductive, flirtatious and sexually precocious, and argued that in five out of six cases the child victim was "a participating member in the sexual act". Bender and Blau (1937) also argued that children's sexual experiences with adult abusers were likely to have minimal negative effects. This theme was echoed over and over in the literature of the early and mid-part of the twentieth century. Indeed, as late as 1975 (Olafson et al., 1993) a standard psychiatric textbook proposed that female victims of incest "do not act as though they were injured" (Henderson, 1975, p. 1536). These comments betray a position which seeks to normalise CSA and minimise its effects on victims, while suggestions that children are sometimes "willing participants" in abuse denies the unequal power relations between abuser and abused.

This neutralising of the effects of adult–child sexual interactions is epitomised most strongly in the famous Kinsey report (Kinsey, Pomeroy, Martin & Gebhard, 1953). Kinsey's research achieved fame and some notoriety because of his findings concerning the high prevalence levels of extra- and pre-marital sex. However, a more startling finding for the contemporary reader is that approximately 25% of Kinsey's respondents, over 1,000 women, reported that they had been victims of CSA by a man who was at least five years older than they. Furthermore, some 80% of these victims reported psychological distress at these experiences. Despite this, Kinsey was sceptical:

It is difficult to understand why a child except for its cultural conditioning should be disturbed at having its genitalia touched, or disturbed

*at seeing the genitalia of other persons, or disturbed at even more spe-
cific sexual acts. (Kinsey et al., 1953, p. 121)*

Thus, a remarkable aspect of Kinsey's data was effectively ignored
(Crewdson, 1988; Herman, 1981). Indeed, views perpetuated by Kinsey's
interpretation of his data manifest themselves in the literature until quite
recently. For example, Yates (cited in Olafson et al., 1993) proposed that
"non-coercive father–daughter incest can in fact produce competent and
notably erotic young women. Childhood is the best time to learn." If
behaviour which flies in the face of contemporary morality about
adult–child relationships is nevertheless observed to occur, even among
members of mainstream society, one way of reconciling this paradox is to
suggest that it is indeed somehow "natural" and of little consequence.

POTENTIAL SOCIETAL FACTORS IN THE INTERMITTENT AMNESIA OF CHILDHOOD SEXUAL ABUSE

In addition to the social psychological processes that bear on the pattern
of representation of abuse and its consequences in recent history, aspects
of the history of society itself, in a social and socio-political sense, has also
played a role in determining the status of CSA and its consequences
among both professionals and the lay population.

In this section we consider two broad societal themes that have
emerged in the literature on CSA; first, gender, in particular its relationship to the role of the professional; and secondly an increasing social focus
on the "self" in the latter part of the twentieth century. Finkelhor (1984,
p. 12) has observed that "sexual abuse is a problem which incriminates a
particular sex — men — a rather uncomfortable fact for many men to deal
with". While this is not to deny that a proportion of CSA is committed by
women (and that Finkelhor's comment arguably reflects the social construction of CSA as primarily a "male problem"), it is significant if we bear
in mind that, over the last 100 years, the social sciences and medicine have
been male-dominated professions. The suggestion has therefore been
made that male-dominated social and medical sciences that emerged in
the late Victorian era consciously or unconsciously may have incorporated self-serving prejudices into their theories, data and discourse about
mental health issues including CSA. Consequently, such prejudice may
have manifested itself as a defence (Gay, 1984) against the idea that misog-
yny and sexual abuse were rife within male society. Furthermore, at the
end of the nineteenth century this misogynistic suppression of CSA may
have been compounded by a professional discourse that regarded the
viewpoints of women and the content of female culture, as backward and

superstitious (Goldstein, 1982). For example, Rieger attacked Freud's seduction hypothesis because it gave credence to the "paranoid drivel" of hysterical women, thus establishing a "deplorable old wives psychiatry" (Masson, 1984; Olafson et al., 1993). Thus, because the male-dominated viewpoint in the social and medical sciences defined the epistemological gaze (Foucault, 1977; Sartre, 1943) for the best part of 80 years until the 1970s, any issue for which the social consequences for men were negative suffered suppression and dilution. Arguably, the vehicles for such suppression and dilution were the social psychological processes discussed above. A culture of silence about CSA and its consequences, the representation of abused and abusers as 'other', the denial of the reality of CSA accounts, and the 'normalisation' of abuse, can all be conceptualised as gender-biased, protective mechanisms for a male-dominated social system. As Herman (1981, p.3) notes, "without a feminist analysis, one is at a loss to explain why the reality of incest was for so long suppressed by supposedly responsible professional investigators".

The rise of the women's movement in the 1970s coincided with the most recent reawakening of awareness of CSA and its consequences in the public and professional domains. Busfield (1996) suggests that the contribution of feminist theorists has been to encourage a critical analysis of the ideological construction of sexual violence, in which men are exonerated by references to the power of the male sex drive. Feminists have also raised awareness of how societal inequalities of power and control are mirrored in the relationship between abuser and abused, and have provided a more complex vocabulary to describe forms of sexual violence and to resist the normalisation of male sexual dominance. This 'consciousness raising' has been a painful and charged business. As Olafson et al. (1993) argue, feminist observation of adult male behaviour, and in particular male professional behaviour, can be thought of as a reversal of the epistemic gaze — a process liable to inspire powerful reactions in the mostly male professional elite. Furthermore, feminism and the associated social changes in patterns of work and domestic life have presented a serious threat to the male-dominated professional monopoly on defining reality and categories such as class, race, gender and normal sexuality. This process has been aided by the rising number of female professionals in the social and medical sciences.

As the contents of this volume testify, one correlate of these recent socio-political changes has been a sharp rise in the number of allegations of CSA. Predominantly, allegations made by women against men and often, though by no means always, within the context of supportive relationships with female therapists. Additionally, a non-trivial proportion of these allegations involves recovered memories. Subsequent denial of these allegations and counter-accusations of 'false memories' of abuse echo the Freudian debate of a century ago. The discourse of the accused males of the modern age is littered with references to the gender issue (Pendergrast, 1996).

The second societal theme that may bear upon the social representation of CSA in modern society relates to discourses about "the self" and the increasing role of psychological concepts in these. Rose (1990) highlights how, in the second half of the twentieth century, the psyche has received progressively more attention, and became a central project of public and private life. Autonomy, self-improvement and personal fulfilment are achieved through choices about work, relationships and lifestyle. In a similar vein, Giddens (1991) describes how life in the late modern age is characterised by high levels of reflexivity and how social identity and meaning are achieved through the conscious construction of the self. Both these writers highlight the proliferation of psychotherapies as a defining feature of the self-oriented society. The last two decades has seen a huge expansion in the range of psychotherapies and quasi-psychotherapies designed not only to help individuals overcome problems, but also to promote 'growth', happiness and self-development. It is now possible to find therapists who specialise in almost any problem you care to name, from sexual problems, to fear of flying, social skills training, relationship counselling, and problems of eating, shopping or drug abuse. Psychological forms of self-exploration have expanded beyond the domain of 'abnormality' and the psychiatric system, into the domains of everyday life. Psychotherapeutic discourse now appears regularly in magazine advice columns, on day-time television, and in the ever-expanding market of 'self-help' books. Rose (1990) describes the progressive seepage of psychological concepts into everyday life as the "psychologization of the mundane". Even people with no formal knowledge of psychology are apt to discuss the events of daily life in terms of psychological processes and subjective experiences (stress, tension, coping strategies, neuroses, phobias and so on). Current society — or at least certain sections of society — is arguably more psychologically aware than it has ever been.

The implications of these changes for the current discussion of CSA revolve around the increased social acceptability of admissions to flaws in the self, and associated engagement in the therapy process. There are specialists and therapy groups available to both victims and perpetrators of CSA, while the media abounds with frank and open discussion of topics such as incest that only 50 years ago carried such rigid taboos that they were effectively non-existent in the public domain. As already noted, even the complexities of the recovered/false memory debate have received in-depth media coverage in television documentaries, fictional dramas, and Sunday supplements. Furthermore, if we consider how this rise in the importance of the self links with other profound social changes associated with late modernity (such as globalisation, the technological revolution, and the breakdown of traditional social institutions), it is difficult to imagine that society will ever again be able to collectively "forget" CSA as it has done in the past. Arguably, the new place of CSA in public consciousness is here to stay.

A number of commentators (e.g. Hughes, 1993; Pendergrast, 1996) have argued that such social changes can be directly implicated in the rise in prevalence of reports of CSA and, more pertinently, in recovered memories of abuse. For example, Hughes (1993) argues in *Culture of Complaint* (p. 7) that 'cult' therapies teach us that

> *we have been given imperfect role models, or shamed of affection, or beaten, or perhaps subjected to the goatish lusts of Papa; and if we don't think we have, it is only because we have repressed the memory and are therefore in even more urgent need of the quack's latest book.*

An equally powerful counter-argument, of course, is that increased social discourse about the self and psychological difficulties has given victims of abuse a platform to talk about their experiences and even to recover memories of those experiences from memory.

LOOKING TO THE FUTURE

In this chapter we have reviewed briefly the psychosocial history of societal and professional representations of CSA and its consequences. We have illustrated how public and professional awareness of CSA and its consequences has waxed and waned over the last century, and identified some possible societal and social psychological reasons for this intermittent amnesia. At the time of writing it seems inconceivable that CSA will once more slip from public and professional consciousness. Despite the contemporary emphasis on the idea that some memories of CSA may be false, the documented, corroborated evidence for a chronically high prevalence of abuse in all sections of society remains as a powerful reminder of the nature and scope of the problem.

The technology of the current age ensures that the spread of information and the accessibility and archiving of that information have reached unprecedented levels. This is also true of information on CSA and the shear breadth and substance of the documentary database on CSA mitigates against any future social and professional 'silence'. Furthermore, contemporary society's increasing concern with the self and with psychological exploration forms part of a spectrum of such profound social changes that such a "reforgetting" of CSA seems unlikely. Shifting social and political patterns over the latter part of the twentieth century mean that, perhaps for the first time, the abused now have a voice that is heard, however reluctantly. This is crucially different from the turn of the nineteenth century where the abused almost exclusively relied on powerful male professionals as arbiters of the truth of their autobiographical narratives. Such professional partiality still occurs, but many mental health and social science professionals who are interested in abuse issues today are women, some of whom themselves have suffered experiences of CSA. This change in the gender profile of the key professions involved in clinical and research aspects of abuse seems certain to play a key role in the maintenance of writing and research on abuse, the development of treatments for the abused, the refinement of social and health structures, and the attraction of funding to investigate CSA further.

REFERENCES

American Psychiatric Association (1987). *Diagnostic and Statistical Manual of Mental Disorders* (3rd edn, revised). Washington: Author.

Bender, L., & Blau, A. (1937) The reaction of children to sexual relations with adults. *American Journal of Orthopsychiatry, 7*, 500–518.

Benedek, E. P. & Schetky, D. H. (1987). Problems in validating allegations of sexual abuse. Part 1: Factors affecting perception and recall of events. *Journal of the American Academy of Child and Adolescent Psychiatry, 26*, 912–915.

Bescherov, D. J. (1985a). An overdose of concern: Child abuse and the overreporting problem. *Regulation: American Enterprise Institute Journal on Government and Society, 27*.

Bescherov, D. J. (1985b). "Doing something" about child abuse. *Harvard Journal of Law and Public Policy, 8*, 539–389.

Bonaparte, M., Freud, A. & Kris, E. (Eds.) (1954). *The Origins of Psychoanalysis: Letters to Wilhelm Fliess, Drafts and Notes by Sigmund Freud*. New York: Basic Books.

Breuer, J. & Freud, S. (1893–95/1955). Studies in Hysteria. In the standard edition of *The Complete Psychological Works of Sigmund Freud* (Vol. 3; trans. J. Strachey). London: Hogarth Press.

Briere, J. (1989). *Therapy for Adults Molested as Children: Beyond Survival*. New York: Springer Publishing Company.

Briere, J. & Zaidi, L. Y. (1989) Sexual abuse histories and sequelae in female psychiatric emergency room patients. *American Journal of Psychiatry, 146*, 1602–1606.

Brownmiller, S. (1975). *Against Our Will: Men, Women and Rape*. New York: Simon & Schuster.

Busfield, J. (1996). *Men, Women and Madness: Understanding Gender and Mental Disorder*. Basingstoke: Macmillan Press.

Coleman, L. (1986). False allegations of child sexual abuse: Have the experts been caught with their pants down? *Forum* (published by the California Attorneys for Criminal Justice), Jan.–Feb., 12–22.

Connell, R. (1995). *Masculinities*. Cambridge: Polity Press.

Cramer, J. (1991, March 4). Why children lie in court. *Time*, p. 76.

Crewdson, J. (1988). *By Silence Betrayed: Sexual Abuse of Children in America*. Boston, MA: Little, Brown & Company.

Dijkstra, B. (1986). *Idols of Perversity: Fantasies of Feminine Evil in Fin-de-Siècle Culture*. New York and Oxford, England: Oxford University Press.

Douglas, M. (1966). *Purity and Danger: An Analysis of the Concepts of Pollution and Taboo*. London: Routledge & Kegan Paul.

Edley, N. & Wetherell, M. (1995). *Men in Perspective: Practice, Power an Identity*. London: Harvester Wheatsheaf.

Elliott, D. M. & Briere, J. (1995). Posttraumatic stress associated with delayed recall of sexual abuse: A general population study. *Journal of Traumatic Stress*, **8**, 629–647.

Ellis, H. (1905). *Studies in the Psychology of Sex* (2 vols). New York: Random House.

Ferenczi, S. (1955). Confusion of tongues between adults and the child: The language of tenderness and passion. In M. Balint (Ed.), *Final Contributions to the Problems and Methods of Psycho-Analysis* (pp. 156–157). London: The Hogarth Press.

Finkelhor, D. (1984) *Child Sexual Abuse: New Theory and Research*. New York: The Free Press, MacMillan.

Finkelhor, D., Hotaling, G., Lewis, I A. & Smith, C. (1990). Sexual abuse in a national survey of adult men and women: Prevalence, characteristics and risk factors. *Child Abuse and Neglect*, **14**, 19–28.

Foucault, M. (1977) *Discipline & Punish: The Birth of the Prison* (translated by A. Sheridan). New York: Pantheon.

Freedman, E. B. (1987). Uncontrolled desires: The response to the sexual psychopath, 1920–1960. *The Journal of American History*, **74** *(1)*, 83–106.

Freud, S. (1963). *Dora: An Analysis of a Case of Hysteria* (Ed. P. Rieff). New York: Collier.

Freud, S. (1896/1962). The aetiology of hysteria. In the standard edition of *The Complete Psychological Works of Sigmund Freud* (Vol. 3; trans. J. Strachey). London: Hogarth Press.

Friedrich, W. N. (1990). *Psychotherapy of Sexually Abused Children and their Families*. New York: W. W. Norton & Company.

Gardner, R. A. (1987) *The Parental Alienation Syndrome and the Differentiation between Fabricated and Genuine Child Sex Abuse*. Creskill, NJ: Creative Therapeutics.

Gay, P. (1984). *The Bourgeois Experience: Victoria to Freud: Education of the Senses*. New York: Oxford University Press.

Gelman, D. (1989, November 13). The sex-abuse puzzle. *Newsweek*, p. 99.

Gervais, M.-C., Morant, N. & Penn, G. (1999) Making sense of "absence": Towards a typology of absence in social representations theory and research. *Journal for the Theory of Social Behaviour*, **29** *(4)*, 419–444.

Giddens, A. (1991) *Modernity and Self-Identity: Self and Society in the Late Modern Age*. Cambridge: Polity Press.

Gilman, S. (1985) *Difference and Pathology: Stereotypes of Sexuality, Race and Madness*. London: Cornell University Press.

Gilman, S. (1988) *Disease and Representation: Images of Illness from Madness to AIDS*. London: Cornell University Press.

Goetz, C. (Ed. & Trans.) (1987). *Charcot the Clinician: The Tuesday Lessons. Excerpts from nine case presentations on general neurology delivered at the Salpêtrière Hospital in 1887–1888*. New York: Raven Press.

Goldstein, J. (1982) The hysteria diagnosis and the politics of anticlericalism in late nineteenth-century France. *Journal of Modern History*, **54**, 209–239.

Gordon, L. (1988). *Heroes of their Own Lives: The Politics and History of Family Violence*. New York: Viking Penguin.

Henderson, D. J. (1975). Incest. In A. M. Freedman, H. I Kaplan & B. J. Sadock (Eds), *Comprehensive Textbook of Psychiatry*, 2nd edn (pp. 1530–1539). Baltimore MD: Williams and Wilkins.

Herman, J. L. (1981). *Father–Daughter Incest.* Cambridge and London, UK: Harvard University Press.

Herman, J.L. (1992). *Trauma and Recovery: From Domestic Abuse to Political Terror.* London: Pandora.

Hughes, R. (1993). *Culture of Complaint: The Fraying of America.* New York: Oxford University Press.

Jacques, E. (1955) Social systems as defence against persecutory and depressive anxiety: A contribution to the psycho-analytical study of social processes. In Klein, M., Heinmann, P. & Money-Kyrle, R. (Eds), *New Directions in Psycho-Analysis* (pp. 478–498). London: Tavistock Publications.

Jodelet, D. (1991) *Madness and Social Representations.* Hemel Hempstead: Harvester Wheatsheaf.

Joffe, H. (1996) The shock of the new: A psycho-dynamic extension of social representations theory. *Journal for Theory of Social Behaviour,* **26**, 197–219.

Kimmel, M. (1987). *Changing Men: New Directions in Research on Men and Masculinity.* Beverley Hills, CA: Sage.

Kinsey, A. C., Pomeroy, W.F., Martin, C. E. & Gebhard, P. H. (1953). *Sexual Behavior in the Human Female.* London: W. B. Saunders.

Loftus, E. F. (1993). The reality of repressed memories. *American Psychologist, 48,* 518–537.

Masson, J. M. (1984). *The Assault on Truth: Freud's Suppression of the Seduction Theory.* New York: Farrar, Strauss & Giroux.

Menzies-Lyth, I. (1960) A case-study in the functioning of social systems as a defence against anxiety: A report on a study of the nursing service of a general hospital. *Human Relations,* **11**, 95–121.

Micale, M. (1989). Hysteria and its historiography: A review of past and present writings. *History of Science,* **27**, 223–267 and 319–351.

Olafson, E., Corwin, D. L. & Summit, R. C. (1993). Modern history of child sexual abuse awareness: Cycles of discovery and suppression. *Child Abuse and Neglect,* **17**, 7–24.

Pendergrast, M. (1996). *Victims of Memory.* London: Harper Collins.

Rabinowitz, D. (1990, May). From the mouths of babes to a jail cell: Child abuse and the abuse of justice: A case study. *Harpers Magazine.*

Rose, D. (1998) Television, madness and community care. *Journal of Community and Applied Social Psychology,* **8**, 213–228.

Rose, N. (1990). *Governing the Soul: The Shaping of the Private Self.* London: Routledge.

Sartre, J. P. (1943). *Being and Nothingness* (trans. H. E. Barnes). London: Methuen.

Schlossman, S. & Wallach, S. (1978). The crime of precocious sexuality: Female juvenile delinquency in the progressive era. *Harvard Educational Review,* **48**, 65–94.

Simpson, A. E. (1988). Vulnerability and the age of female consent: Legal innovation and its effect of prosecutions for rape in eighteenth-century London. In G. S. Rousseau & R. Porter (Eds), *Sexual Underworlds of the Enlightenment* (pp. 181–205). Chapel Hill, NC: University of North Carolina Press.

Summit, R. C. (1988). Hidden victims, hidden pain: Society's avoidance of child sexual abuse. In G. E. Wyatt & G. J. Powell (Eds), *Lasting Effects of Child Sexual Abuse* (pp. 39–60). Newbury Park, CA: Sage Publications.

van der Kolk, B. A. & van der Hart, O. (1989) Pierre Janet and the breakdown of adaptation in psychological trauma. *American Journal of Psychiatry,* **146**, 1530–1540.

Weiss, J. et al. (1955). A study of girl sex victims. *Psychiatric Quarterly,* **29**, 1–27.

Williams, L.M. (1994). Recall of childhood trauma: A prospective study of women's memories of child sexual abuse. *Journal of Consulting and Clinical Psychology,* **62**, 1167–1176.

2

RECOVERED MEMORIES: EFFECTS UPON THE FAMILY AND COMMUNITY

Gisli H. Gudjonsson

INTRODUCTION

In a Survey by the American False Memory Syndrome Foundation (FMSF), Wakefield and Underwager (1992) describe the typical initial reaction of the accused parents as "shock and devastation" (p. 487). Few families had any prior warning of problems and the accusations came as a total surprise. The parents were generally not provided with specific information about what they were supposed to have done and were left wondering what they were being accused of. At the time of the study lawsuits had already been filed in almost 20% of the cases.

Wakefield and Underwager (1992, p.503) provide an insight into the potential consequences of recovered memories:

> *The costs of belief in such memories are devastating to families, society, and the social contract we need to continue our civilization. The anguish and pain generated by these claims is devastating to those accused. The cost to persons believing in the memories are substitution of unknowns for their family relationships. Children may grow up without grandparents. Families may be bankrupted by legal expenses. In some instances criminal charges may be filed. The costs may well include very*

Recovered Memories: Seeking the Middle Ground. Edited by Graham M. Davies and Tim Dalgleish. © 2001 John Wiley & Sons Ltd.

practical realities such as trebling of home owner insurance rates for every citizen.

Following the FMSF survey a number of books have been written on the topic of recovered memories and these provide vivid examples of the damaging effects it has had on families concerned (e.g. Goldstein & Farmer, 1992; Loftus & Ketcham, 1994; Ofshe & Watters, 1994; Wright, 1994; Pendergrast, 1995).

Recently, Leo (1997) has provided an extensive review of the social and legal consequences associated with recovered memory therapy. He concludes,

> *In sum, recovered memory therapy is a mental health tragedy that has caused immense harm and suffering to thousands of people. In addition, thousands of parents have been accused (and presumed guilty) of unspeakably abusive acts that almost certainly did not occur, and in the process have seen their families shattered, their reputations ruined, their finances depleted, and their adult children forever lost to the recovery movement. (p. 688)*

The above quotes by Wakefield and Underwager (1992) and Leo (1997) illustrate the enormity of the potential consequences associated with recovered memories. These authors appear to assume that all recovered memories are false. In contrast, Schooler, Bendiksen and Ambadar (1997) argue, on the basis of their analysis of individual case studies, that there is evidence that some recovered memories of Childhood Sexual Abuse have been independently corroborated. Here it very much depends on the quality of the independent corroborative evidence. Unfortunately, in almost all cases of recovered memories, it is impossible to know precisely where the actual ('ground') truth lies.

Pope and Brown (1996) and Brandon, Boakes, Glaser and Green (1998) note that scientists often take an extreme position with regard to their views on recovered memories. What we do not know is the extent to which beliefs in the veracity or falsehood of recovered memories influence our perceptions of the potential consequences of the accusations for the families and the community at large.

In the present chapter the author presents data from the survey he conducted among members of the British False Memory Society (BFMS). After providing a brief review of the main findings of the survey, the author presents some new data which focuses in more detail on the impact of the accusations of Childhood Sexual Abuse on the families involved. Those readers who wish to read the previous publications from the survey are referred to Gudjonsson (1997a, 1997b and 1997c).

BACKGROUND TO THE BFMS SURVEY AND MAIN FINDINGS

In January 1995 members of the British False Memory Society (BFMS) were sent a questionnaire to complete. The questionnaire was devised and adapted from that used by the False Memory Syndrome Foundation (FMSF) in the USA (Wakefield & Underwager, 1992). It consisted of 24 pages and the questions were classified under five headings: (A) Family Information — Demographics; (B) Family Life; (C) Events Surrounding the Accusations; (D) Accusing Child's Childhood History; and (E) Comment on the Accusing Child's Adult Life.

A total of 403 questionnaires were sent out and 282 (70%) were completed and returned. The proportion of returned questionnaires was substantially higher than the 54% reported in the FMSF survey.

The majority (87%) of the questionnaires were completed by the accuser's parents. The remaining questionnaires were completed by a sibling ($N = 19$), uncles and aunts ($N = 7$), and others (e.g. partners of the accused, grandparents).

The majority of the accusers (87%) were female and the accusations were in over 70% of cases directed against the biological father, who is alleged to have acted either alone or with others. Interestingly, accusations involving stepfathers were found in only 4% of the cases. This is in contrast to studies investigating cases of Childhood Sexual Abuse (CSA) not involving recovered memories where the perpetrators are more likely to be stepfathers than biological fathers (e.g. Russell, 1984). This raises interesting questions about differences in the nature of sexual abuse accusations between stepfathers and biological fathers. Are such differences related to psychological factors or experiences in childhood, such as attachment, bonding, or feelings of bodily intrusiveness, or is the difference merely explained by a sample bias? This is an area that merits further research. Unfortunately, in the FMSF survey the proportion of biological fathers was not reported.

There were 317 accusers and in 254 (90%) of the cases there was one accuser only. This is similar to the 86% figure reported in the USA survey. The average age of the accusers was 33 years (SD = 8.3). The majority of the respondents described the accusations as being of a general nature and many commented that they did not know the specific nature of the accusations. The most common types of specific accusations were rape (30%), sexual intercourse (29%), touching of the genitals (23%), and oral sex (20.5%). Murder was reported to have taken place in 11 (4.5%) of the cases. In nearly half (44%) of the cases the sexual abuse is alleged to have commenced before the child's fifth birthday and 5% allegedly commenced during the child's first year of life.

The respondents were asked if the accusing person claimed that the abuse was allegedly "forgotten" over a certain period of time and then later "recovered". Out of 268 respondents who answered the question, 196 (73%) said that the memory had been allegedly "forgotten" and later "recovered"; 26 (10%) said their case did not involve "recovered memories", and 46 (17%) said they did not know whether or not this was the case.

The accusations had mainly arisen within a therapeutic relationship. Depression and eating disorder were the most common reasons for seeking therapy. In addition, significant relationship problems were the most commonly reported stress factor prior to the accusations being made.

As far as these families were concerned, they were Caucasian, typically well educated and of high socio-economic status, which is consistent with the results from the FMSF (Wakefield & Underwager, 1992) and New Zealand (Goodyear-Smith, Laidlaw & Large, 1997) surveys. No significant differences emerged between the accusers and their siblings in terms of academic success, but significantly more of the accusers were unemployed or worked in the caring professions (Gudjonsson, 1997b). More of the accusers had received psychological or psychiatric treatment in adolescence and during tertiary education than their siblings, but no significant difference was found for treatment in childhood. This suggests that among the grown-up 'children' of members of the BFMS, adult psychological and psychiatric problems, such as depression, eating disorder, and difficulties in interpersonal relationships, are associated with problems in adolescence rather than problems in childhood.

THE IMPACT ON THE FAMILY

Procedure

One of the criticisms of the survey is that some of the cases, as far as the family were aware, did not involve recovered memories. In the present analysis of the data only those 196 cases where recovered memories were reported to be present are included. Excluded were the 46 cases where it was not known whether or not the case involved recovered memories and the 26 cases where the respondent reported that the case did not involve recovered memories.

The data presented are derived from answers given to questions in Section C of the questionnaire, labelled "Events Surrounding the Accusations".

Legal consequences

The 196 respondents were asked if the accusations had been reported to the police. Forty-one (21%) said the accusation had been reported to the police. A further 33 (17%) said they did not know whether or not this was the case.

Out of the 196 cases, 17 (9%) involved criminal proceedings being instigated as a result of the case being reported to the police. One of the cases involved both criminal and civil proceedings. In contrast, in the 26 cases where recovered memory was not alleged, eight (31%) involved legal action being instigated. This difference is highly significant (χ^2 df =1) = 11.21, $p< 0.001$). In only one of the cases of recovered memories was the defendant convicted in contrast to five where no recovered memory had been reported. This difference is significant (Fisher's exact probability test (df = 1) $p = 0.005$). Therefore, in cases of recovered memories, only a small minority are reported to the police and legal proceedings instigated. Where the accusation does not involve recovered memories, the figures are considerably higher, perhaps suggesting the reluctance of the accuser, the police, and the legal profession to proceed with cases of recovered memories (Gudjonsson, 1997c).

From this British survey, the findings suggest that about one in every five cases of recovered memories are reported to the police, but these cases are almost always unsuccessful (i.e. it is almost impossible to obtain a conviction), presumably because of problems of evidential credibility. As far as civil cases are concerned, the survey suggests that they are extremely rare in Britain.

Pope and Brown (1996) argue that it is impossible to estimate the number of cases of recovered memories that appear before the courts, but point to the work of Whitfield (1995) which shows that, in the USA, civil cases outnumber criminal cases about 10 to 1. This is because the standard of proof in criminal cases, "beyond a reasonable doubt", far exceeds the civil standard of "Preponderance of evidence". That is, it is easier to prove a case in civil than criminal proceedings. In view of this, and the findings from the survey by the FMSF, it is perhaps surprising that only one of the cases in the BFMS survey involved civil action, whereas criminal prosecutions were much more common. This probably has much to do with the UK being a less litigious society than the USA. Another reason may relate to the motivations behind the lawsuit. Pope and Brown (1996) suggest several important motivations, including the plaintiff wishing to having her or his story told in court, wanting an amendment from the alleged abuser (e.g. an admission, an apology), and a financial compensation for the damage caused.

Family contact with the accuser

Out of the 196 cases, 112 (57%) involved no contact with the accusing person at all. In other words, contact with the accusing person may have stopped as a consequence of the recovered memory accusations. In the 84 (43%) cases where there was some contact and 47 involved more than one type of contact, the most common contact was face-to-face interaction (65 cases), followed by a telephone conversation (50 cases) and correspondence (27 cases).

The effect on siblings and other relatives

In 80 (41%) cases it was reported that the siblings tried to stay neutral (i.e. not to take sides). In a further 21 (11%) cases only some of the siblings managed to remain neutral. In 107 (55%) cases a sibling allegedly confronted the accusing person "with disbelief".

When asked if the accusations had affected other relatives, such as grandparents, in 116 (59%) cases it was reported that this was the case. When asked how many people were affected by the accusations, on average eight people were reported to have been affected by it (mean = 8.1, SD = 6.3, range 1–50). What we do not know is the ways in which these people have been affected.

Accused person seeking therapy

The respondents were asked if, as a result of the accusations, they had sought treatment or help from a therapist. In 62 (32%) cases it was reported that therapy had been sought because of stress or depression.

What is interesting about this finding is that 145 (74%) of the families reported that they did not think that the accusations would have been made if the accuser had not had therapy. In other words, they were blaming therapists for the recovered memories which resulted in accusations. In spite of this, when under stress of the accusations, almost a third of the accusers had sought therapy themselves.

Contacting a solicitor

In view of the potential legal implications of the accusations, both civil and criminal, it is not surprising that many of the accused persons sought legal advice. In 59 (30%) cases the accused person had consulted a solicitor following the accusation. The cost involved ranged from £10 to £22,500. The typical cost was between £300 and £700.

Effects on marriage

The respondents were asked what effect the accusations had had on their marriages. In 141 (72%) cases it was reported that there had been an effect on their relationship with their spouse. The main effect was to cause pressure on the relationship, and in three cases the accusations had resulted in the couple becoming divorced. In a further three cases the accusations resulted in sexual impotence. In 15 cases, some positive effects were reported, such as the accusations having brought the couple closer together.

When asked if the non-accused partner of an accused person considered at any time that the accusations might possibly be true, 28 (14%) reported this to be the case. This is likely to have caused immense tension within the marriage. In these circumstances it may be very difficult for the non-accused partner to remain neutral and he or she will have to decide who to believe (i.e. the grown-up child or the spouse).

Effects on relationship with friends and extended family

The respondents were asked if the accusations had resulted in changes in the amount of contact they had with their friends and extended family. As far as friends are concerned, in 131 (67%) cases there had been no change in the amount of contact, 20 (10%) had increased contact, and 18 (9%) had reduced contact.

The effects on the extended family were more marked. In 116 (59%) cases there had been no change in the amount of contact, 31 (16%) had increased contact, and 24 (12%) had reduced contact.

These results indicate that in the majority of cases, the amount of contact with friends and the extended family is not affected. Where there had been change, both increased and reduced contact were reported. Increased contact was particularly noted among the extended family. What is not known from the survey is the nature of the change in contact. Does increased contact mean that the accused person is actively seeking support from friends and extended family? Does reduced contact mean isolation from others due to the distress and preoccupation associated with the accusations? In future research it would be important to investigate changes in the nature and quality of the relationship with friends and family.

Distress experienced by the family

Many of the people completing the questionnaire wrote lengthy and emotional letters with the questionnaire where they expressed their distress and devastation upon the family. Examples of their comments are given below:

"Since the allegations we have suffered extreme stress, agitation and financial problems".

"My husband is unable to work due to the accusations and the control the court case has over our life is extremely traumatic for every one".

"My wife and I were devastated and could not obtain help from anybody else at the time".

"Sadly, my wife died very suddenly in 1992. She had been utterly shattered by our daughter's accusations, which are patently false. I had no word from my daughter when her mother died. Last year I had a one-hour long tape from her. She explained to me how she would be happy to resume relations, but that there was an 'entrance fee', the fee being total acceptance of the accusations. I replied that she must know that she is always my beloved daughter and that my, and indeed all the rest of the family's doors are wide open, but that a relationship must not be on the basis of an 'entrance fee'. Since then I have had no word from her.

The accusations have caused us all a great deal of grief and sadness. Our daughter has totally withdrawn and refuses to have any contact with us".

Retraction

At the time of the survey, 9 (5%) of the 196 families reported that the accuser had retracted some of the accusations, and a further 7 accusers (4%) had retracted the accusations fully. These figures are compatible with those reported by de Rivera (1997), where it was claimed that out of 5,851 cases in the USA collected by the FMSF, over 300 (5%) had "come to believe that they made false accusations" (p. 271).

Cases of retracted accusations are interesting in that they may cast light on the process of both the recovered memories and the process of retraction (de Rivera, 1997; Ost, Costall & Bull, in preparation). For example, de Rivera (1997) argues, on the basis of four cases studies, that the patient only continues to believe the abuse reality as long as she remains isolated from the family's reality. Secondly, in order for the patient to be able to believe in the sexual abuse by the parent, she needs to have great faith in the idea that traumatic experiences involving abuse can be completely dissociated from conscious awareness over many years and from the awareness of outside observers with whom the person frequently interacts (e.g. teachers, friends, siblings). Thirdly, the retractors' level of mental functioning deteriorates as the therapy progresses and they improve markedly when they are reunited with their families.

Pope and Brown (1996) discuss the important clinical and forensic issues to be considered by therapists and expert witnesses in relation to cases of recovered memories. These include realising that any clinical case can become a forensic case, avoiding serving as an expert witness in one's patient's case, seeking advice from knowledgeable colleagues, avoiding "intrusive advocacy" (i.e. the therapist unwisely tries to influence whether or not the patient brings a lawsuit), and engaging in safe and competent clinical practice. Brandon et al. (1998) also provide useful guidelines for clinician practitioners in order to avoid the many pitfalls associated with eliciting recovered memories. Careful consideration of these guidelines reduces the likelihood of eliciting false memories and being subsequently sued by the patient or his or her family. Many therapists report that one or more of their clients claim to have recovered memories of childhood sexual abuse (Andrews, this volume; Andrews, Morton, Bekerian & Davies, 1995; Pope & Brown, 1996).

CONCLUSIONS

There are a number of limitations to the data presented from the BFMS survey. First, it only gives the views of the accused family. It does not provide information from the accusers. For a comprehensive picture, research needs to focus on both the accused and the accusers. Both parties are emotionally involved in accusations of a very sensitive nature and this may influence their objective reporting of the case. In addition, the families who completed the questionnaire may have had limited or distorted information about the accusing person and the circumstances surrounding the case. In many instances they were relying on information from a second or third party.

In spite of the limitations of the survey, the findings illustrate the devastating consequences upon the families. The accusations had undoubtedly caused the families immense distress. For the key players involved, as well as the community at large, considerable cost is associated with recovered memories. For the accused, there is typically a breakdown in the relationship with the grown-up child. Where contact exists it tends to be hostile and acrimonious; parents lose contact with their grandchildren; and siblings do not see each other. For the accused there is also a sense of public humiliation, even if no civil or criminal action is taken. The crimes they are being accused of are often very serious, involving rape and sexual indecency of various kinds, and in some cases there are allegations of murder and satanic abuse. The stress upon the family is immense, sometimes resulting in separation or divorce between the couple. Following the accusations, in about one-third of the cases the accused person seeks therapy for stress and depression. Although, in the UK, criminal or civil proceedings are not commonly instigated in these cases, they do take place, particularly in the USA (Wakefield & Underwager, 1992; Pope & Brown, 1996; Leo, 1997). The accusers and the accused are suing each other. Therapists are being sued by the accused parents, and in some cases by the accusers after they have retracted the accusations.

Even when accusations are false they may nevertheless be held with a strong belief which is resistant to change. According to Kihlstrom (cited in Pope & Brown, 1996), one of the most striking features of the phenomenon of recovered memories is the extent to which the accuser avoids confrontation with any evidence that might challenge the belief and memory regarding the accusation. The accusation takes on a life of its own, which is encapsulated and resistant to change. The accusers often appear to become totally preoccupied by the recovered memories, which undoubtedly makes it difficult for them to focus on interpersonal relationships and employment. Gudjonsson (1997b) found that significantly more of the accusers than their siblings remain unemployed, which means a loss of their contribution to the economy.

It appears that only a small minority, probably around 5%, of the accusations are fully retracted. This means that in the majority of cases, the accuser continues to believe and recall childhood sexual abuse, which may or may not have taken place. A false belief that one has been sexually abused in childhood is likely to be experienced as painful and potentially traumatising. Research should focus on the nature of the psychological symptoms, including possible post-traumatic stress disorder, reported by the accusers of childhood sexual abuse involving recovered memories and contrast the symptoms with those reported by persons who claim to have always remembered the abuse (i.e. the accusation does not involve recovered memories).

The present data highlight some of the consequences upon the families involved in the accusations. What is needed are studies which focus in detail in both the short-term and long-term consequences of the accusations on all the key players involved, as well as the effects on the community as a whole. Irrespective of the veracity or falsehood of the accusations, there are no winners, only sufferers.

REFERENCES

Andrews, B., Morton, J., Bekerian, D. A. & Davies, G. (1995). The recovery of memories in clinical practice: Experiences and beliefs of British Psychological Society practitioners. *Psychologist*, **8**, 209–214.

Brandon, S., Boakes, J., Glaser, D. & Green, R. (1998). Recovered memories of Childhood Sexual Abuse. Implications for clinical practice. *British Journal of Psychiatry*, **172**, 296–307.

de Rivera, J. (1997). The construction of false memory syndrome: The experience of retractors. *Psychological Inquiry*, **8**, 271–292.

Goldstein, E. & Farmer, K. (1992). *Confabulations: Creating False Memories, Destroying Families*. Boca Raton, FL: SIRS Books.

Goodyear-Smith, F. A., Laidlaw, T. M. & Large, R. G. (1997). Surveying families accused of Childhood Sexual Abuse: A comparison of British and New Zealand results. *Applied Cognitive Psychology*, **11**, 31–34.

Gudjonsson, G. H. (1997a). Accusations by adults of Childhood Sexual Abuse: A survey of the members of the British False Memory Society (BFMS). *Applied Cognitive Psychology*, **11**, 3–18.

Gudjonsson, G. H. (1997b). The members of the BFMS, the accusers and their siblings. *The Psychologist*, **10**, 111–115.

Gudjonsson, G. (1997c). Members of the British False Memory Society: The legal consequences of the accusations for the families. *Journal of Forensic Psychiatry*, **8**, 348–356.

Leo, R. A. (1997). The social and legal construction of repressed memory. *Law and Social Inquiry*, **22**, 653–693.

Loftus, E. & Ketcham, K. (1994). *The Myth of Repressed Memory*. New York: St Martin's Press.

Ofshe, R. & Watters, E. (1994). *Making Monsters. False Memories, Psychotherapy, and Sexual Hysteria*. London: Charles Scribner's Sons.

Ost, J., Costall, A. & Bull, R. (in preparation). A perfect symmetry? Retractors' experiences of recovering and then retracting Abuse Memories.

Pendergrast, M. (1995). *Victims of Memory*. Vermont: Upper Access.

Pope, K. S. & Brown, L. S. (1996). *Recovered Memories of Abuse. Assessment, Therapy, Forensics*. Washington, DC: American Psychological Association.

Russell, D. E. H. (1984). The prevalence and seriousness of Sexual Abuse: Stepfathers versus biological fathers. *Child Abuse and Neglect*, **8**, 15–22.

Schooler, J. W., Bendiksen, M. & Ambadar, Z. (1997). Taking the middle line: Can we accommodate both fabricated and recovered Memories of Sexual Abuse? In M. A. Conway (Ed.), *Recovered Memories and False Memories* (pp. 251–292). Oxford: Oxford University Press.

Wakefield, H. & Underwager, R. (1992). Recovered memories of alleged sexual abuse: Lawsuits against parents. *Behavioral Sciences and the Law*, **10**, 483–507.

Whitfield, C. L. (1995). *Memory and Abuse*. Deerfield Beach, FL: Health Communications.

Wright, L. (1994). *Remembering Satan: A Case of Recovered Memories and the Shattering of an American Family*. New York: Alfred A. Knopf.

3

RECOVERED MEMORIES OF ABUSE: THE EFFECTS ON THE INDIVIDUAL

Adrian E.G. Skinner

INTRODUCTION

The purpose of this chapter is to provide examples of the kinds of memories that can resurface after long periods of time and the effect that these memories can have on those who experience them. We also attempt to set those memories in the context of the theoretical understanding of the effects of abuse and the possible mechanisms for forgetting and retrieval.

The language of psychological treatment is rich in metaphor and simile; this both represents an opportunity to express difficult ideas with clarity and force and a dangerous temptation to expand these ideas beyond their range of application. Bearing this warning in mind, it is nevertheless appropriate to liken the task of the clinician dealing with clients who have been involved in actual or alleged sexual abuse to the job of the bomb disposal officer. There is the sense of alert at the first dull gleam of the memory of abuse, and the hasty donning of protective clothing.

Like the bomb disposal officer, psychologists need the appropriate equipment to deal with the situation in front of them. Their equivalent of the heavy helmet and shielding is a clear conceptual framework concerning memory and trauma and the skill to apply that knowledge. It is the lack of such a framework that has contributed to the storm of external criticism

Recovered Memories: Seeking the Middle Ground. Edited by Graham M. Davies and Tim Dalgleish. © 2001 John Wiley & Sons Ltd.

that surrounds work in this area. For instance, Bass and Davis (1988), in their much-criticised work *The Courage to Heal* list innumerable symptoms of psychological disturbance that can result from sexual abuse; from here it is but a short step to the syllogistic conclusion that the presence of these symptoms implies that abuse took place.

For the clinician it is more helpful and almost certainly more reliable to classify abuse as an example of a trauma and to view the client's presentation as an example of post-traumatic stress disorder (Meichenbaum, 1994). In this kind of disorder the two most prevalent sorts of symptoms will be intrusion and avoidance, together with habitual behaviours and cognitive patterns that have arisen over a period of years as a result of the client's attempts to cope with these feelings.

The most systematic and widely accepted list of symptoms that occur in post-traumatic stress disorder is that enumerated in the *Diagnostic and Statistical Manual* of the American Psychiatric Association (DSM-IV). Its companion in the field of categorisation, the World Health Organisation's *International Classification of Diseases* (ICD-10) is less precise. For subjects to satisfy these criteria they must experience symptoms from each of three categories: Re-experiencing, Avoidance and Hyperarousal.

Typical symptoms of re-experiencing include intrusive thoughts, dreams and/or nightmares, flashbacks, and distress provoked by reminders. Avoidance is connected with stimuli associated with their recollection of the trauma, and might include physical and mental avoidance, *including making memories inaccessible.* This avoidance can also 'leak' into outside life with a decreased interest in significant events and feelings of detachment from others and a withdrawal from life. Subjects also experience symptoms of hyperarousal with sleep difficulties, problems of concentration, a tendency to impulsive anger and physiological symptoms of increased arousal such as increased heart rate, sweatiness, etc. These physiological symptoms tend to be in response to stimuli related to the trauma either closely or more distantly.

Importantly, for a formal diagnosis to be made these symptoms must have a significant effect on a person's social or occupational functioning.

Since clinicians will occasionally be called upon to justify their clinical findings to third parties, it is worth noting that the DSM lays down detailed specifications on the variety and severity of symptoms that must be experienced before a formal assessment of post-traumatic stress disorder may be made. If a subject suffers from such symptoms but does not have sufficient symptoms to qualify for such a diagnosis, then the "lower level" diagnosis of Adjustment Disorder is available.

Adherence to these criteria will assist clinicians in communicating their findings both to professional colleagues and to outside bodies such as Courts of Law, and lessen the chance of a diagnosis being challenged.

Such an assessment is well supported by the appropriate use of a variety of psychometric tools. In particular, the Clinician-Administered PTSD Scale (CAPS-1; Blake et al., 1995) can be used as part of a structured interview and helps to elicit both the presence or absence of symptoms and the extent of the distress and disturbance they cause the subject.

It can also be helpful to use a symptom checklist, such as the SCL-90(R) (Derogatis, 1983) in order to compare the severity of the subject's symptoms to clients suffering from other forms of psychological disorder. Subscale scores on such checklists can help to guide and monitor the progress of therapy as well as giving an indication of any other measures that are appropriate, such as antidepressant medication.

The two key psychological elements of post-traumatic syndromes are re-experiencing and avoidance. These phenomena can appear in a variety of guises in the clinical situation.

RE-EXPERIENCING AND INTRUSION

Intrusive thoughts of trauma can take a variety of forms ranging from ruminations about the trauma itself and preoccupation with its perceived consequences to frank flashbacks.

A key element of intrusive thoughts is the element of re-experiencing the traumatic event or events. The feeling that the client is going through the trauma afresh tends not to occur with ruminations but does happen in dreams and nightmares, and particularly if there is an element of re-enacting. For instance, clients for whom the traumatic experience has been sexual frequently and unsurprisingly report difficulties in this area. The combination of reminders of the traumatic situation (nakedness, bodily position, smell, etc.), and the fact that sexual pleasure is associated with deliberate loss of control, is often a powerful stimulus for memories of sexual abuse.

This association can include "flashbacks", during which the abuse is recalled *as if it is happening again*. Such experiences can have a profound negative effect on the capacity of the client to make and maintain adult sexual relationships, and it is in this connection that they often seek treatment.

For victims, this phenomenon can interfere with their sexual relationships and wreck their sexual response. One client said, "If my partner approaches me in a way that reminds me of the abuse, I tend to go right back to it and I freeze. He has had to learn only to make love to me, or suggest lovemaking, in ways with which I am comfortable."

It is not only the overtly sexual side of the relationship that can be affected; often victims find that seemingly trivial stimuli, such as a hand on the shoulder, can re-awaken a particular memory from their abusive history and cause a dramatic response. These victims' partners learn that they have to be extremely careful in the way they behave.

Clients frequently report that these situations can result in recovery of a memory. Childhood sexual abuse often results in avoidance of sexual contact for many years; the eventual formation of a sexual relationship can then re-awaken memories of what happened many years previously. It is a moot point whether this process of reminding constitutes the recovery of a memory that was in fact inaccessible prior to the reminder or that the memory was available but not accessed.

Bass and Davis (1988) 'reverse engineer' this phenomenon and suggest that the existence of such sexual problems implies that sufferers were in fact abused. There is no evidence that this is the case, and clinicians should be wary of making this assumption and also of clients making similar assumptions when exposed to material about sexual abuse outside the consulting room.

However, there is no doubt that the awakening of such memories can result in these memories once again becoming active and being a powerful intrusion into the life of the client, interfering both with daily activities and relationships. Clients frequently report that the intrusive thoughts are so powerful that they make such everyday activity impossible.

The consequences of intrusion include a variety of generalised psychological symptoms such as depression and anxiety, as well as more specific phenomena such as dissociation (both in memory and in the present). Before we move on to accounts of symptoms it is important to note that abuse and memories of abuse can also give rise to other symptoms, although the precise relation of such symptoms to traumatic memories is less clear.

Dissociation can be associated with memories of abuse, both at the time of the abuse and during later life. Dissociation was first cited as a defence mechanism by Janet in the last century (Janet, 1889), and refers to the phenomenon of two or more mental processes taking place simultaneously without being integrated in consciousness.

This is an interesting and tempting notion from a number of viewpoints. Firstly, it is an experience familiar in some form to all of us who have driven a car or shopped in a supermarket and, secondly, it provides an obvious model for making memories inaccessible, and also for their reappearance if and when the dissociative state is re-entered. It also seems an entirely plausible reaction to a situation that is intolerable for the subject.

Less satisfactory, however, is the extension of this phenomenon into the formal diagnosis of dissociative identity disorder (DID), formerly multiple personality disorder (MPD). This disorder involves the coexistence of two or more personalities in the same person, and often involves other personality problems as well (e.g. self-harm). Although these two phenomena may well be linked, it is not clear if there is a spectrum or distribution with transient dissociation at one end and DID at the other.

Indeed, Pope, Oliva, Hudson, Bodkin and Gruber (1999) found in their survey that only about one-third of their respondents (American psychiatrists) believed that dissociative amnesia and dissociative identity disorder should be included without reservations in DSM-IV; a larger proportion replied that these categories should be included only as proposed diagnoses. It is not obvious that peritraumatic dissociation and multiple personalities represent the same underlying phenomenon.

Nevertheless, it is well established that dissociation can and does take place during trauma (e.g. Terr, 1991), and clinical experience as well as intuition tells as that victims frequently report such experiences during abusive episodes.

In cases where material is retrieved as treatment proceeds, the clinician also needs to be aware of the freshly traumatic effect of access to material that the client has previously not had available.

Case Example

K was a woman in her middle forties who was referred urgently for psychological treatment following a history of frequently presenting to her family doctor with a variety of minor physical disorders and breaking into tears on more than one occasion.

K had moved to the locality some two years previously and had had psychiatric treatment including group therapy some years previously. She had been brought up by an uncle and aunt, her mother having died when she was young and her father being unable to look after her. Her father had remarried and she had several half-siblings but had never lived with them and had no contact with her family.

She had left her uncle's home as soon as she had finished school and moved to a large city, where she got a room in a lodging house. She obtained clerical employment and went to night school, eventually qualifying as a lawyer. She married in her middle twenties disastrously, her husband being physically and sexually violent towards her and having several affairs. She eventually left him and had lived on her own since.

During treatment she complained initially of depression, isolation and an inability to make and maintain relationships. When she thought of herself with other people she felt worthless and depressed (her father and uncle had often told her she was worthless). If she attempted to relate to a man she experienced thoughts of the sexual and physical abuse meted out to her by her husband.

As the treatment progressed she began to access memories of sexual abuse by her father and uncle. It was difficult for K and the psychologist to decide whether these memories were 'recovered' in the sense of being fully hidden; she had certainly been aware of the abuse all along but had not felt that she could talk about it before. However, once she began to discuss what had happened to her she began to recall more and more detail.

For K, the intrusive thoughts were of the physical taunts and the sexual abuse. In some situations she experienced actual flashbacks; for instance, if she were in the bath she would recall episodes of abuse which had started with her father bathing her.

Terr (1991) draws a distinction between what she describes as Type I and Type II trauma. In the former the traumatic event is single and discrete, whereas Type II traumatic experiences are sustained and repeated, and are also of different varieties. According to Terr, memories of Type II are characterised by being "spotty" because of dissociation during the traumatic event or events, and this clearly happened here. However, it is difficult to ascribe particular significance to this as memories for repeated events are known to reduce the accuracy for a particular occurrence — one may have had a number of delicious meals in a favourite restaurant but be hard pressed to identify a particular menu, whereas a restaurant visited once on holiday may well provide a more detailed and complete memory.

K clearly reported such dissociation both during the abuse and since. Indeed, it had become an habitual defence mechanism functioning, for instance, in those situations in which she allowed herself sexual involvement. However, this dissociation also clearly contributed towards her sense of detachment and distance from others. It was important to acknowledge in treatment that this dissociation fulfilled both positive and negative functions. K had become a successful lawyer and, some years after her disastrous marriage, had formed a long-term relationship with a kind and gentle man who provided a high level of nurturance as well as adapting to K's sexual anxieties in an accepting way without ever pressuring her as to their origin. K had presented for therapy because she worried that her memories would 'break through' in some way and destroy everything she had so painfully striven to achieve.

During therapy, K made progress both in reducing the impact of the intrusive images through the use of Eye Movement Desensitisation and Reprocessing (EMDR), and in integrating the dissociated parts of herself.

Originally developed in the USA by Francine Shapiro, EMDR is a specific treatment aimed at eliminating intrusive images by enabling those images to be "reprocessed" by the subject and therefore no longer 'unprocessed' and intrusive. Subjects are asked to track a rapidly moving pen visually while experiencing the image, and there is convincing evidence that this reduces the frequency and intensity of such images (e.g. Wilson, Becker

& Tinker, 1997). What is less clear is why this happens, although there are competing theories involving the artificial creation of cognitive or emotional states such as REM sleep or the orienting response (MacCulloch & Feldman, 1996).

However, the large number of memories (and therefore images) that K experienced complicated this process.

AVOIDANCE

Avoidance is an example of a conditioned response. Emotionally and cognitively a previously neutral stimulus comes to possess negative connotations. Behaviourally, instrumental conditioning occurs as approach behaviour is associated with anxiety and avoidance with relief of that anxiety. Such avoidance responses may be total (e.g. avoidance of any contact with men) or specific and bizarre (e.g. a negative response to beards in a case where the abuser was bearded). Avoidance is chiefly a behavioural response complicated by cognition, emotion and habit formation.

Case Example

J was a man in his early seventies. He had served in the British Army during World War II, and been involved in the Battle of Kohima Ridge. This battle on the edge of the northern Indian plain had been one of the turning points of the war and marked the end of the British retreat towards India and also the end of the Japanese advance through the sub-continent.

J had been conscripted during the war and entered an infantry regiment. After initial training his regiment was sent straight out to the Indian sub-continent to help try to stem the Japanese advance. His regiment became embroiled in bitter hand-to-hand fighting. He recalled that at one point in the battle the Japanese had occupied the Governor's house while the British had occupied the garden. The British had taken the house by moving a tank to the door and firing through it.

He had spent several days advancing and retreating, and on one occasion the Japanese had overrun his position. He has sustained a variety of wounds himself and had seen comrades and enemies killed, wounded and dismembered. He himself was wounded at the height of the fighting and evacuated first to a field hospital before eventual repatriation.

After the battle he had been returned to England and was "demobbed" at the end of the war. He had married and worked until retirement as a postman.

He had only sought help on the fiftieth anniversary of the end of the war. Up until that time he had been scrupulous in avoiding contact with reminders of the battle in which he had been involved. He had joined the local branch of the British Legion (an organisation providing support to veterans as well as a local social club) but had not come across any other members of his regiment. He also found that fellow Legion members tended not to talk about their particular experiences.

However, during the activities marking the anniversary he had found that people talked more about what they had done during the war and also that there were an increased number of television programmes about the conflict, and in particular a programme about the campaign on the sub-continent. This programme, which he watched without intending to do so, contained vivid footage of the fighting at Kohima as well as interviews with those who had been there and recounted in detail the fighting and its consequences. As he watched he began to access memories and have images of his own experiences, the most vivid of which was the noise of battle, in particular artillery barrages.

After the length of time that had passed he had not been aware that he had developed an avoidance strategy; however, as he watched he started to experience physiological symptoms of anxiety amounting to panic and had to leave the room.

From that time the avoidance behaviour generalised and he also started to dream about the war; he no longer visited the Legion club and he began to avoid friends from the club. His friends initially visited him but eventually gave up.

Case Example

M was a woman in her early thirties who had been referred for psychological treatment by her family physician. She had presented at the surgery complaining of weight problems linked to "comfort eating" (her own words) and concerns about the effect of her weight gain on her marital relationship. Her doctor had referred her to the practice nurse for dietary control advice but was concerned about her emotional state.

At the time she sought treatment M had been married for about five years and the couple lived in an isolated country district. She worked as a senior executive in local government in a nearby town at the head of a large and busy department dealing with the public.

M and her husband had moved to the area just after they married, primarily as a result of her husband's career. They had previously lived in a large city, where M's large extended family still lived.

The psychologist was initially uncertain that this referral would be helpful for two reasons. Firstly, they were aware that psychotherapy has not proved particularly helpful for weight control and, secondly, the relationship problem seemed to indicate conjoint therapy. However, M was keen to proceed on the basis of having "a bit of extra help" to control her food intake and manage her stress levels at work. Four sessions over two months were therefore devoted to looking at behavioural cues to snacking, addressing issues of stress, and engaging the support of the husband at one remove.

At the fifth session M presented in a nervous and distressed state and asked if she could talk about something else. She had, she said, been to visit her family and had found out that her father (separated from her mother) had been baby-sitting for an 8-year-old girl. Tearfully, she said that this had brought back memories of what her father had done to her when she was that age. She gave an account of systematic abuse stretching over about five years visited on her and her two brothers. This involved both physical sexual abuse and exposure to lurid pornography.

The abuse had stopped at the time that her parents had split up and she and her brothers had gone to live with her mother. She remembered telling her mother about the abuse but did not know whether this had been a factor in her parents' separation. M had always remembered that she had been abused, but the discovery of her father's baby-sitting had led her to recall material that she had forgotten.

M's agenda was quite clear at this point; she was 'confessing' to her psychologist that she had not been telling everything about her over-eating and relationship difficulties, and she wanted advice as to the likelihood that her father was abusing the girl he was minding.

The psychologist said that at this point they had to distinguish between the urgent and the important. Addressing the former issue, M was advised that she was correct to suspect that her father might be abusing his new charge. M and the psychologist decided that she should contact the childcare authorities in her former place of residence as it was their task to ascertain if the child was at risk.

Both the care authorities and the police then interviewed M. The former prevented her father from continuing to act as a baby-sitter while the latter mounted a prosecution. M's brothers were interviewed and confirmed her story.

The treatment sessions during this period focused on helping M through the repeated long journeys to legal interviews as well as using cognitive techniques to help her with the renewed intrusive thoughts which had been stirred up. She actually found the criminal investigation helpful as it allowed her to feel at last that she was not responsible for what happened to her.

Meanwhile the psychologist was asked repeatedly by lawyers about the techniques used to 'recover' these memories. M's father had denied all the allegations and there was the clear implication that these memories had been implanted in some way during treatment, in spite of the fact the events that had led to the recall had occurred outside the treatment room.

M herself had now discussed her past with her husband. This, combined with the fact that she felt she could relinquish responsibility for the past and the techniques to challenge the negative thoughts, led to much improvement in her self-esteem and she terminated therapy.

MEMORY FUNCTION

What can these case examples tell us about the functioning of memory during abuse and the recovery of memories in later life?

Leskin, Kaloupek and Keane (1998) describes three models that help to account for the forgetting of traumatic experiences: biological, behavioural and cognitive. Viewed from a biological angle, traumatic experiences are allied with changes in biochemistry associated with anxiety and arousal. It is known that these changes can interfere with some basic bodily processes at the same time as they assist with others, and it seems logical to assume that the arousal associated with trauma could interfere with memory registration. It is known that other memories associated with altered physiological states can be unreliable, such as 'flashbulb' memories of witnessing a crime. It seems unlikely that such a mechanism could be involved when the traumatic experiences are of Terr's Type II. For the cases quoted above, the traumatic experiences lasted from a period of several weeks (for J) to many years (for K and M). The latter in particular reported that their physiological anxiety responses decayed as the abuse went on, and it cannot therefore be assumed that all the memories were registered at a time of physiological arousal.

The behavioural model offers a more promising analysis of forgetting and recovering. The avoidance response experienced by J can be interpreted using a conditioning framework. Material connected with his wartime experiences were clearly associated with a conditioned anxiety response and were avoided. His re-experiencing was sparked by watching a television programme containing material which 'cued' the memories of his own suffering.

However, this explanation seems a bit thin in terms of offering a comprehensive analysis of the processes involved. Why were TV pictures effective triggers for memory, while the military ephemera and his comrades at the British Legion were not? Viewing the pictures clearly posed no threat and was only a reminder of his own war, so why the anxiety response?

The behaviour of memory in these circumstances requires a more complex and multi-level explanation, which is available if the process is viewed from a cognitive viewpoint. Brewin and Andrews (1998) discuss a variety of cognitive mechanisms that might be wholly or partly responsible for the inaccessibility of traumatic memories.

In terms of longevity, the original mechanism for such forgetting is the concept of repression. In its original Freudian form this represents material which is registered, classified as unacceptable, and therefore intentionally repressed. The psychology of memory decrees that there must be two varieties of repression; that which occurs at the same time as the trauma and represents a failure to encode information, and the suppression of material that has already been processed.

The fact that all three subjects quoted above accessed their memories at some stage clearly contradicts the view that the material was repressed on input. Any such process must have taken place after the memory had been stored.

The related phenomenon of dissociation is clearly relevant here; K, in particular, reported that she defended herself against the horror of the traumatic experience by "spectating". Later in life she purposely developed an alternative persona who was tasked with being 'different' to the 'unacceptable' abused individual. On recalling the abuse, K tended to go back into the other, unacceptable, self.

It is also possible that 'ordinary forgetting' has a role to play in the inability to recall trauma. However, it seems unlikely that this phenomenon would be relevant in the case of long-term abuse where there are very many episodes, but might well play a part where the trauma was related to a single incident only.

What was the relevance of 'false memories' in these three cases? Is there any reason to suppose that the material recalled did not correlate to events in the outside world? Is there any evidence that material was implanted by a treatment process that took a particular view of the world?

It can be seen that there is no report for these three clients of any cueing of memories during treatment interviews; this is because such cueing did not take place. Many criticisms of recovered memories have hinged upon the view that they represent the therapist's view of what went on rather than the client's own recall. In cases involving satanic ritual abuse (SRA), the critical observation has been made that the reported memories are mainly stereotypical accounts of popular views of SRA within the therapy community.

All three clients had interesting comments on the accuracy of their memories. For K, all her memories were recalled spontaneously or through reminders in the environment. She was aware of literature about sexual abuse, had read stories in the press, and was aware of the dangers of 'interference' and 'construction'. Nevertheless, despite her strong history of dissociating both during the abuse and subsequently, she felt that her recall was strictly hers alone.

However, client M reported a slightly different experience; when she underwent her interviews with the child care authorities and police she was asked a variety of questions along the lines, "Did you ever experience...?". She reported that several sessions along these lines ended with her "in a muddle". She was no longer certain that all her memories were intact and complete; she felt uncertain about small details. Nevertheless, she was completely certain that key core events were still fully remembered and that such interference occurred only with peripheral items.

J was more specific in his concerns; when he began to watch the TV film of the war in India he specifically started to wonder if he was combining his own memory for events with what he was seeing on the film. He was concerned that some of his memories were "more like newsreel".

The importance of the appropriate handling of such reports within treatment cannot be overestimated. Clinicians will be aware that memory is a constructive process and the process of recall results in a narrative whose essential completeness will be the result of processing the information during recall as well as on storage. While the Japanese Government was clearly not going to accuse J of confabulating, this was a possibility for both K and M. In the case where there was in fact a legal process, M decided that it was necessary for her to establish at an early stage that parts of her recall were bitty and incomplete, but that other parts were clear. It was also important that she was able to check her recall with others, thus obtaining corroboration for her recalled view of events.

THE OTHER VICTIMS?

Before we close this chapter it is important to view these problems from the 'other side' and to report on some of the unique difficulties of such work.

B was a man in his sixties who lived with his wife in the suburbs of a small town. The letter of referral from his doctor said that he was distressed and depressed by allegations that he had abused his daughter when she was younger.

At his first interview, B described the distressing situation in which he and his wife had found themselves. They had moved to the area when he retired from his work as a health professional. They had three adult children and three grandchildren, two from the marriage of his elder son and one from the marriage of his daughter. His younger son was unmarried. The children lived in different parts of the country.

He recounted that the children's' upbringing had been "normal"; he had worked long hours at his hospital job and his wife had carried the main burden of child rearing. The children had all done well at school and had gone to college and got good jobs in their turn.

The children had had their share of problems — his elder son had a conviction for smoking cannabis — but he felt that these problems were no greater than for any other family. He described their relationship as "warm".

His relationship with his daughter had, however, always been problematical. She had never told him things and they had clashed frequently during her teenage years. She had had a succession of relationships with "unsuitable men" (his words). She had left home to go to University and had not lived with B and his wife since. She had married without consulting them although they had attended the wedding and other family celebrations such as christenings.

B was aware that his daughter had had psychological problems — there had been some question of a suicide attempt when she was at University and he knew that she had had counselling. However, it had come as a shock when she wrote to him and his wife to say that she knew that he had abused her when she was younger and she no longer wanted to see him, and also forbade contact with her own daughter.

B's initial response had been to contact his sons and to "get them make their sister see sense". He said that both of them had talked to her but she remained adamant. He had made unsuccessful attempts to contact her and his wife had spoken to her daughter on one or two occasions, but they both found this very difficult.

B had then visited his family lawyer. He told the psychologist that he did this because he wanted to find out if he could stop his daughter broadcasting falsehoods about him and his behaviour to the family and beyond (she had told her brothers about the abuse and this was making those relationships uncomfortable). He was also worried that she would bring a prosecution against him.

His lawyer had alerted him to the existence of 'false memory syndrome' and he had done some reading and contacted a support group.

At this point the psychologist was uncertain as to B's agenda. The referral from the family doctor had been a request for assistance with the distress caused by the allegations, but this did not seem to be the reason that B was presenting — he seemed in fact to deny abnormal emotions. When asked the question directly, B said that he had been advised by his lawyer to see a psychologist for two reasons; firstly, to try to obtain hints on how the 'false memories' had been implanted in his daughter and, secondly, to try to establish his 'psychological fitness'.

The psychologist told B that he was happy to provide information about memory and its function and assist in discussing the issue of false memory. He could not provide any statement about his opinion whether B could or could not have been an abuser as he did not and could not hold an opinion on this.

After discussing the issue of false memory over two sessions B terminated the appointments. He said that he understood the psychologist's position and that there was no way to say that he had or had not abused his daughter. He appreciated the chance to discuss the whole question of memories of abuse. His agenda remained the same — he was intent on trying to get his daughter to retract her allegations or at least to stop broadcasting them, and was going to try legal means to get access to his grandchild.

CONCLUSIONS

What implications do scientific findings have for the debate about recovered memory? What do these cases, and this analysis, tell us about the effect of recovering memories upon the individual?

The key questions in the scientific debate are, firstly, whether subjects can 'remember' events that did not occur and, secondly, whether the forgetting of traumatic incidents can take place. This debate can move away from the scientific and towards the clinical, political and legal when individuals are involved.

It is clear from the accounts above that individuals can gain access to material of which they were not previously aware. In our accounts it is apparent that the subjects possessed at least partial memory before treatment, and that the recall of additional material occurred outside treatment or without specific prompting or 'memory recovery' techniques such as hypnosis. These subjects had good reason not to remember, and there is a variety of scientific psychological explanations for the process. It is likely that different mechanisms are responsible for different forgetting — repression, dissociation and ordinary forgetting. The view that it is not possible to forget something as traumatic as sexual abuse does not stand up to examination.

Secondly, it also clear that such memories can reappear, cued by a variety of well-understood psychological processes such as cueing. It is much less clear that people can remember events that did not happen at all, although this is clearly theoretically possible. What is not at all certain is how often this has actually happened.

In order to help the clinician navigate through this tricky territory we have set traumatic memories in context as part of the spectrum of post-traumatic phenomena, centring on post-traumatic stress disorder (Meichenbaum, 1994), although extending to include other varieties of clinical problem. Examples are provided of the emergence, effects and treatment of particular memories.

To deal with emerging memories in a particular subject, the clinician should bear in mind that the experience is traumatic and should be fitted into that theoretical framework. This has the advantage of enabling both the clinician and the client to understand and make predictions about feelings, thoughts and behaviour.

Secondly, as soon as memories of illegal activity emerge, the clinician needs to be aware of the possibility that other people and agencies may become involved in the case. This knowledge will also need to be shared with the client. This knowledge should also guide clinical activity. 'Memory recovery' techniques (whatever they are) should be eschewed.

Thirdly, it is possible that the nature of the memories will alter as they emerge. Memory is a constructive process and tends to form a Gestalt or whole. The clinician needs to be aware of this process and its consequences for the client, the process of treatment, and in any outside action such as a legal process.

REFERENCES

Bass, E. & Davis, L. (1988). *The Courage to Heal: A Guide for Women Survivors of Child Sexual Abuse*. New York: Harper & Row.

Blake, D. D., Weathers, F.W., Nagy, L., Kaloupek, D. G., Gusman, F. D., Charney, D. S. & Keane, T. M. (1995). The development of a clinician-administered PTSD scale. *Journal of Traumatic Stress*, **8**, 75–90.

Brewin, C. R. & Andrews, B. (1998). Recovered memories of trauma: Phenomenology and cognitive mechanisms. *Clinical Psychology Review*, **18**, 949–970.

Derogatis, L. R. (1983). *SCL-90-R: Administration, Scoring and Procedures Manual*. Towson, MD: Clinical Psychometric Research.

Janet, P. (1889). *L'automatisme Psychologique*. Paris: Felix Alcan.

Leskin, G. A., Kaloupek, D. G. & Keane, T. M. (1998). Treatment for traumatic memories: Review and recommendations. *Clinical Psychology Review*, **18**, 983–1001.

MacCulloch M. J. B., Feldman, P. (1996). Eye movement desensitisation treatment utilises the positive visceral element of the investigatory reflex to inhibit the memories of post-traumatic stress disorder: A theoretical analysis. *British Journal of Psychiatry*, **169**, 571–9.

Meichenbaum, D. (1994). *Treating Post-Traumatic Stress Disorder: A Handbook and Practice Manual for Therapy*. Chichester: Wiley.

Pope, H. G. Jr, Oliva, P. S., Hudson, J. I., Bodkin, J. A. & Gruber, A. J. (1999). Attitudes toward DSM-IV dissociative disorders diagnoses among board-certified American psychiatrists. *American Journal of Psychiatry*, **156**, 321–323.

Terr, L. C. (1991). Childhood traumas: An outline and overview. *American Journal of Psychiatry*, **148**, 10–20.

Wilson, S. A., Becker, L. A. & Tinker, R. H. (1997). Fifteen month follow-up of eye movement desensitisation and reprocessing (EMDR) treatment for post-traumatic stress disorder and psychological trauma. *Journal of Consulting Clinical Psychology*, **65**, 1047–1056.

4

RECOVERED MEMORIES: THE LEGAL DILEMMAS

Eilis Magner and Patrick Parkinson

RECOVERED MEMORY IN THE FORENSIC CONTEXT

Debates about the validity of recovered memory in a legal context take on a different complexion from those that have occurred in the psychological and psychiatric literature. Debates among psychologists and psychiatrists have largely occurred at a level of generality. Is it possible for memories of traumatic events to be repressed? If so, by what mechanisms does repression occur? How common is total amnesia as a response to traumatic events? How reliable are recovered memories of traumatic events?

These are important questions, and numerous scientific studies have now been conducted which address them. However, few such studies are of assistance to lawyers in dealing with the questions that we have to answer. Lawyers typically ask different questions from scientists and have different understandings of the notion of proof.

For the lawyer, the issue is not whether and how often the phenomenon of traumatic amnesia occurs, but whether it has occurred in a given case where the issue has arisen. It is the particular question that has to be answered. If recent scientific studies had confirmed the assertion of Holmes (1990) that there is no evidence to support the idea of repression, then that scientific finding would have been conclusive of the question whether a witness's account of abuse based upon recovered memories

Recovered Memories: Seeking the Middle Ground. Edited by Graham M. Davies and Tim Dalgleish. © 2001 John Wiley & Sons Ltd.

should be treated as probative in court. This view must now be regarded as untenable in the light of the research evidence available. This research includes well-constructed prospective studies that begin from a baseline of substantiated and officially recorded abuse (Widom & Morris, 1997; Widom & Shepard, 1996; Williams, 1994).

Now the debate within the scientific literature has shifted from the existence of the phenomenon of traumatic amnesia to issues, inter alia, about the reliability of such memories and the role which suggestion might play. Here too, scientific studies are of limited assistance to lawyers, for they can only provide evidence of the likelihood that an account is true or false as a matter of statistical probabilities. Williams (1995) and Dalenberg (1996) found that there were no significant differences in the reliability of continuous and recovered memories. Dalenberg reported that the overall accuracy rate of both was about 75%, among those who submitted evidence, which supported the recovered memories (70% of sample). These findings may demonstrate that a particular account of abuse may well be true, but they are of no assistance in determining whether in fact the story *is* true. Lawyers deal in probabilities, but not statistical probabilities. In any case, even given a statistical likelihood that a story is true, there remains the possibility that the memory of the abuse is inaccurate, at least in relation to some of the details.

Understanding the differences between the questions lawyers need to ask and the questions which have been asked in the scientific research literature helps to explain why lawyers must be so cautious in dealing with recovered memories of abuse. Issues about the validity of memory become contested in an environment in which the general scientific debates are rehearsed in the context of individual innocence or guilt, individual exoneration or liability.

THE NATURE OF RECOVERED MEMORY

A further issue in the legal treatment of recovered memory evidence concerns the nature of recovered memories. A considerable body of scientific evidence indicates that traumatic memory is different from other types of memory — verbal autobiographical memory, semantic memory and procedural memory (Brown, Scheflin & Hammond, 1998). When recovered memories first come into consciousness, they are often experienced as somato-sensory in nature. Fragments of the memory intrude in the form of nightmares or flashbacks, and later the affective component of the memory predominates (van der Kolk & Fisler, 1995). Van der Kolk and van der Hart (1991, p. 447) summarize the nature of what they call dissociated traumatic memory:

Traumatic memories are the unassimilated scraps of overwhelming expe-
riences, which need to be reintegrated with existing mental schemes, and
be transformed into narrative language. It appears that, in order for this
to occur successfully, the traumatized person has to return to the
memory often in order to complete it.

While many people coming for therapy have some partial memory of the traumatic experience, or have begun to experience intrusive recollections before seeking therapeutic assistance (Harvey & Herman, 1994), part of the therapeutic process involves integration of the dissociated memories. Thus the transformation of a traumatic memory to narrative language involves a process of reconstruction of the fragments of memory assisted often by a third party, the therapist.

That all the details might not be clear or even accurate is not necessarily of great importance in the therapeutic setting. The goal of therapy is the resolution of the symptoms of trauma. The truth of the remembered account is of course very important, for the form of therapeutic intervention is likely to depend on the basic validity of the memories. But it is the essence of the remembered story which matters and the focus on therapy is on the present distress rather than the past details.

By way of contrast, in the courtroom, the details matter. Where child sexual assault by a parent is alleged, it is not enough for the prosecution, or a plaintiff in a civil case, to prove in a general way that the abuse occurred. Survivors of intrafamilial child abuse in free recall may recount their history of abuse in terms of a pattern of experiences over a given period of time. However, the law constructs sexual abuse not in terms of abusive relationships but in terms of abusive events (Jones & Parkinson, 1995). Each 'event' of sexual assault is analysed discretely and forms the basis of a separate charge. Each act of molestation is a separate criminal act, just as each robbery or car theft is a separate criminal act. Each element of the offence must be proven. Thus, if the offence charged involves sexual intercourse with a minor, the prosecution must prove that the defendant violated the bodily integrity of the child in a manner that satisfies the definition of sexual intercourse within the meaning of the legislation. Furthermore, the witness to the abuse must describe each act of sexual violation with sufficient specificity that each individual incident is proven beyond reasonable doubt. The witness does not have to give exact dates, but there must be a sufficient level of specificity in the allegations to give to the defendant an opportunity to rebut them (*S v. The Queen*).

Recovered memories may be problematic in the legal context for four reasons. First, because the fragments of memory may not present a sufficiently clear picture of specific events to form the basis of criminal charges (or civil action). Secondly, because the process of reconstruction may also affect the reliability of the memories even without any therapeutic mal-practice or inappropriate suggestion. In this reconstructive process, there is the possibility for autosuggestion as the person seeks to 'complete' the memory (Lindsay & Read, 1994). When the judge or jury must be satis-fied of the truth of the allegations beyond reasonable doubt, the fact that the memories, which form the basis of the testimony, have been recovered after a period of amnesia may itself be a reason for sufficient doubt. Thirdly, where the accusing witness has been assisted in dealing with the traumatic memories by a therapeutic process, there is a further possibil-ity that the psychiatric or therapeutic process has affected the content of the memory. Finally, repeated narrating of the memory may well change its content as the meaning for the individual also changes.

RECOVERED MEMORY AND THE COURTROOM

These issues were brought prominently to public attention by two trials in the United States of America. These were the trial of Franklin on the charge of murder and the trial of the claim by Gary Ramona against the therapists who had treated his daughter Holly.

George Franklin was tried and convicted of murder in 1990. The pros-ecution charged Franklin with the rape and murder of a schoolgirl 20 years earlier. The principal evidence against George Franklin was the tes-timony of his daughter, Eileen Franklin Lipsker. Lipsker had first experi-enced her memories as a "flashback" when sitting in her own living room with her 5-year-old daughter. She then underwent hypnosis and subse-quently testified as to her memories of the event. At the trial in November 1990, Lenore Terr and Elizabeth Loftus testified as to the validity of recov-ered memories. Lenore Terr, a prominent clinician who later wrote studies of recovered memory (Terr, 1991, 1994), testified for the prosecution to the effect that recovered memories could have validity. Elizabeth Loftus, an experimental psychologist who had conducted and written numerous studies of eyewitness memory (Loftus, 1979; Loftus & Ketcham, 1994) tes-tified for the defence about the unreliability of memory. Franklin was con-victed. In 1995 the Franklin conviction was reversed with an order that would have allowed a new trial. In 1996 the case was dismissed for lack of prosecution (Johnstone, 1997, pp. 5, 380).

In *Ramona v. Isabella*, a father brought action against his daughter's ther-apists after she recovered memories of years of horrific sexual abuse by her father several months into her treatment for bulimia. The daughter confronted Gary Ramona with an accusation in the office of one of her therapists. He denied the charges. Four years later, after losing his job and going through a messy divorce, Ramona sued his daughter's therapist, the practitioner who conducted a sodium amytal interview of his daughter and the hospital in which both the interview and the confrontation took place. The daughter was told by her therapist that sodium amytal was a truth drug. In fact the drug induces a state of suggestibility. At the trial the daughter testified for the defence, as did Lenore Terr. Elizabeth Loftus was called to testify for the plaintiff. The jury found for the plaintiff. But, faced with a claim for damages of $8.5 million, the jury awarded damages of only $0.5 million (Johnstone, 1997). The decision was not appealed because the costs of the appeal were not justified by the size of the damages award (Brown et al., 1998, p. 558).

The legal dilemmas that are illustrated by these two cases arise in all common law jurisdictions, and in both criminal and civil trials. Should a witness who has undergone hypnosis, or a sodium amytal interview, or indeed therapy of any kind, be allowed to testify as to memories recovered by that means or at all? Should expert witnesses be allowed to testify as to the validity of these memories? Should independent support for the testimony about the incident based on recovered memory be necessary before a decision can be reached? Should the court be informed about the process by which the memory was recovered? Other questions arise in civil proceedings. For example, there are questions about whether the lapse of time should bar proceedings based on the recovered memory and about whether an action lies against the therapist.

Questions about repressed and recovered memories will arise in court not only if a criminal prosecution or civil action is brought on the basis of recovered memories, or if a therapist is sued for professional malpractice. Another way in which issues about recovered memories may arise is where the recovered memory has incidental relevance. For example in *HG v. The Queen*, Australia's highest court had to determine whether a rape shield provision (which prohibits the introduction of evidence of past sexual history) prevented the defence from alleging that an 8-year-old child who complained of sexual abuse had in fact been sexually assaulted by her natural father five years earlier. There was no evidence to suggest this, but the defence argued that the child had repressed her memories of such an assault and wanted to call the evidence of a psychologist who would rely on evidence about the child's behaviour patterns. The High Court of Australia held that such evidence was inadmissible.

CIVIL OR CRIMINAL ACTION BASED ON RECOVERED MEMORIES

Individuals who, after a course of therapy, recover memories of childhood sexual abuse or obtain the ability to deal with their memories of this abuse frequently turn to the courts. The trial that results may be on criminal charges where the sanction, if guilt is proved, will be a criminal penalty. Alternatively, the survivor of childhood sexual abuse may seek a remedy in damages by bringing a civil action for assault, battery, or infliction of emotional distress (Kanovitz, 1992).

The difficulties for "complainants" in the criminal process lead many victims to pursue civil remedies. A civil action for damages may avoid many of the problems inherent in the criminal justice system, chief of which is the higher standard of proof required for success. It can be settled by agreement so it is more concerned with achieving justice between the putative victim and offender. Des Rosiers (1998) has also argued cogently that such proceedings operate therapeutically.

EFFECT OF LIMITATION PERIODS

In Australia and in Great Britain major criminal charges are not time-barred but Limitations Acts apply to require that civil actions be brought within a set period. In the United States of America speedy prosecution provisions apply to require criminal proceedings to be dealt with expeditiously but limitations periods on civil actions are often subject to exception. Until recently civil actions brought by survivors of childhood abuse were frequently barred by limitation periods, which typically required that actions to recover damages in tort be brought within a period of three to five years. In advance of statutory amendment, some courts, particularly in the United States of America, were persuaded to extend the period of limitations on the basis of arguments that the plaintiff was not able to bring the action until the memory was recovered (Kanovitz, 1992, pp. 1201–1202; *Johnson v. Johnson*; *Daly v. Derrick*; *Callahan v. State*). The argument used was that, although the plaintiff always remembered the incidents, psychological problems delayed their realisation that the abuse had caused serious emotional harm (Kanovitz, 1992, p. 1202; *DeRose v Carswell*).

Statutory amendments in many jurisdictions have specifically conferred power on the courts to extend the limitation period. These powers can be exercised where the plaintiff did not know that the injury had been sustained or was unaware of the nature or extent of personal injury suffered; or was unaware of the connection between the personal injury and the defendant's act or omission. As at mid-1997, 37 American states had either legislatively or judicially provided an extension of time for adult survivors of child sexual abuse in at least some circumstances (Brown et al., 1998; p. 591). Similar reforms have been adopted in several other jurisdictions (Limitation Act 1969 (NSW) s. 60F).

EVIDENTIAL ISSUES IN CRIMINAL OR CIVIL ACTION AGAINST AN ALLEGED OFFENDER

Whenever the question of recovered and repressed memory arises in the case in court there are a number of evidentiary issues that will need to be resolved. Courts in different common law jurisdictions provide varying solutions to these problems, but they are all conscious of the same problems.

Admissibility of testimony after therapy

The question of how therapeutic assistance affects the admissibility of evidence has been examined mainly in relation to the issue of whether testimony can be received from a witness whose memory for the events has been hypnotically refreshed. Common law courts have adopted a variety of approaches to the question. One solution has been to hold that the hypnotic session was irrelevant on the basis that if the witness would otherwise have been competent, the witness remains competent (*Roughley, Marshall and Haywood v. R*). On the other end of the spectrum, it has been held that the hypnotic session makes the evidence completely inadmissible (*People v. Guerra*; *People v. Shirley*). The preferable approach appears to be a case-by-case assessment in which the exercise of certain precautions is relevant and the failure to exercise such precautions leads to the exclusion of the evidence as inadmissible. The defendant does not need to establish that the process adversely affected the memory (*R v. Mcfelin*; *R v. Jenkyns*). Provisions in the Californian Evidence Code mandate this approach. These provisions have been influential in many judicial decisions in other jurisdictions (*R v. Browning*; *R v. Mcfelin*; *R v. Jenkyns*).

The New South Wales Court of Criminal Appeal in *R v. Tillott* rejected the argument that this approach should be confined to cases where hypnosis is used. In that case an appeal was allowed because the trial judge had ruled that the failure to observe the precautions was irrelevant to the question of whether a witness could give evidence after a session of Eye Movement Desensitisation and Reprocessing (EMDR). Abadee J, stated that sufficient meaningful similarities of dangers, inherent dangers, and risks had been identified to support the view that the same safeguards as apply to memory affected by hypnosis should apply to memory, the subject of the EMDR process. It was not relevant to determine whether the procedures used were the same, if the procedures used held similar dangers. This reasoning makes this decision potentially applicable to any other psychological therapy in which memory is explored. Donald Spence (1982, pp. 91–94) has argued persuasively that any form of psychotherapy presents the same dangers. It is suggested here that this implies that the reasoning in *R v. Tillott* could be applied to exclude the testimony of a patient who has recovered memories after any form of psychotherapy where precautions have not been taken, whether or not hypnosis, sodium amytal, or EMDR are employed.

Kanovitz (1992) argued that, where hypnosis has been used for therapeutic rather than forensic purposes, the approach of the courts should be different (p. 1261). This argument was based on several grounds. One point Kanovitz made was that the memory errors that hypnosis laboratory experiments demonstrate are mistakes about details of events not about whether an event occurred (pp. 1234–1238). She also suggested that hypnotisability is a stable trait that could be measured and identified, and introduced as evidence going to credibility (pp. 1238–1241). Finally she suggested that the presence of clinical symptoms provided evidence that there was a memory to be retrieved and minimised the danger that a memory could be implanted in the absence of information (pp. 1241–1242).

Such an argument was accepted in the context of a trial before a single judge in Western Australia (*The Queen v. Jumeaux*). It was rejected by the Court of Criminal Appeal in *R v. Tillott*. It was also considered and rejected in the American case of *Borawick v. Shay*. In this case the appellate court affirmed the decision of the lower court, dismissing the civil case as a consequence of the ruling that the plaintiff could not testify as to her memories of abuse following therapeutic hypnosis. The plaintiff had no memory of abuse before or immediately after she underwent 12 to 14 sessions of therapeutic hypnosis. She did have a history of disturbance and psychiatric treatment lasting over a period of three years before hypnosis was used. The trial judge had found that the hypnotist was not properly qualified and the hypnotist had stated that he kept no permanent records of the sessions.

The appellate court reviewed the law concerning the admissibility of hypnotically refreshed testimony generally before turning to the argument founded on Kanovitz's suggestion. The appellate court stated that, while it appreciated the force of many of the arguments presented by Kanovitz, it was not willing to assume that the risks of suggestibility, confabulation, and memory hardening are significantly reduced when the hypnosis that triggers the testimony is used for therapeutic purposes (*Borawick v Shay* p. 607). The court indicated that an approach, which would admit such evidence without pause, was inadequate to protect defendants from unfounded charges in either criminal or civil suits. They refused to hold that the observance of safeguards would always determine the admissibility of the evidence. Instead, following the decisions in *Sprynczynatyk v. General Motors Corp* and *McQueen v. Garrison*, the court indicated that a pre-trial hearing should determine whether in all the circumstances the testimony was sufficiently reliable and whether its probative value outweighed any prejudicial effect (*Borawick v. Shay*, p. 608). Applying this approach, the court held that the evidence should be excluded not merely because the proper precautions had not been used in the hypnotic sessions but also because Borawick had levelled a series of similar accusations against numerous persons other than the defendants.

Whether or not the observance of precautions is deemed conclusive, it appears that the conditions under which the therapeutic session is conducted will be relevant to determining whether the testimony is admissible. There are a number of statements that outline relevant safeguards; of these, the most thorough are those outlined by McConkey and Sheehan (1995) in their book *Hypnosis, Memory and Behavior in Criminal Investigation*. These guidelines were used as the basis for the guidelines adopted by the Australian Psychological Society (1995; McConkey, 1995; Magner, 1995).

Admissibility of expert testimony

In the context of both criminal and civil litigation in which reliance is placed on recovered memory evidence, questions arise concerning the admissibility of expert evidence about witness memory. It will be necessary to show that witnesses called to offer factual information and opinion evidence about the performance of memory have appropriate qualifications and requisite expertise. There is some uncertainty about the ability of clinicians to offer such evidence. The legal system also incorporates rules that restrict evidence about the credibility of a witness.

It is a basic premise of the common law trial system that witnesses should testify only to their primary observations. The drawing of inferences and conclusions is the task of the tribunal of fact. Opinion evidence is, on this basis, normally excluded. It is clear, however, that the courts will receive expert testimony in certain circumstances. Where expert testimony is relevant to a question before the court, the qualifications of the expert can be established, and the basis of the expert testimony can be explained, then the testimony will normally be received. It may still be excluded by the court pursuant to a policy of the law or in the exercise of discretion.

The statutory provisions adopted recently in certain Australian jurisdictions stipulate that if a person has specialised knowledge based on training, study or experience, the opinion rule does not apply to evidence of an opinion that is wholly or substantially based on that knowledge (Evidence Act 1995 (Cth) and (NSW), s. 79). In the United States of America, Rule 702 of the Federal Rules of Evidence permits expert testimony pertaining to "scientific, technical or other specialised knowledge". In the case of *Daubert v. Merrell Dow Pharmaceuticals, Inc.*, the Supreme Court of the United States of America held that the trial judge, in applying Rule 702, had a duty to ensure that "any and all scientific testimony or evidence admitted is not only relevant, but reliable". Further the Supreme Court indicated that 'scientific' implied "a grounding in the methods and procedures of science" (*Daubert v. Merrell Dow Pharmaceuticals, Inc.*, pp. 589–590) while 'knowledge' connoted "more than subjective belief or unsupported speculation".

The question of whether expert evidence about recovered memory was admissible under the tests adumbrated in *Daubert* has been explored but not concluded. In *United States v. Bighead*, the appellate court, by a majority, held that the evidence of a witness, who was the director of forensic services at a Children's Advocacy Centre, held degrees in nursing and was licensed as a therapist, was admissible. The witness testified after cross-examination had challenged the accusing witness's ability to recall and recount the incidents. The expert testimony was confined to the general characteristics of such witnesses, and the timing of reports and their ability to recall the abuse. The majority, citing *United States v. Cordoba*, held that the tests for the admissibility of expert scientific testimony do not require exclusion of expert testimony that involves specialised knowledge rather than scientific theory (*United States v. Bighead*, p. 1331). A strong dissent was recorded on the basis that the test for the admissibility of expert evidence requires the court to examine the methodology of the expert and to exclude statements of subjective belief or unsupported speculation (*United States v. Bighead*, p. 1335).

It has been suggested that, on the one hand, when experts invoke science by suggesting that their opinions are grounded in the knowledge of a larger professional community, the testimony may be excluded if the court concludes that the knowledge does not meet the court's threshold for reliability. On the other hand, the suggestion is that when experts rest their opinion on their own clinical judgement, courts frequently admit the opinion evidence after looking only to the credentials of the witness (Sales, Shuman & O'Connor, 1994).

Setting aside questions about the qualifications and methodology of the expert witness, there are questions as to the admissibility of evidence going to the issue of the credibility of the witness testifying on the basis of recovered memories (Magner, 1989). The basic approach in common law jurisdictions is to assume that a witness is credible until that credibility is challenged in cross-examination (Evidence Act 1995 (Cth) and (NSW), ss. 102–108). On the basis that credibility of a witness is a question peculiarly within the province of the jury, and that the jury may be particularly apt to adopt and apply uncritically expert evaluations of witness credibility, the courts tend to be particularly restrictive of expert evidence in this area. The position frequently taken is that an expert witness will be allowed to testify generally about processes and factors that are relevant to determinations as to the victim's credibility, but prevented from testifying that a particular witness is or is not telling the truth (*Farrell v. The Queen; United States v. Rouse*).

Whenever the question of suggestibility and recovered memory is squarely raised in a court case, experimental psychologists will be able to testify in order to explain the studies that establish that witnesses are suggestible. Whether clinical psychologists will be able to testify that memories can be repressed and recovered is more problematic, both because it is harder to show that such evidence is reliable and because the jury's function of deciding whether witnesses are credible is jealously preserved.

Burden of proof and independent support

In a civil case the burden is borne by the party who has asked the court for a remedy. The court must find that the case of a party is proved if the court is satisfied that the case has been proved on the balance of probabilities. When criminal charges have been brought, the prosecution must prove its case beyond reasonable doubt.

In common law jurisdictions, the normal rule is that a decision, even a decision in a criminal case, can be reached on the basis of the testimony of one witness alone. Exceptions to that rule are created where, for one reason or another, the law deems it relevant to look for independent support for the principal witness. The term 'corroboration' is sometimes used to connote such independent support. Speaking generally, where the law deems independent support to be desirable but not essential, the practice is to require the trial judge to warn the jury that they should be careful about convicting on unsupported testimony that is considered to be unreliable for some reason. If, in such a case, the judge fails to warn the jury an appeal will be allowed. However, if the judge gives the warning the jury may convict even where the independent support is less than satisfactory. Where the law deems independent support to be essential, the corroboration requirement is strengthened and the judge is required to intervene to prevent the jury considering the case unless independent support exists.

The modern trend, as exemplified by the Evidence Act recently adopted in Australia, is to abolish any rule based on the view that independent support is essential (Evidence Act 1995 (Cth) and (NSW), s. 164). Instead, emphasis is put on providing an appropriate warning to the jury whenever the facts of the case require it (*Longman v. The Queen (1989) 168*

CLR 79; Evidence Act 1995 (Cth) and (NSW) s. 165(2)). There is authority for the proposition that such a warning will be required whenever criminal charges are based on recovered memory whether or not that fact is explored in the course of the trial (*R v. Hyatt*). This is the approach that is supported by Lewis and Mullis (1999) in their recent article in the *Law Quarterly Review*.

There is, however, a question as to whether a warning is sufficient in this context. A warning puts the matter into the hands of the jury. Long before criminal charges fall to be decided by the jury, the defendant will have suffered incalculable damage. Were corroboration essential, the matter will be disposed of much more quickly. The prosecuting authorities will consider the question of whether corroboration exists before bringing charges and will decline to proceed in the absence of corroboration. Even if the discretion of the prosecuting authorities miscarries, the trial judge will intervene and dismiss the charges as soon as the absence of corroboration becomes apparent. To make corroboration essential to found a charge, legislative intervention would be necessary. Such intervention is unlikely.

Another approach is to require independent support or corroboration before testimony can be received from a witness who has undergone therapy, as in *Borawick v. Shay*. This approach may be taken in both civil and criminal cases. The effect is to make corroboration mandatory without legislative action. Given the problems with recovered memories from a legal perspective, discussed in the first part of this chapter, requiring corroboration for recovered memory evidence is strongly recommended. Even if the majority of recovered memories can be shown to be essentially reliable, the case at hand may be in the minority of cases where the memory is not reliable. In such a case the fragmentary nature of recovered memories means that crucial details from a legal perspective may be the product of confabulation.

In Australia, it is unlikely that a prosecution will succeed without corroborative evidence. Even if a conviction is secured from a jury, an appellate court has the power to set aside a conviction if it is of the opinion that the verdict of the jury is unreasonable or cannot be supported, having regard to the evidence. In 1997 the New South Wales Court of Appeal used this power to set aside a conviction which relied on recovered memory (*R v. Eishauer*). The decision was reached by a majority of two to one in circumstances where in fact there appeared to be independent support for the conviction. Sperling J stated that the decision should not be taken as indicating that "a case of sexual abuse of a child can never be made out where a memory of events is absent for some time and later comes to be experienced. Every case must turn on its own facts." Nonetheless, the decision suggests that it may in future be very difficult to obtain a conviction in a case where the prosecution is based on a recovered memory. The Franklin case was also ultimately disposed of by the exercise of similar powers vested in an appellate court.

Disclosure

It may appear that many of the more cumbersome precautions that the legal system brings into play when dealing with recovered memory could be avoided by omitting to mention that the memory is recovered. There are strong ethical objections to concealing from an opponent in the context of any litigation the fact that the memory relied upon has apparently been lost and then recovered. In the context of the criminal law there is a strong obligation on the prosecution to disclose relevant material to the defendants (*R v. Maguire; Alister v. The Queen (1984) 154 CLR 404*). Where the disclosure obligations are not discharged (as in *R v. CPK*) the appellate court will have no difficulty in allowing the appeal. Further penalties may follow under the court's power to deal with contempt.

Given that the common law trial system is adversarial it does not follow from the obligation to disclose the facts to the opponent that these facts will necessarily be put into evidence. There is an instance of a recent case (*R v. Hyatt*) in which the facts were not put into evidence as a result of a deliberate choice of the defence. The prosecution resulted from a memory recovered by the niece of the defendant. Memory recovery occurred when her daughter told the accusing witness of an indecent assault by her great-uncle. The defence chose not to raise the issue of recovered memory at the trial because the trial judge had ruled that such questions would allow into court evidence of what the daughter had told her mother. An appeal against conviction was dismissed.

ACTION AGAINST THE THERAPIST

Therapists who go beyond assisting clients to recover and deal with their memories of childhood abuse may be liable for professional negligence in actions brought by their clients. In order to succeed in an action for negligence the plaintiff must establish four things. The plaintiff must show (1) that a duty of care was owed by the defendant to the plaintiff, (2) that that duty was breached, (3) that damage resulted from the breach and (4) that the damage was reasonably foreseeable. Negligence in professional practice is assessed with reference to the prevailing standards that the relevant profession observes at the time when the breach of duty is alleged to have occurred. For this reason therapists would be well advised to observe the precautions recommended by their professional association as representing "best practice" in dealing with recovered memories. The courts faced with a negligence action will consider advice given in the reports of professional bodies, such as that of the Working Party of the British Psychological Society (1995).

Two American cases in which the therapist was found liable for professional malpractice in the context of alleged recovered memories illustrate the circumstances in which such liability might be found. In *Joyce-Couch v. De Silva* the therapist was found liable in negligence after she conducted 141 to 171 sodium pentothal interviews with an adult client thought to be a survivor of childhood sexual abuse. The therapist had failed to reveal to the client the information gathered through the interviews, had continued the injections of pentothal even while the client's condition worsened and had lied about the treatment and its effect in response to direct questions. In another case an action against the therapist succeeded after the therapist had subjected a 9-year-old child to great pressure to induce her to identify her rapist as her father (*James W v. Superior Court*). The child had clearly stated that the rapist was not her father and there was extrinsic evidence suggesting that a stranger had committed the rape.

Much more problematic is the liability of the therapist to persons who are not clients. In *Ramona v. Isabella* the therapists were held liable to the alleged abuser. This case has caused considerable concern to therapists. It should be noted, however, that the finding against the therapists was based on the fact that they were involved in various ways in bringing the father into the process by helping to arrange the confrontation. One therapist was present at the meeting. This meant that they owed a duty of care to the father as someone directly involved in their therapeutic work. Therapists who heed the warnings the Ramona case contains should have no difficulty in avoiding liability.

As a matter of precedent, the *Ramona* case was a liberal interpretation of the liberal Californian laws on professional negligence (Brown et al., 1998, pp. 556–567). It is clearly, therefore, exceptional. To the extent that it is a precedent, there are good arguments why it should not be followed. Bowman and Mertz (1996, p. 638) argue strongly that therapists should not be held liable to third parties against the wishes of the therapist's client. It is their view that the courts should not allow malpractice claims when fully competent adult patients or clients do not believe that they have suffered malpractice. Instead they suggest that the third party's remedy should lie against the source, the survivor whose false memories have occasioned the damage rather than the therapist. One reason why it is problematic to say that the therapist owes a duty of care to the alleged abuser is that this duty may conflict with the therapist's duty to the client. In North America, this is likely to be seen as a fiduciary duty (Frankel, 1993). A fiduciary owes a duty of loyalty to the client and must refrain from having an inconsistent loyalty or obligation. If the therapist owed a duty of care to an alleged abuser then it would be impossible to reconcile this duty with his or her duty to the client. In Britain and Australia, such a case would probably not be analysed in terms of fiduciary obligation, but the same argument could be made as a matter of tort law.

CONCLUSION

There are some reasons to suggest that in the legal realm the middle ground on recovered memories has been found. The problems that arise out of the recognition that memory is not immutable and that psychiatric and psychological therapies can affect memory have not always been handled well. The courts are now tending to take an approach that will prevent the application of criminal sanctions where no other evidence is available, but will allow for the possibility of criminal sanctions where there is other evidence.

Civil actions are not formally subject to the same constraints in this regard. However, it is reasonable to expect that the demands of the system in the shape of costs and the realistic assessment of claims will tend to put an emphasis on independent support for evidence in the civil process as well. The nature of the question in the legal context dictates that caution should be taken with recovered memories, and that only where there is corroborative evidence should recovered memories be used as the basis of legal sanctions.

Lewis and Mullis (1999) suggest that there is a choice to be made between two uncomfortable positions. Either some innocent men will be the victims of the miscarriage of justice or some abused women will see their abusers walk free. The latter, they say, is extremely undesirable, but the former is intolerable. We agree completely with these sentiments.

Bowman and Mertz (1996) suggested that inquiry into remembered childhood sexual abuse is better suited to the interpretative methods of the social sciences than to the legal arena. We can endorse this suggestion and the suggestion that the legal system should foster and protect a slow and careful therapy process, giving therapist and client time to rethink and develop interpretations.

REFERENCES

Acts

Limitation Act 1969 (NSW).
Evidence Act 1995 (Cth) and (NSW).

Cases

Alister v. The Queen (1984) 154 CLR 404.
Borawick v. Shay, 68 F 3d 597; 1995 US App LEXIS 29707 (2nd Cir, 1995).
Callahan v. State, 464 NW 2d 268 (Iowa 1990).
Daly v. Derrick, 281 Cal Rptr 709 (Ct App, 1991).
Daubert v. Merrell Dow Pharmaceuticals, Inc. (1993) 509 US 579, 589, 125 L Ed 2d 469, 113 S Ct 2786.
DeRose v. Carswell, 242 Cal Rptr 368 (Ct App, 1987).
Farrell v. The Queen (1998) 155 ALR 652; 22 ALJR 1292.
HG v. The Queen [1999] HCA 2 (9 February 1999).
James W v. Superior Court (Goodfriend) 21 Cal Rptr 2d 169, 170 (Ct App, 1993).
Johnson v. Johnson, 701 F Supp 1363 (1988).
Joyce-Couch v. De Silva, 602 NE 2d 286 (Ohio Ct App 1991).
Longman v. The Queen (1989) 168 CLR 79.
McQueen v. Garrison, 814 F 2d 951 (4th Cir, 1987).
Molien v. Kaiser Foundation Hospitals (1980) 616 P 2d 813 (Cal 1980).
People v. Guerra, 37 Cal App 3d 385; 690 P 2d 635 (Cal SC 1984).
People v. Shirley, 31 Cal 3d 18; 723 P 2d 1354 (Cal SC 1982).
R v. Browning (*The Independent*, 17 May 1994); (1995) Crim LR 227.
R v. CPK (1995) No. 60330/94 (21 June 1995) (NSW CCA) unreported.
R v. Eishauer, No 60593/96 (19 September 1997) (NSW CCA) unreported.
R v. Hyatt (1998) 4 VR 182.
R v. Jenkyns (1993) 32 NSWLR 712.
R v. Mcfelin (1985) 2 NZLR 750.
R v. Tillott (1995) 38 NSWLR 1.
Ramona v. Isabella, No. 61898 (Cal Super Ct, 13 May 1994)
Roughley, Marshall and Haywood v. R (1995) 78 A Crim R 160.
S v. The Queen (1989) 168 CLR 266.
Sprynczynatyk v. General Motors Corp, 771 F 2d 1112 (8th Cir, 1985).
The Queen v. Jumeaux (WA Supreme Court, 23 September 1994, unreported).
United States v. Bighead, 128 F 3d 1329; 1997 US App LEXIS 32237 (9th Cir, 1997)
United States v. Cordoba, 104 F 3d 225 (9th Cir, 1996).
United States v. Rouse, 111 F 3d 561; 1997 US App LEXIS 6659 (8th Cir, 1997).

Books and articles

Australian Psychological Society (1995). Guidelines relating to the reporting of recovered memories. *Bulletin of the Australian Psychological Society*, **17**, 20–21.
Bowman, C. G. & Mertz, E. (1996). A dangerous direction: Legal intervention in sexual abuse survivor therapy. *Harvard Law Review*, **109**, 549–639.
British Psychological Society (1995). *Recovered Memories: The Report of the Working Party of the British Psychological Society*.
Brown, D., Scheflin, A. W. & Hammond, D. C. (1998). *Memory, Trauma Treatment and the Law*. New York: W. W. Norton & Co.
Dalenberg, C.J. (1996). Accuracy, timing and circumstances of disclosure in therapy of recovered and continuous memories of abuse. *Journal of Psychiatry and Law*, **24**, 229–275.
Des Rosiers, N. (1998). *Rethinking credibility from a therapeutic perspective*. Paper presented to XXIIIrd International Congress on Law and Mental Health, Paris.

Frankel, T. (1993). Fiduciary relationship in the United States today. In D Waters (Ed.), *Equity, Fiduciaries and Trusts* (pp. 173–194). Toronto: Carswell.

Harvey M. & Herman, J. (1994). Amnesia, partial amnesia and delayed recall among adult survivors of childhood trauma. *Consciousness and Cognition,* **3,** 295–306.

Holmes, D. (1990). The evidence for repression: An examination of sixty years of research. In J. Singer (Ed.), *Repression and Dissociation: Implications for Personality, Theory, Psychopathology and Health* (pp. 85–102). Chicago: Univ. of Chicago Press.

Johnstone, M. (1997). *Spectral Evidence: The Ramona Case, Incest, Memory and Truth on Trial in Napa Valley.* Boston: Houghton Mifflin Co.

Jones E. & Parkinson P. (1995). Child sexual abuse, access and the wishes of children. *International Journal of Law and the Family,* **9,** 54–85.

Kanovitz, J. (1992). Hypnotic memories and civil sexual abuse trials. *Vanderbilt Law Review,* **45,** 1185–1262.

Lewis, P. & Mullis, A. (1999). Delayed criminal prosecutions for childhood sexual abuse: Ensuring a fair trial. *Law Quarterly Review,* **115,** 265–295.

Lindsay D. & Read, J. (1994). Incest resolution psychotherapy and memories of childhood sexual abuse. *Applied Cognitive Psychology,* **8,** 281–338.

Loftus, E. F. & Ketcham, K. (1994). *The Myth of Repressed Memory: False Memories and Allegations of Sexual Abuse.* New York: St Martin's Press.

Loftus, E. F. (1979). *Eyewitness Testimony,* Cambridge, Mass.: Harvard University Press.

Magner, E. S. (1989). Expert testimony as to credibility. *Australian Bar Review,* **5,** 225–242.

Magner, E. S. (1995). Recovered memories: The Australian position. *Expert Evidence,* **3,** 151–154.

McConkey K. M. & Sheehan, P. W. (1995). *Hypnosis, Memory and Behavior in Criminal Investigation.* New York: The Guilford Press.

McConkey, K.M. (1995). Hypnosis, memory and the ethics of uncertainty. *Australian Psychologist,* **30,** 1–10.

Sales, B. D., Shuman, D. W. & O'Connor M. (1994). In a dim light: Admissibility of child sexual abuse memories. *Applied Cognitive Psychology,* **8,** 399–406.

Spence, D. R. (1982). *Narrative Truth and Historical Truth: Meaning and Interpretation in Psychoanalysis.* New York: W. W. Norton & Co.

Terr, L. (1991). Childhood traumas: An outline and overview. *American Journal of Psychiatry,* **148,** 10–20.

Terr, L. (1994). *Unchained Memories: True Stories of Traumatic Memories, Lost and Found.* New York: Basic Books.

van der Kolk, B. A. & Fisler, R. (1995). Dissociation and the fragmentary nature of traumatic memories: Overview and exploratory study. *Journal of Traumatic Stress,* **8,** 505–525.

van der Kolk, B. A. & van der Hart, O. (1991). The intrusive past. The flexibility of memory and the engraving of trauma. *American Imago,* **48,** 425–454.

Widom C. S. & Morris, S. (1997). Accuracy of adult recollections of childhood victimization: Part 2: Childhood sexual abuse. *Psychological Assessment,* **9,** 34–46.

Widom C. S. & Shepard R. L. (1996). Accuracy of adult recollections of childhood victimization: Part 1: Childhood physical abuse. *Psychological Assessment,* **8,** 412–421.

Williams, L. M. (1994). Recall of childhood trauma: A prospective study of women's memories of child sexual abuse. *Journal of Consulting and Clinical Psychology,* **62,** 1167–1176.

Williams, L. M. (1995). Recovered memories of abuse in women with documented child sexual victimization histories. *Journal of Traumatic Stress, 8*, 649–673.

PART II

EVIDENTIAL ASPECTS

5

THE RECOVERED MEMORIES CONTROVERSY: WHERE DO WE GO FROM HERE?

D. Stephen Lindsay and J. Don Read

The greatest psychological controversy of the 1990s (and perhaps of the latter half of the twentieth century) concerned cases of "recovered memories" of childhood sexual abuse (CSA). Debate focused on cases in which women who initially believed they had not experienced CSA reported recovered memories of sexual abuse after exposure to CSA-memory-oriented psychotherapy. Especially in the early years of the debate, perspectives on such cases were highly polarized, with critics of CSA-memory-oriented psychotherapies claiming that recovered-memory experiences are iatrogenic illusions (e.g. Ofshe & Watters, 1994) and counter-critics suggesting that such claims are motivated by a desire to minimize CSA and protect perpetrators (e.g. Pope, 1996). This topic, which was the focus of hundreds of publications in the 1990s, featured prominently in the popular media and in prestigious psychology journals (e.g. *American Psychologist*, the flagship journal of the American Psychological Association, and *The Psychologist*, that of the British Psychological Society). Major professional societies representing a variety of constituencies in a number of countries produced

Recovered Memories: Seeking the Middle Ground. Edited by Graham M. Davies and Tim Dalgleish. © 2001 John Wiley & Sons Ltd.

policy statements and guidelines on recovered memories (see Grunberg & Ney, 1997, for a review of 10 such publications). Recovered memory cases led to legislative reforms, civil and criminal prosecutions of alleged abusers, and law suits against therapists by former clients and parents (see Underwager & Wakefield, 1998).

As discussed by Lindsay and Briere (1997), numerous psychological and sociological factors converged to make the public and professional debate about recovered memories deeply divisive and fiercely contentious. Happily, as the 1990s draw to a close the fury of the "memory wars" is gradually subsiding, and professionals engaged in the debate are increasingly emphasizing points of consensus. In this chapter, we first briefly summarize these emerging points of agreement and then turn to a consideration of the numerous scientific questions left in the wake of the controversy. It is our hope and belief that the painful and destructive controversy of the last decade of the twentieth century will bear fruit in the form of exciting new research in the first decade of the twenty-first.

WHERE HERE IS

There is near-universal agreement that individuals who experienced sexual abuse in post-infancy childhood sometimes do not remember in adulthood that they were abused, and that such individuals can sometimes remember the long-forgotten abuse when appropriately cued (e.g. Freyd, 1997, p. 1; Loftus, 1997, p. 191; Pendergrast, 1996, pp. 89–94, 536; Underwager & Wakefield, 1998, p. 402.). Similarly, there is near-universal agreement that suggestive influences can sometimes lead adults who were not sexually abused during childhood to believe, falsely, that they did experience such abuse, and that highly suggestive practices must be avoided in trauma-oriented psychotherapy (e.g. Briere, 1997, pp. 26–27; Courtois, 1997). It is not so much that agreement on these points is new, but rather that professionals on each side of the controversy have come increasingly to acknowledge and even highlight in their published and spoken statements the legitimate concerns of those on the other. Modest as these points of consensus may appear, embracing both of them provides the essential foundation for a shift away from polarized debate and toward constructive engagement with the research questions raised by accurate and illusory recovered memory experiences: How and why does each of these phenomena occur, how prevalent is each, and what are their practical implications (e.g. for psychotherapy and for legal practice)?

HOW AND WHY

It is fittingly ironic that the decade of the recovered memories contro-versy was also the vaunted "Decade of the Brain" in the United States.[1] Technological breakthroughs enabling measurement of the active human brain (e.g. functional magnetic resonance imaging and event-related potential encephalography), harnessed in well-funded interdisciplinary collaborations between research psychologists, neurologists, and tech-nologists, have greatly sped the acquisition of knowledge of the brain's structure and functions, including memory. Concurrently, cognitive psy-chologists have developed formal models of mental processes, some-times instantiated in connectionist computer networks that well simulate human performance of certain memory tasks.

The rate of progress in the science of memory has been dramatic, but despite the wealth of beautifully coloured images of the brain during performance of memory tasks, and despite the proliferation of sophisti-cated cognitive models of memory, science is still far short of an under-standing of how memory works. We can point to certain brain structures (e.g. the hippocampus, particular regions of the frontal lobes, etc.) and say with considerable confidence that they play particular roles in various memory tasks, and we can enumerate the neurotransmitters secreted in those areas and describe the operation of the cellular gates by which electrochemical activation is transmitted from one neuron to another, but we have little idea of how these cells and chemicals give rise to recollections of past experiences.

What exactly is going on in the brain when, for example, you remem-ber the first time you rode a bicycle? Various densely interconnected con-stellations of neurons increase or decrease their rates of action potentials, consequently increasing or decreasing the activation of other neurons and, *voilà!* you experience an echo of the butterflies and the pride mingled with fear of that long-past event, and see yourself (perhaps from an exter-nal perspective quite different from that of the experience itself) peddling madly away. To date, neuroscience can explain memory phenomena such as this only in the most vague terms (cf. Bub, 2000). Similarly, formal mathematical models of memory perform quite well at fitting data from highly constrained memory tasks (e.g. yes/no decisions as to whether or not words on a test list had previously appeared on a study list), but at this point it is difficult to choose between competing models and in any case none provides anything like a satisfying account of autobiographical reminiscence. Cognitive psychologists specializing in autobiographical

---

[1] (for the Presidential Proclamation of the Decade of the Brain, see http://lcweb.loc.gov/loc/brain/proclaim.html).

memory have identified a number of general principles and hypothesized various mechanisms (see, e.g., Cohen, 1996; Stein, Ornstein, Tversky & Brainerd, 1997), but at this stage these theories are not well specified and hence do not enable precise predictions.

In short, the contemporary science of memory leaves ample room for debate as to accounts of forgetting, remembering, and confabulating memories of CSA in adulthood, and there are many questions sorely in need of empirical investigation. The following paragraphs highlight some of these questions.

HOW AND WHY DO SOME PEOPLE WHO EXPERIENCED CSA COME TO FORGET THAT THEY WERE ABUSED?

The mystery of memory would be considerably simplified if forgetting did not occur. Memory researchers would still have to grapple with questions such as how experience is represented and stored in the brain and how it is retrieved, but without the problem of forgetting, the task of understanding memory would be much easier. People do forget, however, and the question of how and why individuals remember some things and forget others is a central issue for memory scientists.

Everyday experience and research evidence converge in demonstrating that a person who appears to have forgotten a particular event when tested under one constellation of conditions may reveal excellent memory for that event when tested under other conditions. You may, for example, find that you cannot now recall the name of the man who became Prime Minister of Israel in 1999. Receiving additional cues (e.g. being told that the name begins with the letter "B") might enable you to recall the name. Even if cues do not enable recall—and even if you have the subjective sense that you simply do not know this information—you may immediately recognize "Barak" as the correct name. If so, the memory information was available (i.e. represented in the brain) and although it was not accessible under the conditions of the recall tests, it was accessible under the conditions of the recognition test. Furthermore, under a given set of testing conditions one may remember some aspects of a particular past experience but not others (e.g. remembering that a particular event happened but not when or where; Johnson, Hashtroudi & Lindsay, 1993). Relatedly, an individual may know that he or she had a particular experience (e.g. a tonsillectomy) in the past yet not recollect any episodic details of that experience (e.g. Gardiner & Java, 1991). Research on "implicit" memory demonstrates that even when memories of past events do not give rise to a feeling of remembering or knowing on a recognition test, they may nonetheless influence performance on indirect tests of memory. For example, prior auditory exposure to polysemous words in a disambiguating context (e.g. "taxi fare") can bias spelling of the critical words on a subsequent dictation task (e.g. "fare" rather than the more common "fair") even when individuals do not recognize the items from the initial word list (Eich, 1984). Interestingly, manipulations at study, at test, or between study and test that affect memory on one kind of test may have no effect (or even opposite effects) on other kinds of memory tests (for review, see Kelley & Lindsay, 1996). Thus forgetting is far from an all-or-none phenomenon: We may forget a particular event in some senses and/or in some contexts but not in others, and multiple mechanisms may contribute to various forms of forgetting.

It is likely, therefore, that there is no single answer to the question of how some adults come to forget CSA. This is partly because there are various senses in which a person might be said to have forgotten abuse (e.g. not recalling the abuse because cues had not been encountered or had not been sufficiently specific; remembering some details or episodes of the abuse while forgetting others; failing to remember any episodic details of the abuse while retaining knowledge that it occurred; forgetting in such a way that the abuse would not be recollected under any conditions but the memories of it might nonetheless influence behaviour and experience; entirely forgetting, in such a way that the system is unaffected by the past experience). Different mechanisms may be involved in different kinds or senses of forgetting.

Even for a given definition of forgetting, it may be that different mechanisms are involved in different sorts of CSA cases. For example, forgetting of abuse that occurred during the first two years of life can be attributed to infantile amnesia (Eacott, 1999; Eacott & Crawley, 1998; Fivush, 1998; Fivush & Hamond, 1990), which appears to be related to developmental changes in brain structure and function more than to psychosocial factors. In post-infancy, some forms of abuse may be experienced as ambiguous or confusing but not particularly salient or meaningful, whereas other forms of abuse may be experienced as overtly traumatic, and different mechanisms may account for forgetting of cases along this continuum. Forgetting of abuse that occurred early in childhood outside of the child's regular environment may differ from forgetting of familial abuse. So too, abuse that occurred repeatedly, in a regularly scripted pattern, may be forgotten via different mechanisms (and/or in different senses) than isolated instances of abuse. Finally, even given a specific definition of forgetting and a well-specified category of abuse cases, there may be variation across individuals in forgetting mechanisms.

A central question raised by the recovered memories controversy is whether or not forgetting of CSA entails the operation of a special traumagenic amnesia mechanism, qualitatively distinct from the mechanisms that underlie forgetting of other sorts of childhood experiences (e.g. poor encoding, lack of rehearsal, lack of appropriate external and internal cues). The points made in the preceding paragraph suggest that ordinary mechanisms of forgetting may be sufficient to explain at least some cases of forgetting of CSA (e.g. failures to recall isolated instances of non-violent abuse that occurred in early childhood). There is room for debate as to whether or not a special traumagenic forgetting mechanism underlies forgetting of other forms of CSA and, if so, what kinds of abuse histories can be forgotten only via such a special mechanism.

The question of whether or not forgetting of CSA entails a special mechanism is analogous to the controversy regarding so-called flashbulb memories—unusually vivid and detailed recollections of the circumstances in which one learned of a very surprising and personally significant event (e.g. John Lennon's murder). Brown and Kulik (1977) proposed that humans are biologically equipped with a special mechanism that engages on such occasions and creates extremely vivid and durable memories. Debate continues as to whether flashbulb memories reflect the operation of a special mechanism or the "ordinary" effects of such factors as salience, distinctiveness, and rehearsal. People often experience extraordinarily detailed, long-lasting recollections of significant events, but critics of the flashbulb-mechanism hypothesis note that such recollections are not necessarily accurate, are affected by the same variables that affect other recollections, and are not restricted to momentous events (see, e.g., Winograd & Neisser, 1992, for reviews). These critics argue that flashbulb events foster the use of ordinary mechanisms that lead to vivid (albeit imperfect) memories: In the words of Christianson (1989), flashbulb memories are "special, but not so special." Some cognitive psychologists, however, argue that flashbulb memories cannot be explained entirely in terms of ordinary mechanisms of memory (e.g. Conway, 1995).

Returning to the question of the mechanisms that underlie forgetting of CSA, intuition suggests that there are limitations on the kinds of CSA histories that could be forgotten via ordinary mechanisms of forgetting. For example, it seems counter-intuitive that a person could "simply forget" having been forcibly raped as a young child. It does seem likely that there are limits on the sorts of histories that can be forgotten via ordinary mechanisms, but it may be that a systematic bias leads people to have inaccurate intuitions about the likelihood of forgetting dramatic childhood experiences: People can recollect all of the important, dramatic childhood experiences that they can recollect, and they rarely encounter evidence of the important, dramatic childhood experiences that they have forgotten. Ongoing research in our labs indicates that forgetting of significant childhood and adolescent experiences may be substantially more common than intuition would suggest (Lindsay, Read, Hyman & Schooler, 1999; see also Henry, Moffitt, Caspi, Langly & Silva, 1994; Loftus, 1993; Read, 1997).

Given the limitations of intuition, it is clear that we must instead rely on carefully conducted empirical investigations of the forgetting of CSA. Unfortunately, most studies that have attempted to shed light on the mechanisms by which CSA is forgotten suffer from two major limitations. One limitation is that most of the studies have used a retrospective design, in which adults who currently report having experienced CSA are asked about prior periods during which they did not remember the abuse. One problem with this approach is that it necessarily excludes individuals who experienced abuse but do not currently remember it. Furthermore, it is not clear what it means when individuals in such studies report prior periods of not remembering (e.g. do they mean that they avoided thinking about the abuse, that they had not encountered cues that would have led them to think of it, or that they were completely unaware of having such a history even though they encountered relevant cues?). Melchert and Parker (1997) found that 20% of their sample who reported a CSA history also reported prior periods without memory for the abuse, but these respondents often indicated that they were referring to intentional avoidance of thinking about the abuse rather than to amnesia for it; Williams (1995) likewise reported that some of the women in her sample who reported prior periods of not remembering a documented instance of CSA indicated that they were referring to times during which they avoided thinking about the abuse.

Even if researchers devised questionnaires that would adequately clarify what respondents mean when they report prior periods of not remembering, there are reasons to be sceptical of people's ability to make accurate retrospective assessments of prior non-remembering. For example, Schooler, Ambadar and Bendiksen (1997) reported two cases in which individuals who reported newly recovered memories had apparently told others about the abuse during the time when they were allegedly unaware of their abuse histories. Furthermore, Belli, Winkielman, Read, Schwarz and Lynn (1998) and Read and Lindsay (2000) reported evidence that, having recently engaged in efforts to remember childhood events, can dramatically alter an individuals assessment of his or her ability to remember. Therefore, the fact that all or many of the respondents in several of the retrospective self-report studies published to date had previously been involved in CSA-memory-oriented psychotherapy further complicates the interpretation of their results. Because of the ambiguities of retrospective self-report designs, prospective designs, such as those employed by Williams (1994) and Widom (1997), have much greater potential informativeness.

The second major limitation of existing research on the mechanisms of forgetting CSA is that hardly any of the studies have included assessment of forgetting of non-CSA events. Such studies have implied that reports of prior periods of partial or complete forgetting of CSA can be taken as evidence of partial or complete traumagenic amnesia for CSA. As noted by Read (1997) and Read and Lindsay (2000), it is essential to include appropriate controls if one wishes to test hypotheses about the special nature of forgetting of CSA. For example, Read found that a non-trivial minority of a community sample reported prior periods of partial or complete lack of memory for a wide variety of kinds of childhood events (e.g. music lessons). The point here is not to dismiss the hypothesis that there is a special traumagenic amnesia mechanism, but rather merely to point out the need for more and better research on this issue (i.e. prospective designs with appropriate control conditions).

Just as in the debate about flashbulb memories, it will likely prove difficult to bring definitive evidence to bear on the question of whether or not a special mechanism underlies forgetting of CSA. For one thing, "ordinary" mechanisms of memory are complex, interactive, and as yet incompletely understood, making it difficult to distinguish them from a hypothesized traumagenic amnesia mechanism. For another thing, some of the hypothesized "special mechanisms" bear a striking resemblance to "ordinary mechanisms". It may be difficult, for example, to draw a clear distinction between the clinical construct of dissociation and the "ordinary" cognitive constructs of divided attention and poor encoding.

The cases that most demand the postulation of a special mechanism of forgetting, if they are to be accepted as accurate, are those in which individuals report new memories of a horrific history of years of violent abuse of which they were previously utterly unaware. For example, the case that engaged our interest in the recovered memories controversy involved a middle-aged woman who had by all accounts been on good terms with her father throughout her adult life, and had no memories or beliefs about abuse, but who then experienced (over the course of two years of intensive therapy with a CSA-memory-oriented counsellor) new memories of multiple instances of bizarre and tortuous abuse by her father and neighbourhood men. Although the limitations of "ordinary" mechanisms of forgetting are not known, it seems unlikely that they could account for such cases. Our opinion is that such cases are best understood in terms of illusory memories and false beliefs, rather than in terms of mechanisms of forgetting. It must be acknowledged, however, that current scientific knowledge does not enable us to draw a clear line between CSA histories that could v. could not plausibly be forgotten and then recovered.

GIVEN FORGETTING OF CSA, HOW AND WHY WOULD MEMORIES BE RECOVERED?

The notion of "transfer appropriate processing" (TAP) (Roediger, Weldon & Challis, 1989) provides a useful framework for understanding memory recovery. According to TAP, the likelihood that memories of a past experience will be accessed is determined by the degree of similarity between current cognitive processes and cognitive processes performed when the event occurred. For example, if your current cognitive processes become similar to those you performed at breakfast this morning, you may experience recollections of breakfast. Mentally processing information related to breakfast (e.g. reading the word "breakfast", smelling bacon, experiencing a hunger pang, stepping into your kitchen, etc.) causes current cognitive processes to resemble those performed at breakfast, and if the similarity is sufficiently great and distinctive it will cue recollections of breakfast. Thus any factor that increases the similarity of current cognitive processing to processing performed during a particular past experience (e.g. providing verbal or environmental cues that reconstitute aspects of cognitive processing during the past experience; inducing an affective state similar to that of the past experience, etc.) will increase the likelihood that memories of that experience will be accessed.

Cognitive principles of memory such as those described above have been implemented in the Cognitive Interview, a technique designed to maximize the amount of accurate information that eyewitnesses provide to forensic investigators (e.g. Fisher, 1995). Research on the Cognitive Interview indicates that techniques such as context reinstatement and instructions to recall witnessed events from a variety of perspectives can substantially increase the amount of accurate information recalled, without affecting (or, in the case of children, only slightly increasing) the incidence of false recall (see Memon, 1998).

These ideas are also consonant with those offered by some CSA-memory-oriented clinicians. The TAP perspective suggests that some forms of psychotherapy may encourage essentially accurate recollections of long-forgotten CSA, because such therapies orient clients toward thinking about their childhoods, may present rarely discussed cues associated with long-forgotten events, and may re-establish rare affective and cognitive states that facilitate retrieval of memories of prior occurrences of similar states (Lindsay & Briere, 1997).

It is important to emphasize that the subjective experience of remembering does not arise necessarily and exclusively from "retrieval" of memory "traces". Accessing information about a past experience is not a matter of moving an object from one spatial location in the brain to another, but rather a matter of partially reinstating the pattern of cognitive processing performed during the past experience. Also people can reactivate and use memory information about a specific past event without having the feeling of remembering (as in involuntary plagiarism and other examples of implicit memory), and can have the feeling of remembering events that never occurred in their pasts (as in *déjà vu* and other sorts of illusory memories).

These and related findings led Jacoby, Kelley and Dywan (1989) to argue that the subjective experience of remembering arises when people attribute aspects of their current mental experience to memory (see also Johnson et al., 1993). Several factors are thought to be involved in determining whether a mental event is experienced as a memory rather than as a product of perception, inference, or fantasy. For example, because using memory typically facilitates processing (e.g. it is easier to form an image of a face by reactivating memories of a previously seen face than by using imagination to construct an image of a never-seen face), people have a bias to attribute fluent images to memory. The person's current orientation and expectations also matter: People are more likely to experience an image or idea as a memory if they are trying to remember something when it comes to mind than if they are otherwise oriented. Thus a vivid image that is fluently generated during an attempt to remember is likely to be experienced as a memory. This hypothesis is supported by studies in which manipulations that cause non-studied items to come fluently to mind at test sometimes lead people to mistake those thoughts as memories (e.g. Kelley & Jacoby, 1998; Lindsay & Kelley, 1996; Whittlesea, 1993; Whittlesea & Williams, 1998).

In summary, existing evidence and theory suggest that long-forgotten memories of CSA may be remembered (i.e. "recovered") if conditions lead individuals to (a) partially reinstate patterns of cognitive processing that are similar to those performed during the abuse and (b) be oriented toward attributing thoughts, feelings, and images to memory. Considerable research is needed, however, to assess the extent to which these ideas, which are based primarily on laboratory research, can indeed be generalized to real-world recovered memory cases.

HOW AND WHY CAN NON-ABUSED ADULTS COME FALSELY TO BELIEVE THAT THEY WERE ABUSED?

This question has been the focus of prior publications by a number of cognitive psychologists (e.g., Hyman & Billings, 1998; Lindsay & Read, 1994; Loftus, 1993, 1997), and space considerations prohibit a detailed review of the relevant theories and data here. Briefly, a century of research on eyewitness suggestibility effects and other memory errors demonstrates that people sometimes experience illusory recollections of events that did not really occur. Research indicates that false memories are most likely when suggestive influences are strong and concern an event or time period that is poorly remembered. Suggestions increase in strength if they are given by an authority figure, are perceived as plausible and are not perceived as overtly misleading, are encountered repeatedly, or are presented in ways that evoke vivid images or encourage the recipient to accept thoughts, images, and feelings as accurate memories. Some individuals may be more susceptible to suggestive influence than others (perhaps because they are more responsive to authority, less analytically critical in their thinking style, or have more vivid imagery than other individuals) (Eisen & Carlson, 1998; Heaps & Nash, 1999; Hyman & Billings, 1998; Schooler & Loftus, 1993).

It was noted above that remembering of long-forgotten events occurs when current conditions lead an individual to (a) partially reinstate patterns of cognitive processing that are similar to those performed during the abuse and (b) be oriented toward attributing thoughts, feelings, and images to memory. So too, illusory memories occur when conditions lead an individual to (a) create patterns of cognitive processing (via imagination, perhaps blended with veridical memories) like those that would have occurred during abuse and (b) be oriented toward attributing such mental events to memory. Ironically, many of the same conditions that would probably assist an individual in recovering essentially accurate memories (e.g. use of guided imagery to mentally reinstate context, encouragement to work at remembering and not to be critical or doubtful about the historical accuracy of whatever comes to mind) would also promote illusory memory experiences.

Although extant research enables us to identify numerous factors that modulate the likelihood that suggestive influences will lead to false beliefs, much remains to be discovered about how these factors interact with one another. For example, comparisons both across and within studies demonstrate that, all else being equal, it is easier to create false memory reports regarding a peripheral detail in a passively witnessed event than to create false memory reports regarding a dramatic life event. Furthermore, it has been demonstrated that if suggestive influences are sufficiently strong, and if the suggested event is said to have happened long ago, false memory reports of fairly dramatic childhood life events can be obtained in a substantial minority of adult participants (e.g. Hyman & Billings, 1998; Loftus & Pickrell, 1995; Porter, Yuille & Lehman, 1999; Spanos, Burgess, Burgess, Samuels & Blois, 1999; see also Gudjonsson's [e.g. 1992] work on interrogative suggestibility and false confessions; for a recent review of related suggestibility effects in children, see Poole & Lindsay, 1998). Yet we are far short of a detailed understanding of the way the various factors that determine the strength of suggestive influences combine with one another and interact with the content of the suggestions and with individual differences. Specific claims regarding the likelihood that a particular constellation of suggestive influences would lead to particular kinds of false memory reports in specific individuals must await the development of such an understanding.

It would be unethical to conduct experiments designed to assess the likelihood that particular forms of suggestive influences will lead to particular kinds of false memories of CSA. Therefore researchers can only (a) conduct experiments using analogue suggestions that meet ethical requirements yet can plausibly be generalized to false memories of CSA (e.g. Hyman & Billings, 1998; Loftus & Pickrell, 1995; Porter et al., 1999; Spanos et al., 1999) and (b) use survey and case study methodologies to assess the extent to which the principles appear to fit actual cases of illusory recovered-memory experiences (e.g. Dalenberg, 1997; de Rivera, 1997; Gudjonsson, 1992). Given the limitations of these approaches, experts on both sides of this issue will have to continue to be cautious in their claims regarding specific recovered memory cases.

Most if not all published experimental studies of suggestibility have used suggestions of quite specific events. For example, Hyman and his co-workers have suggested to young adults that when they were 5 years old they knocked over a punch bowl at the head table at a wedding reception. Clients receiving CSA-memory-oriented psychotherapy may be exposed to comparably specific suggestions (e.g. by hearing or reading other people's accounts of CSA), but it is likely that CSA-memory-oriented therapies usually impart much more general suggestions regarding a broad category of events (i.e. suggestions that the client experienced some form of CSA). On the one hand, highly specific suggestions provide detailed external support for images that could subsequently be misidentified as memories. On the other hand, more general suggestions are less likely to be dismissed as implausible, and leave more room for the free use of imagination and for the intermingling of veridical memories and products of imagination. Research is needed comparing the effects of highly specific versus general suggestions on illusory memories.

Although discussions of suggestibility have emphasized false memories, it is worth noting that real-world cases in which reports of CSA emerged via highly suggestive therapies may not always involve false memories per se. It is clear that some individuals do experience vivid and perceptually detailed pseudomemories (e.g. of satanic ritual abuse or alien abductions), but others may simply come to believe that suggested events happened, without experiencing pseudomemories of those events. This, too, is an area in need of investigation.

To date, little is known about the impact of misleading suggestions to the effect that an event had *not* occurred. It may be harder to "erase" recollections than to create pseudomemories, because a suggestion that X did not occur would be a good cue to retrieve memories of X's occurrence (leading recipients immediately to reject the suggestion as inaccurate); in contrast, failing to retrieve memories in response to a positive suggestion would not provide a basis for rejecting the suggestion as inaccurate (unless recipients were sure they would remember the suggested event if it had occurred).

We are aware of only two studies on the effects of "erasing" suggestions. In a study by Pezdek and Roe (1997), some 4- and 10-year-old children who were touched innocuously during an interaction with the experimenter later received a suggestion that no touching had occurred. Other children received a suggestion to the effect that a different form of innocuous touching had occurred. Yet other children were not touched at all, and some of these received a suggestion to the effect that they had been touched. Only the changed-touch suggestion distorted children's reports of touching during a final interview, perhaps because the event to which the suggestion pertained was very recent and/or because the suggestibility manipulation was quite weak (i.e. a passing comment). In contrast, Wright, Loftus and Hall (2001) found that when a scene in a previously witnessed event was omitted from a post-event narrative description of that event, participants were subsequently less likely to recall or recognize that scene on a final memory test, and that this "erasure" effect was comparable in size to that of post event suggestions that added false information. This is yet another area in need of vigorous research activity.

HOW OFTEN?

Prevalence of forgetting CSA

A number of studies have reported data that could be used to estimate the prevalence of prior periods of non-remembering of CSA among adults who report a CSA history (see Scheflin & Brown, 1996). Findings range dramatically, from a low of 16% in Williams's (1995) prospective study to a high of 77% in Roe and Schwartz (1996). Unfortunately, such studies suffer from the limitations discussed in the preceding section on mechanisms of forgetting CSA (e.g. uncertainty regarding what respondents mean when they report prior periods of non-remembering, questions about the validity of such retrospective self-reports, concerns about subject-selection procedures and about reactivity). In the two prospective studies published to date, Williams (1994) found that 12% of the 129 women with a documented history of CSA did not report any CSA when interviewed 17 years after the documented abuse, whereas Widom (1997) found that 37% of 94 women with documented histories of CSA denied having experienced CSA when interviewed 20 years later. These different findings may reflect differences in the actual CSA histories of the two samples (e.g. it may be that those in Williams's study had experienced more CSA, or experienced CSA at a later age), differences in the interviewing techniques (e.g. Williams's participants may have been more disclosing or better cued), or any of a number of other differences between the studies. Further research using prospective designs and careful assessments of memory for abuse is needed.

HOW PREVALENT ARE RECOVERED-MEMORY EXPERIENCES?

How commonly do people have recovered memory experiences of various kinds, and in what circumstances? A number of published studies of diverse kinds of restricted samples shed various degrees of light on this question, including:

- surveys of psychotherapists' perceptions of memory recovery phenomena in their clients (e.g. Andrews et al., 1995; Andrews, 1997; Bottoms, Shaver & Goodman, 1996; Palm & Gibson, 1998; Polusny & Follette, 1996; Poole, Lindsay, Memon & Bull, 1995; Pope & Tabachnick, 1995);
- studies of clients who received CSA-memory-oriented therapies (e.g. Briere & Conte, 1993; Dalenberg, 1997; Gold, Hughes & Hohnecker, 1994; Herman & Shatzow, 1987);
- research by specialists in Dissociative Identity Disorder (formerly Multiple Personality Disorder) (e.g. Coons, 1994; Ross et al., 1991);
- surveys of individuals who self-selected on the basis of memory for childhood CSA or other trauma (e.g. Albach, Moorman & Bermond, 1996; Dale & Allen, 1998; Hovdestad & Kristiansen, 1996; van der Kolk & Fisler, 1995);
- Williams's (1994, 1995) prospective study, in which women who reported the documented instance of CSA were asked about prior periods during which they did not remember it;
- Elliott and Briere's (1995) general population self-report survey of 505 US respondents;
- case studies of individuals who experienced recovered memories (e.g. Cheit[2]; Corwin & Olafson, 1997; Schooler et al., 1997);
- self-report surveys of samples from restricted populations, such as undergraduate students (e.g. Melchert & Parker, 1997; Sheiman, 1993), women in a drug rehabilitation program (Loftus, Polonsky & Fullilove, 1994), therapists (Feldman-Summers & Pope, 1994), "retractors" (i.e. individuals who recovered memories that they subsequently decided were illusory—e.g. de Rivera, 1997), and accused parents (e.g. Gudjonsson, 1997).

---

[2] http: / /www.brown.edu/Departments/Taubman[rule]Center/Recovmem/.

Given the conceptual complexity, methodological difficulty, and emotional/political sensitivity of the issues at hand, it is perhaps not surprising that such studies have yielded diverse findings and interpretations regarding the frequency of recovered memory experiences. There is a need for large-scale surveys of the general population to estimate the prevalence of recovered memory experiences and to characterize those experiences along a variety of dimensions (e.g. How often are the memories perceived as false v. accurate by the person who experienced memory recovery, and by others? What if any personality characteristics or situational variables are associated with memory recovery? How often do recovered memory experiences include specific memory images?). To the best of our knowledge, the only general-population survey designed to shed light on any of these issues was that conducted by Elliott and Briere (1995); this is an impressive study in many ways, but like any single study it has limitations (e.g. vague definition of "amnesia", lack of information about how memory recovery came about, etc.).

We suspect that the dramatic sorts of memory recovery experiences that have been the focus of debate, in which individuals who initially believed they experienced no CSA come to remember multiple instances of extreme forms of abuse, are rare in the general population. On the one hand, existing research suggests that only a minority of the population suffers severe forms of CSA (see, e.g., Finkelhor, 1994) and that most people who experienced such abuse remember it (see Alpert et al., 1996; Koss, Tromp & Tharan, 1995). It is also probable that only some of those who do forget ever recover memories of the abuse. Thus it is likely that essentially accurate recovered memory experiences involving severe abuse are quite rare. On the other hand, existing research also indicates that people are unlikely to develop illusory memories of CSA unless they are exposed to quite powerful suggestive influences, and so it is likely that essentially false recovered memory experiences are also rare in the general population, and that they are becoming more rare as use of highly suggestive approaches to memory recovery work diminishes. Although we believe these speculations to be well grounded, systematic research is needed on these issues.

IMPLICATIONS

Is it beneficial for clients to remember CSA?

Despite the widespread popularization of CSA-memory-oriented approaches to psychotherapy in the 1990s, there is little empirical support for such approaches. Indeed, we have not been able to find any published study that tested the hypothesis that adults who initially have no recollections of CSA but who present with certain symptoms thought to be associated with a CSA history benefit from attempts to uncover memories of such events. There are empirical data supporting the idea that adults who are aware of recent sexual assault can benefit from therapies that include attention to and desensitization of abuse memories (e.g. Foa, Rothbaum, Riggs & Murdock, 1991; Resick & Schnicke, 1992), and it may be that CSA-memory-oriented therapies can be helpful for adults who were sexually abused as children, but this is an issue desperately in need of empirical work.

If systematic research does reveal benefits of CSA-memory-oriented therapies for adults (relative to appropriate control treatments), a host of related questions will become pressing. Can procedures be developed to identify which clients are more or less likely to benefit from CSA-memory-oriented therapy? Which approaches to fostering CSA memories are associated with favourable outcomes, and which are not? Are CSA-memory-oriented therapies still effective if steps are taken to reduce risks (e.g. informed consent, limited number or duration of techniques)? How can therapists best support clients who report concerns about a possible CSA history in the absence of memories? Professional organizations (see Grunberg & Ney, 1997) and individual professionals (e.g. Courtois, 1997, 1999) have offered a variety of thoughtful opinions on these issues, together with guidelines for dealing with CSA-memory issues in therapy, but the empirical foundation of such recommendations requires substantial strengthening.

HOW CAN PSYCHOLOGISTS IMPROVE SUPPORT FOR SEQUELAE OF RECOVERED MEMORIES?

Individuals who experience recovered memories of CSA often report that memory recovery was a traumatic experience (e.g. Courtois, 1999). The popular literature promoting CSA-memory-oriented therapy addresses the need for healing from sequelae of recovering memories, including developing alternative forms of social support for people who terminate contact with family members and sever friendships with those who doubt the accusations (e.g. Bass & Davis, 1988; Frederickson, 1992). Further development of effective supports for people who recover memories may benefit from systematic research.

Some people who recover memories later come to doubt or even reject the belief that they were sexually abused, and it is likely that this process also involves considerable psychological stress, especially if the individual had previously confronted a family member with allegations. Thus there is a need for research on efficacious treatment interventions for such people. Similarly, parents accused of having sexually molested their off-spring may also experience psychological suffering, largely attributable to the destruction of their families but also sometimes to stress associated with public humiliation, financial strains imposed by civil suits, or even threats to liberty. The suffering of accused parents may be genuine even when the accusations are partly or entirely valid. There is a need for research on effective psychotherapies for such individuals, as well as for the development of ways of helping families to cope with disintegration and, where appropriate, reintegration. Finally, therapists who work with CSA issues face tremendous stress, and systematic research and theory development may assist in devising approaches to practice that minimize that stress and provide resources and support for practitioners while max-imizing care for clients (Arvay & Uhlemann, 1996; Courtois, 1999).

ARE THERE RELIABLE MEANS OF POSTDICTING THE ACCURACY OF RECOVERED-MEMORY REPORTS?

Research indicates that it is possible crudely to estimate the accuracy of recovered-memory reports by weighing a constellation of kinds of evidence including (a) the presence / absence of converging evidence; (b) how the memories came about (the less evidence of suggestive memory recovery work the greater the confidence); (c) the nature and clarity of the memories (with more credence given to detailed, integrated recollections than to vague feelings); (d) the likelihood of the alleged events being for-gotten if they had actually occurred (e.g. when and how often the abuse is said to have occurred; probability that the person would have encoun-tered reminders, overall memorability of the alleged events, etc.); (e) the plausibility of having memories to recover (e.g., less credence given to reports of events said to have occurred before two years of age); and (f) the base rate of the alleged type of abuse. Future research may also enable the development of valid and reliable individual difference measures that might be useful, along with other information, in evaluating recovered memory reports (Read & Winograd, 1998).

   At this point, it is not known exactly how these factors should be weighted, nor how well this approach would work: It is likely that even an optimal solution would sometimes erroneously reject essentially accu-rate memory reports as false and sometimes erroneously accept essen-tially illusory memory reports as accurate. Systematic research on this issue will be difficult and will doubtless require converging evidence using a variety of paradigms—for example, experimental research using analogue events and suggestions (which enable researchers to know exactly which memory reports are accurate and which are not) and studies of real-world cases in which individuals report various kinds of recovered memories (see Read, 1999, for citations).

SUMMARY

The fiercely polarized contentiousness of the early years of the recovered-memories debate has given way to more balanced and constructive perspectives. With regard to the politics of the recovered memory issue, it has become clear that there is no contradiction between being concerned about childhood sexual abuse and being concerned about the risks of suggestive forms of CSA-memory-oriented therapies. From the perspective of memory science, it has become clear that both essentially accurate and essentially illusory recovered memory experiences are genuine phenomena urgently in need of rigorous empirical investigation. The memory wars of the 1990s have already provided the impetus for exciting new research on a wide range of empirical and theoretical fronts, and new research in the 2000s will greatly advance our understanding of the questions raised in this chapter and elsewhere (e.g. Berliner & McDougall, 1997; Lindsay & Briere, 1997; Schooler & Hyman, 1997). In addition to its intrinsic intellectual value, the knowledge gained through such research will enhance psychologists' ability to support adults who were sexually abused as children while minimizing the risk of iatrogenic illusory memories or false beliefs.

REFERENCES

Albach, F., Moorman, P. P. & Bermond, B. (1996). Memory recovery of childhood sexual abuse. *Dissociation*, **IX**, 261–273.

Alpert, J. A., Brown, L.S., Ceci, S. J., Courtois, C.A., Loftus, E. F. & Ornstein, P.A. (1998). Final report of the American Psychological Association working group on investigation of memories of childhood abuse. *Psychology, Public Policy and Law*, **4**, 931–1078.

Andrews, B., Morton, J., Bekerian, D. A., Brewin, C. R., Davies, G. M. & Mollon, P. (1995). The recovery of memories in clinical practice: Experiences and beliefs of British Psychological Society practitioners. *The Psychologist*, May, 209–214.

Andrews, B. (1997). Forms of memory recovery among adults in therapy: Preliminary results from an in-depth survey. In J. D. Read & D. S. Lindsay (Eds), *Recollections of Trauma: Scientific Evidence and Clinical Practice* (pp. 455–460). New York: Plenum.

Arvay, M. J. & Uhlemann, M. R. (1996). Counsellor stress in the field of trauma: A preliminary study. *Canadian Journal of Counselling*, **30**, 193–210.

Bass, E. & Davis, L. (1988). *The Courage to Heal: A Guide for Women Survivors of Child Sexual Abuse*. New York: Harper & Row.

Belli, R. G., Winkielman, P., Read, J. D., Schwarz, N. & Lynn, S. J. (1998). Recalling more childhood events leads to judgments of poorer memory: Implications for the recovered/false memory debate. *Psychonomic Bulletin and Review, 5*, 318–323.

Berliner, L. & McDougall, J. (1997). Agenda for research: Clinical approaches to recollections of trauma. In J. D. Read & D. S. Lindsay (Eds), *Recollections of Trauma: Scientific Evidence and Clinical Practice* (pp. 523–529). New York: Plenum.

Bottoms, B. L., Shaver, P. R. & Goodman, G. S. (1996). An analysis of ritualistic and religion-related child abuse allegations. *Law and Human Behavior, 20*, 1–34.

Briere, J. (1997). An integrated approach to treating adults abused as children with specific reference to self-reported recovered memories. In J. D. Read & D. S. Lindsay (Eds), *Recollections of Trauma: Scientific Evidence and Clinical Practice* (pp. 25–41). New York: Plenum.

Briere, J. & Conte, J. (1993). Self-reported amnesia for abuse in adults molested as children. *Journal of Traumatic Stress, 6*, 21–31.

Brown, R. & Kulik, J. (1977). Flashbulb memory. *Cognition, 5*, 73–99.

Bub, D. N. (2000). Methodological issues confronting PET and fMRI studies of cognitive function, with special reference to human brain function. *Cognitive Neuropsychology, 17*, 467–484.

Christianson, S. A. (1989). Flashbulb memories: Special but not so special. *Memory and Cognition, 17*, 435–443.

Cohen, G. (1996). *Memory in the Real World.* Psychology Press: East Sussex, England.

Conway, M. A. (1995). *Flashbulb Memories.* Mahwah, NJ: Lawrence Erlbaum.

Coons, P. M. (1994). Confirmation of childhood abuse in child and adolescent cases of multiple personality and dissociative disorder not otherwise specified. *Journal of Nervous and Mental Disease, 182*, 461–464.

Corwin, D. & Olafson, E. (1997). Videotapes discovery of a reportedly unrecallable memory of child sexual abuse: Comparison with a childhood interview video-taped 11 years before. *Child Maltreatment, 2*, 91–112.

Courtois, C. A. (1997). Informed clinical practice and the standard of care: Proposed guidelines for the treatment of adults who report delayed memories of childhood trauma. In J. D. Read & D. S. Lindsay (Eds), *Recollections of Trauma: Scientific Evidence and Clinical Practice* (pp. 337–361). New York: Plenum.

Courtois, C. A. (1999). *Recollections of Sexual Abuse: Treatment Principles and Guidelines.* New York: W. W. Norton.

Dale, P. & Allen, J. (1998). On memories of childhood abuse: A phenomenological study. *Child Abuse and Neglect, 22*, 799–812.

Dalenberg, C. J. (1997). The prediction of accurate recollections of trauma. In J. D. Read & D. S. Lindsay (Eds), *Recollections of Trauma: Scientific Evidence and Clinical Practice* (pp. 449–454). New York: Plenum.

de Rivera, J. (1997). Understanding false memory syndrome. *Psychological Inquiry, 8*, 330–341.

Eacott, M. J. (1999). Memory for events of early childhood. *Current Directions In Psychological Science, 8*, 46–49.

Eacott, M. J. & Crawley, R. A. (1998). The offset of childhood amnesia: Memory for events that occurred before age 3. *Journal of Experimental Psychology: General, 127*, 22–33.

Eich, E. (1984). Memory for unattended events: Remembering with and without awareness. *Memory and Cognition, 12*, 105–111.

Eisen, M. L. & Carlson, E. B. (1998). Individual differences in suggestibility: Examining the influence of dissociation, absorption, and a history of childhood abuse. *Applied Cognitive Psychology, 12*, S47–S61.

Elliott, D. & Briere, J. (1995). Post traumatic stress associated with delayed recall of sexual abuse: A general population study. *Journal of Traumatic Stress, 8*, 629–647.

Feldman-Summers, S. & Pope, K. S. (1994). The experience of "forgetting" childhood abuse: A national survey of psychologists. *Journal of Consulting and Clinical Psychology, 62*, 636–639.

Finkelhor, D. (1994). Current information on the scope and nature of child sexual abuse. *The Future of Children, 4*, 31–53.

Fisher, R. P. (1995). Interviewing victims and witnesses of crime. *Psychology, Public Policy, and Law, 1*, 732–764.

Fivush, R. (1998). Children's recollections of traumatic and nontraumatic events. *Developmental Psychology, 10*, 699–716.

Fivush, R. & Hamond, N. R. (1990). Autobiographical memory across the preschool years: Toward reconceptualizing childhood amnesia. In R. Fivush & J. A. Hudson (Eds), *Knowing and Remembering in Young Children* (pp. 223–248). New York: Cambridge University Press.

Foa, E. B., Rothbaum, R. O., Riggs, D. S. & Murdock, T. B. (1991). Treatment of posttraumatic stress disorder in rape victims: A comparison between cognitive-behavioral procedures and counseling. *Journal of Consulting and Clinical Psychology, 59*, 715–723.

Frederickson, R. (1992). *Repressed memories: A journey to recovery from sexual abuse.* New York: Simon & Schuster.

Freyd, P. (1997, May). Dear friends. *FMSF Newsletter, 6* (6), 1. (http://advicom.net/~fitz/fmsf/fmsf-news/0053.html)

Gardiner, J. M. & Java, R. I. (1991). Forgetting in recognition memory with and without recollective experience. *Memory and Cognition, 19*, 617–623.

Gold, S. N., Hughes, D. & Hohnecker, L. (1994). Degrees of repression of sexual abuse memories. *American Psychologist, 49*, 441–442.

Grunberg, F. & Ney, T. (1997). Professional guidelines on clinical practice for recovered memory: A comparative analysis. In J. D. Read & D. S. Lindsay (Eds), *Recollections of Trauma: Scientific Evidence and Clinical Practice* (pp. 541–555). New York: Plenum.

Gudjonsson, G. H. (1992). *The Psychology of Interrogations, Confessions and Testimony.* New York: John Wiley & Sons.

Gudjonsson, G. H. (1997). The members of the BFMS, the accusers and their siblings. *Psychologist, 10*, 111–115.

Heaps, C. & Nash, M. (1999). Individual differences in imagination inflation. *Psychnomic Bulletin and Review, 6*, 313–318.

Henry, B., Moffitt, T. E., Caspi, A., Langly, J. & Silva, P. (1994). On the "remembrance of things past": A longitudinal evaluation of the retrospective method. *Psychological Assessment, 6*, 92–101.

Herman, J. L. & Schatzow, E. (1987). Recovery and verification of memories of childhood sexual trauma. *Psychoanalytic Psychology, 4*, 1–14.

Hovdestad, W. E. & Kristiansen, C. M. (1996). A field study of "false memory syndrome": Construct validity and incidence. *Journal of Psychiatry and Law, 24*, 299–338.

Hyman, I. E., Jr. & Billings, F. J. (1998). Individual differences in the creation of false childhood memories. *Memory, 6*, 1–20.

Jacoby, L. L., Kelley, C. M. & Dywan, J. (1989) Memory attributions. In H. L. Roediger III & F. I. M. Craik (Eds), *Varieties of Memory and Consciousness: Essays in Honour of Endel Tulving* (pp. 391–422). Hillsdale, NJ: Erlbaum.

Johnson, M. K., Hashtroudi, S. & Lindsay, D. S. (1993). Source monitoring. *Psychological Bulletin*, **114**, 3–28.

Kelley, C. M. & Jacoby, L. L. (1998). Subjective reports and process dissociation: Fluency, knowing, and feeling. *Acta Psychologica*, **98**, 127–140.

Kelley, C. M. & Lindsay, D. S. (1996). Conscious and unconscious forms of memory. In E. L. Bjork & R. A. Bjork (Eds), *Handbook of Perception and Cognition: Memory* (Vol. 10; pp. 31–63). New York: Academic Press.

Koss, M. P., Tromp, S. & Tharan, M. (1995). Traumatic memories: Empirical foundations, forensic and clinical implications. *Clinical Psychology: Science and Practice*, **2**, 111–132.

Lindsay, D. S. & Briere, J. (1997). The controversy regarding recovered memories of childhood sexual abuse: Pitfalls, bridges, and future directions. *Journal of Interpersonal Violence*, **12**, 631–647.

Lindsay, D. S. & Kelley, C. M. (1996). Creating illusions of familiarity in a cued recall remember/know paradigm. *Journal of Memory and Language*, **35**, 197–211.

Lindsay, D. S. & Read, J. D. (1994). Psychotherapy and memories of childhood sexual abuse: A cognitive perspective. *Applied Cognitive Psychology*, **8**, 281–338.

Lindsay, D. S., Read, J. D., Hyman, R. E. Jr & Schooler, J. W. (1999, July). *Explorations of distant memories*. Paper presented at the meeting of the Society for Applied Research on Memory and Cognition, Boulder, CO.

Loftus, E. F. (1993). The reality of repressed memories. *American Psychologist*, **48**, 518–537.

Loftus, E. F. (1997). Dispatch from the (un)civil memory wars. In J. D. Read & D. S. Lindsay (Eds), *Recollections of Trauma: Scientific Evidence and Clinical Practice* (pp. 171–194). New York: Plenum.

Loftus, E. F. & Pickrell, J. (1995). The formation of false memories. *Psychiatric Annals*, **25**, 720–724.

Loftus, E. F., Polonsky, S. & Fullilove, M. T. (1994). Memories of childhood sexual abuse: Remembering and repressing. *Psychology of Women Quarterly*, **18**, 67-84.

Melchert, T. P. & Parker, R. L. (1997). Different forms of childhood abuse and memory. *Child Abuse and Neglect*, **21**, 125–135.

Memon, A. (1998). Telling it all: The Cognitive Interview. In A. Memon, A. Vrij & R. Bull (Eds), *Psychology and Law: Truthfulness, Accuracy and Credibility* (pp. 170–187). New York: McGraw-Hill.

Ofshe, R. & Watters, E. (1994). *Making Monsters: False Memories, Psychotherapy, and Hysteria*. New York: Charles Scribner & Sons.

Palm, K. M. & Gibson, P. (1998). Recovered memories of childhood sexual abuse: Clinicians' practices and beliefs. *Professional Psychology: Research and Practice*, **29**, 257–261.

Pendergrast, M. (1996). *Victims of Memory: Incest Accusations and Shattered Lives* (2nd ed.). Hinesburg, VT: Upper Access.

Pezdek, K. & Roe, C. (1997). The suggestibility of children's memory for being touched: Planting, erasing, and changing memories. *Law and Human Behavior*, 21, 95–106.

Polusny, M A. & Follette, V. M. (1996). Remembering childhood sexual abuse: A national survey of psychologists' clinical practices, beliefs, and personal experiences. *Professional Psychology: Research and Practice*, **27**, 41–52.

Poole, D. A. & Lindsay, D. S. (1998). Assessing the accuracy of young children's reports: Lessons from the investigation of child sexual abuse. *Journal of Applied and Preventative Psychology*, **7**, 1–26.

Poole, D. A., Lindsay, D. S., Memon, A. & Bull, R. (1995). Psychotherapy and the recovery of memories of childhood sexual abuse: U.S. and British practitioners' opinions, practices, and experiences. *Journal of Consulting and Clinical Psychology,* **63**, 426–437.

Pope, K. S. (1996). Memory, abuse, and science: Questioning claims about the False Memory Syndrome epidemic. *American Psychologist,* **51**, 957–974.

Pope, K. S. & Tabachnick, B. G. (1995). Recovered memories of abuse among therapy patients: A national survey. *Ethics and Behavior,* **5**, 237–248.

Porter, S., Yuille, J. C. & Lehman, D. (1999). The nature of real, implanted, and fabricated childhood emotional events: Implications for the recovered memory debate. *Law and Human Behavior,* **23**, 517–537.

Read, J. D. (1997). Memory issues in the diagnosis of unreported trauma. In J. D. Read & D. S. Lindsay (Eds), *Recollections of Trauma: Scientific Evidence and Clinical Practice* (pp. 79–100). New York: Plenum.

Read, J. D. (1999). The recovered/false memory debate: Three steps forward, two steps back? *Expert Evidence,* **7**, 1–24.

Read, J. D. & Lindsay, D. S. (2000). "Amnesia" for summer camps and high school graduation: Memory work increases reports of prior periods of remembering less. *Journal of Traumatic Stress,* **13**, 129–147.

Read, J. D. & Winograd, E. (Eds) (1998) *Individual differences and memory distortion.* Special issue of *Applied Cognitive Psychology,* **12** (SI).

Resick, P. A. & Schnicke, M. K. (1992). Cognitive processing theory for sexual assault victims. *Journal of Consulting and Clinical Psychology,* **60** 748–756.

Roe, C. M. & Schwartz, M. F. (1996). Characteristics of previously forgotten memories of sexual abuse: A descriptive study. *Journal of Psychiatry and Law,* **24**, 189–206.

Roediger, H. L. III., Weldon, M. S. & Challis, B. H. (1989). Explaining dissociations between implicit and explicit measures of retention: A processing account. In H. L. Roediger & F. I. M. Craik (Eds), *Varieties of Memory and Consciousness: Essays in Honour of Endel Tulving* (pp. 355–389). Hillsdale, NJ: Erlbaum.

Ross, C. A., Miller, S. D., Bjornson, L., Reagor, P., Fraser, G. & Anderson, G. (1991). Abuse histories in 102 cases of multiple personality disorder. *Canadian Journal of Psychiatry,* **36**, 97–101.

Scheflin, A. W. & Brown, D. (1996). Repressed memory or dissociative amnesia: What the science says. *Journal of Psychiatry and Law,* **24**, 145–188.

Schooler, J. W., Ambadar, Z. & Bendiksen, M. (1997). A cognitive corroborative case study approach for investigating discovered memories of sexual abuse. In J. D. Read & D. S. Lindsay (Eds), *Recollections of Trauma: Scientific Evidence and Clinical Practice* (pp. 379–388). New York: Plenum.

Schooler, J. W. & Hyman, I. E. Jr (1997). Investigating alternative accounts of veridical and non-veridical memories of trauma. In J. D. Read & D. S. Lindsay (Eds), *Recollections of Trauma: Scientific Evidence and Clinical Practice* (pp. 531–540). New York: Plenum.

Schooler, J. W. & Loftus, E. F. (1993). Multiple mechanisms mediate individual differences in eyewitness accuracy and suggestibility. In J. M. Puckett & H. W. Reese (Eds), *Mechanisms of Everyday Cognition* (pp. 177–203). Hillsdale, NJ: Erlbaum.

Sheiman, J. A. (1993). 'I've always wondered if something happened to me.' Assessment of child sexual abuse survivors with amnesia. *Journal of Child Sexual Abuse,* **2**, 13–21.

Spanos, N. P., Burgess, C. A., Burgess, M. F., Samuels, C. & Blois, W. O. (1999). Creating false memories of infancy with hypnotic and non-hypnotic procedures. *Applied Cognitive Psychology,* **13**, 201–218.

Stein, N. L., Ornstein, P. A., Tversky, B. & Brainerd, C. (Eds) (1997). *Memory for Everyday and Emotional Events*. Mahwah, NJ: Lawrence Erlbaum.

Underwager, R. & Wakefield, H. (1998). Recovered memories in the courtroom. In S. J. Lynn & K. M. McConkey (Eds), *Truth in Memory* (pp. 394–434). New York: Guilford Press.

van der Kolk, B. A. & Fisler, R. (1995). Dissociation and the fragmentary nature of traumatic memories: Overview and exploratory study. *Journal of Traumatic Stress*, **8**, 505–525.

Whittlesea, B. W. A. & Williams, L. D. (1998). Why do strangers feel familiar, but friends don't? A discrepancy-attribution account of feelings of familiarity. *Acta Psychologica*, **98**, 141–165.

Widom, C. S. (1997). Accuracy of adult recollections of early childhood abuse. In J. D. Read & D. S. Lindsay (Eds), *Recollections of Trauma: Scientific Evidence and* (pp. 49–70). New York: Plenum.

Whittlesea, B. W. A. (1993). Illusions of familiarity. *Journal of Experimental Psychology: Learning, Memory, and Cognition*, **19**, 1235–1253.

Williams, L. M. (1994). Recall of childhood trauma: A prospective study of women's memories of child sexual abuse. *Journal of Consulting and Clinical Psychology*, **62**, 1167–1176.

Williams, L. M. (1995). Recovered memories of abuse in women with documented child sexual victimization histories. *Journal of Traumatic Stress*, **8**, 649–673.

Winograd, E. & Neisser, U. (Eds) (1992). *Affect and Accuracy in Recall: Studies of "Flashbulb" Memories (Emory Symposium on Cognition)*. New York: Cambridge University Press.

Wright, D. B., Loftus, E. F. & Hall, M. (2000). Now you see it, now you don't: Inhibiting recall and recognition of scenes. *Applied Cognitive Psychology*, **15**, 471–482.

6

DISCOVERING FACT AND FICTION: CASE-BASED ANALYSES OF AUTHENTIC AND FABRICATED DISCOVERED MEMORIES OF ABUSE

Katharine K. Shobe and Jonathan W. Schooler

For over a decade the psychological community has been in the midst of a debate over the status of recovered memories of childhood sexual abuse (CSA). Although practitioners often consider these recovered memories as accurate depictions of events that occurred long ago (Briere, 1992; Courtois, 1988; Herman, 1992), many experimental psychologists have expressed skepticism over the accuracy of such memories and have challenged the notion of concepts like repression (Brenneis, 1997; Kihlstrom, 1996, 1998; Loftus & Ketcham, 1992). While there are likely to be many different reasons for the gulf between experimental researchers and clinical practitioners in this debate, it seems likely that one central factor has been the types of evidence upon which the two traditions have historically relied. Practitioners have a long history, dating back to Freud, of relying on case reports and personal experience to inform theory. In contrast,

Recovered Memories: Seeking the Middle Ground. Edited by Graham M. Davies and Tim Dalgleish. © 2001 John Wiley & Sons Ltd.

experimental psychologists rely primarily on controlled experimental data. The difference in these traditions has colored the manner in which each has viewed the evidence put forth by the "other side". For example, practitioner researchers have argued that the experimental literature on the influence of suggestion on memory provides "no evidence to suggest that psychotherapists have the degree of power and influence that would be required to produce this [fabricated memories] effect" (Harvey & Herman, 1994, p. 296). From the opposite perspective, experimental researchers, trained to rely on solid experimental evidence, have dismissed case-based evidence as "unconfirmed clinical speculations, certainly not as evidence for repression" and have argued that "there is no controlled laboratory evidence for repression" (Holmes, 1990, p. 97).

How are we to make headway on this issue if participants from both sides of the "fence" reject out of hand the forms of evidence provided by the other side? Clearly, we cannot expect individuals to ignore their training and professional experience. Clinicians, many of whom have encountered individuals who they believe to have recovered actual memories, cannot be expected to entirely abandon their intuitive judgment on the basis of seemingly remote experimental studies, many of which involve the rather mundane memories of introductory psychology students. On the other hand, experimental researchers cannot be expected to ignore the well-grounded biases that can confound conclusions not founded in controlled experimentation (e.g. Dawes, 1989). Nor can we ask them to abandon their deep respect for the importance of controlled experimentation in drawing conclusions about basic memory processes. What we might expect from both sides, however, is a willingness to at least explore the possible value of evidence that differs from that for which they were originally trained to use. Clinicians need to consider the implications to their research of experimental findings on memory suggestibility. And experimental researchers need to consider case-based evidence that may provide insights into phenomena that for a combination of pragmatic and ethical reasons cannot be fully captured in the lab.

This chapter represents an effort by the authors, both of whom were trained in basic experimental psychology, to go beyond their customary forms of evidence and explore how case-based data may illuminate the mechanisms that lead individuals to believe they have discovered long forgotten memories of abuse. Although we will focus on an uncustomary type of data, we will maintain the theoretical vantage of experimental researchers. In particular we will consider the data from the perspective of the four phases of memory routinely considered when assessing the veracity of memories: encoding, retention interval, retrieval, and post-retrieval. As we hope to demonstrate, these four fundamental phases of memory models provide an invaluable heuristic for (1) defining the key constructs involved in this controversy, (2) evaluating the evidence supporting these constructs, and (3) considering potential mechanisms underlying them.

ASSUMPTIONS UNDERLYING RECOVERED MEMORIES OF ABUSE

In addition to the clash between the kinds of evidence associated with the practitioner and experimental traditions, another factor which has contributed to the recovered memory controversy has been the loose use of terms and a concomitant and consistent failure to explicate the assumptions underlying those terms. For example, the term "repression" is sometimes used to describe a phenomenon, i.e. cases in which individuals have remembered seemingly forgotten trauma. However, other times it is used to describe a mechanism, a dynamic unconscious defense mechanism that is hypothesized to actively keep the memory from consciousness. Indeed, even within these two general categories usages differ. For example, as a phenomenon, repression is sometimes used to characterize any forgetting of sexual abuse, whereas at other times it is limited to the forgetting of extensive repeated abuse. In its usage as a mechanism, repression is sometimes described as exclusively unconscious forgetting while at other times it includes motivated suppression.

In order to progress on this issue it is critical that we clearly identify the assumptions underlying our terms. Towards this end it is helpful to consider four fundamental phases of memory — the encoding, retention interval, retrieval (which are considered in virtually all discussions of memory) and post-retrieval phase (which is often overlooked but in cases of memory accuracy is equally important). By considering implicit/explicit assumptions of terms in light of these four phases we can be much more precise in identifying core claims and thus establishing what types of evidence might support or contradict those claims.

Encoding assumptions

The first element in any characterization of memory formation is the encoding phase, which corresponds to the situations surrounding the original formation of the memory. In the context of characterizing a memory as "recovered" the critical encoding assumption is that the experience actually occurred. As will be discussed, in many cases there seems to be good reasons to believe that recovered memories were never actually experienced. In other cases, it has been possible to find relatively compelling evidence that supports at least the gist of abuse claims associated with so-called recovered memories. However, even if the details of the event are generally accurate, individuals' construal of the experience may fundamentally change. As will be argued, the reframing of experiences may play a central role in the experience of "recovering" memories, particularly given that they often involve adults' recollections of childhood events. In short, the notion that a recovered memory, even if it corresponds to a real event, necessarily represents a recovery of the original memory is highly questionable.

Retention interval assumptions

The second phase in the fate of any memory is the retention phase, which corresponds to the period between the time a memory is encoded and the time in which it is retrieved. The retention interval assumptions underlying the claim of a recovered memory are even more daunting than are the encoding assumptions. During the retention interval it is assumed that, for at least a considerable period of time, the memory had been completely forgotten. In this context, however, it is conceptually difficult to define what exactly is meant by forgotten. If a memory had not been thought about for some period of time, does that make it necessarily forgotten? What if a memory came to mind, but its retrieval was subsequently forgotten? What "completely forgotten" typically means is that at the time of recollection, the individual had the *impression* that the memory was previously unavailable. The basis of this impression may involve a variety of factors including (1) an inability to explicitly recall previous acts of remembering, (2) folk theories about the types of experiences that individuals should always remember, and (3) the sense of surprise associated with the recollective experience (Schooler, in press).

Given the vagueness of the construct of complete forgetting, the corroboration of forgetting is equally elusive. Since remembering is often a personal process, it is simply not clear how one could ever document that a memory never came to mind. Moreover, even if a memory had not come to mind for some period, it is still difficult to distinguish whether it was truly unavailable, or, like many memories from our distant past, simply did not have occasion to be remembered. Perhaps the most persuasive evidence of forgetting involves cases in which individuals are explicitly asked about their abuse during the retention interval phase and fail to report it (cf. Williams, 1994). However, even here real questions surround whether a lack of report can be characterized as forgetting. A failure to report an experience may occur because the individual is embarrassed and does not want to talk about it. It may also occur because the question does not cue the expected experience. For example, Joslyn, Carlin, and Loftus (1998) found that many individuals who initially responded "no" when asked if they had ever been sexually abused as a child, subsequently recalled being the victims of particular actions (e.g. being fondled in a way that made them feel uncomfortable). This was not simply a definitional issue, as these individuals often subsequently indicated that the type of specific experience that they reported did in fact constitute sexual abuse. Such a finding suggests that individuals may fail to report abuse memories not because they are entirely inaccessible, but simply because (for a variety of reasons, some of which will be explored later) a query about sexual abuse does not cue their memories.

Retrieval assumptions

The third key phase in discussions of the fate of memories is the retrieval stage in which a recollection corresponding to the original event is brought to mind. The key assumption associated with claims of recovered memories is that at some point the individuals had retrieval experiences in which they perceived themselves to have discovered a long-lost memory. Even if individuals are inaccurate in their assessments of their forgetting, they may still have authentic discovery experiences in the sense that they genuinely *perceive themselves* to have found a previously unknown memory. As will be argued, individuals may have profound discovery experiences corresponding to memories of experiences of which they are known to have possessed some prior knowledge. This point illustrates the need to consider the authenticity of the perception of the discovery of the memory separately from that of the forgetting itself. It also focuses us on what we believe is the defining attribute of memories that are typically characterized as recovered — namely, they are *associated with the perception that an individual has made a fundamental discovery about the contents of his or her own memories.*

Post-retrieval assumptions

Although most discussions of memory typically end with a consideration of the retrieval assumptions, in the context of enduring personal memories, there is a fourth critical stage that needs to be considered, namely, the fate of the memory after it has been retrieved. In eyewitness situations, post-retrieval factors turn out to be critical to individuals' final construals of their memories. For example, with the passage of time and particularly following hearing the input of other witnesses, individuals typically become increasingly confident in their recollections, overestimating their original confidence. In the present context, the critical assumption underlying the characterizing of a memory as recovered is that individuals' construal of what they did and did not know about the memory prior to recalling it is currently the same as it was when the memory was originally recalled. However, it seems quite plausible that in many cases individuals' beliefs about the nature and magnitude of their discoveries may change with time. For example, they might come to believe that they were more shocked at the discovery than they were originally. Alternatively, they may confuse the nature of the discovery, increasingly recalling the discovery of a new interpretation of an experience with a discovery of the memory for the experience itself.

Discovered memories of abuse

In sum, the characterization of a memory as recovered involves a variety of assumptions regarding the encoding, retention interval, retrieval, and post-retrieval phases of memory. When considered together and taken to their most stringent levels, these assumptions set a target that may simply be impossible for any recollection to live up to. In short, when we carefully decompose the assumptions underlying the classification of a memory as recovered, we quickly see that it is highly unlikely that any memory (or at least not ones that occur naturally over extended durations with standard forms of documentation) will ever fully pass muster on all of the criteria. This leaves us with a phenomenon that is easily dismissed before it is even investigated (which indeed seems to have often been its fate). However, if we focus on what appears to be the truly defining characteristic of "recovered" memories, namely that individuals perceive themselves to have made profound discoveries about their past, we can begin to get a handle on tractable research questions — namely, investigating the various encoding, retention interval, retrieval, and post-encoding factors that can contribute to individual's perceptions that they have discovered long lost memories of abuse. In this context, we believe that the term "discovered memory" more aptly defines the phenomenon in question (Schooler, Ambadar & Bendiksen, 1997a; Schooler, 2000). By discovered memory, we simply mean situations in which individuals sincerely *perceive* themselves to have discovered memories of experiences of which they think they had previously been unaware.

The term "discovered memory" keeps open the possibility that individuals could have discovery experiences corresponding to memories that were not, at least in some sense, entirely forgotten. The term "discovered" also maintains agnosticity regarding the precise mapping between what is discovered and what actually occurred. Individuals could in principle discover memories that were entirely veridical, entirely false, or, as may often be the case, somewhere in between. Most importantly, the term "discovered memory" focuses us on the seemingly defining characteristic of these memories, namely that they are associated with the sense that something very profound has been discovered in one's memory. Armed with the basic construct of discovered memories we can consider actual cases of discovered memories within the context of the critical encoding, retention interval, retrieval, and post-retrieval factors that may characterize each case. In the following analysis we first consider cases of discovered memories that appear to have at least some correspondence to real events. We then consider discovered memories that seem more likely to be the product of suggestion. As will be seen, although there are obviously fundamental differences between discovered authentic and false memories, there are also some important sources of overlap. Moreover, the encoding, retention interval, retrieval, and post-retrieval phase distinctions provide an invaluable heuristic for considering the evidence for and mechanisms surrounding both types of "memories".

DISCOVERED AUTHENTIC MEMORIES

With the above definitional and evidentiary considerations we (Schooler, 1994, in press; Schooler, Ambadar & Bendiksen, 1997a; Schooler, Bendiksen & Ambadar, 1997b) have sought to investigate cases of individuals who reported discovering seemingly forgotten memories of abuse and for which there appeared to be some corroborative evidence that some abuse actually took place. The present discussion includes seven cases. The first six cases have been discussed previously by Schooler et al. (1997a), and Case 7 by Schooler (in press).

These cases were identified through modest networking and are not in any sense a representative sample. In each case, Schooler and colleagues sought to document the individuals' characterization of the encoding, retention interval, retrieval, and post-retrieval of the memory. In addition, they sought independent corroboration of the central claims associated with each stage. The term "corroboration" in these cases is used in its traditional meaning of "to make more certain; confirm; to strengthen" (Costello et al., 1991). Just as a particular experimental result can support a scientific hypothesis without "proving" it, so, too, can corroborative evidence strengthen historical claims without providing incontrovertible documentation.

At the encoding phase, the key issue surrounds documenting the alleged abuse (usually by contacting other individuals who the victim indicated had prior knowledge of either the abuse itself or the abusive tendencies of the alleged perpetrator). Of course, the memories of corroborators might also be in error. However, if such corroborative reports involve longstanding memories then they are less vulnerable to the concern that they were the products of a recent suggestion. Indeed, even those who are generally skeptical of recovered memories do not question the abuse recollections of individuals who report having maintained longstanding intact memories of abuse (Loftus, 1994). In short, if the recollections of individuals who report discovered memories of abuse can be corroborated by others who have maintained intact memories, then we may have greater confidence that the discovered memories correspond to actual events.[1]

At the retention interval phase the key issue is evidence that might speak to the availability of the memory during that phase. As noted, evidence in confirming the unavailability of memories is potentially suspect for a variety of reasons; nevertheless, it is sometimes possible to find disconfirming evidence (i.e. evidence that the memory was in fact available at a time in which it was perceived to be inaccessible).

At the retrieval interval phase, evidence surrounding the authenticity of the characterization of the discovery is also considered. This usually entails the reports of others who heard about the recovery soon after it occurred.

At the post-retrieval phase, evidence surrounds consideration of the time that passed between the alleged occurrence of the discovery and its subsequent investigation, such as evidence from others that the construal of the discovery may have changed.

In the following discussion we first describe the encoding, retention interval, retrieval and post-retrieval characteristics and evidence surrounding the seven cases. We then consider the more general encoding, retention interval retrieval, and post-retrieval mechanisms that might have contributed to these cases.

Case 1

JR is a 39-year-old male whose memory discovery occurred at age 30.

Encoding

JR reported that at approximately age 12 he went on a camping trip with a priest, who during the night fondled his genitals and lay on top of him. JR further alleged that this abuse continued intermittently over the next several years. Corroboration of this abuse comes from several sources. First, JR reported that when he confronted the priest, he acknowledged the molestation and tried to assuage him by indicating that he had sought treatment for sexually abusive clergy following an incident with another individual. JR also reported that several of his brothers had indicated that

---

[1] Of course, if a discovered memory cannot be corroborated this does not imply that the memory is necessarily false. By the very nature of abuse, many cases may occur without any incriminating evidence to subsequently corroborate it. Indeed, as will be mentioned later, one form of abuse that may be particularly difficult to corroborate (i.e. that which occurs surreptitiously in the home at night) may also be especially prone to forgetting.

the priest had approached them. In addition, subsequent to JR's memory recovery and attempted lawsuit, another individual reported that he too had been sexually approached by the priest. This individual indicated that he had maintained an intact memory of the abuse all of his life, but had previously failed to discuss the memory due to his embarrassment.

Retention interval

Prior to the recovery experience, JR believes that he had no recollection whatsoever about this history of sexual abuse. He stated with confidence that if asked if he had ever been sexually abused he would have unhesitantly said "no". JR further believed that he forgot the memory of each episode of sexual abuse right after it happened so that when he woke up the next morning he did not have any sense of what had occurred the night before. JR suggested that his immediate forgetting of the incidents accounts for why he continued to willingly go on subsequent trips with the priest. Although it is quite difficult to assess the full extent of JR's forgetting throughout the entire period during which he claims to have forgotten his history of abuse, there is some evidence suggesting that this memory may not have been accessible to him during some periods in his life. Specifically, several years prior to his recovery experience, JR was in therapy with ND regarding an entirely unrelated difficulty. Although the issue of sexual abuse was never raised in these sessions, ND indicated that JR discussed many other intimate aspects of his life, leading ND to conclude that JR was truly unaware of possessing the memories of abuse.

Retrieval

JR provided the following characterization of his retrieval experience. One night JR went to see a movie where the main character grapples with memories of sexual molestation. As the movie went on, JR found himself more and more agitated without understanding why. Hours later, when he was in bed, he remembered the experience of being abused (genital fondling) by a parish priest on a camping trip when he was 12 years old (18 years prior). The memory came "fairly suddenly" with great vividness. As JR described it: "I was stunned, I was somewhat confused you know, the memory was very vivid and yet I didn't know one word about repressed memory." Over the following six to ten months after the first memory was recovered, JR remembered at least 10 other incidents of abuse by the same individual that he estimated occurred over the next several years, all of which were recalled as occurring while the two were on trips to different places.

One possible concern with JR's characterization of his retrieval experience is that JR ultimately pursued legal recourse in this case. Thus, skeptics might argue that JR's recovered memory report was simply a ruse to get past statute of limitation laws. However, it is important to note that at the time of his recovery (1986) there were no cases in which memory repression had been successfully used as an argument for overturning statute of limitation laws, and indeed it was such laws that ultimately prevented the prosecution of this case. Thus, the recovery of this memory did not occur in an environment in which the possible legal advantages of characterizing it as having been "recovered" would have been appreciated. In addition, further evidence for the authenticity of JR's retrieval experience comes from the accounts of ND. According to ND, JR described his recovery experience to him soon after it occurred in a manner much the same as it was described to us. At that time, JR was very upset about the memory recollection and completely unaware of the phenomenon of recovered memories. As a good friend of JR, ND sees it as inconceivable that JR would have feigned this extremely emotional discovery experience.

Post-retrieval

JR apparently described and re-described his experience to many individuals through out the nine-year duration between the time his memory discovery originally occurred and the time that we interviewed him. Thus there is certainly the possibility that his recollections of the original discovery could have evolved with the passage of time. Nevertheless, the fact that ND recalls JR describing the experience in largely the same terms throughout this duration suggests that post-retrieval factors were at most only modest.

Case 2

WB is a 40-year-old female whose memory discovery occurred at age 40.

Encoding

WB described her original abuse experience as involving forced sexual intercourse while she was hitchhiking at age 16. WB indicated that following her rape experience she described it to several of her co-workers at the camp at which she was working at the time. Corroboration of the rape came from one of those co-workers who was an individual whom she later married. In a separate interview, MB's former husband recounted the day in which she had returned from her day off and reported having had a "bad experience" in which she had sex "involuntarily" but had not protested. A few days later she described it as "something like rape".

Retention interval

WB fluctuated in her characterization of her forgetting. In her initial characterization of her recovery experience (written two days after the experience) WB observed, "In a way, I have managed to repress the *meaning* of what happened all of these years. I may have not completely forgotten the experience ... but I have pushed it away, minimized it It wasn't a real rape." Several months later in an interview, when asked if there was ever a time in which she would have honestly believed that she had not been raped had she been asked directly, she observed, "I actually think this is the case." Although WB believed she might have entirely forgotten the memory, in an independent interview her ex-husband disclosed that during the years that they were married WB mentioned in passing several times that she had been raped, but totally without affect. Interestingly, WB has no recollection whatsoever of having mentioned her rape to her ex-husband during their marriage, and was quite startled to learn that she had done so.

Retrieval

The night after a friend described another woman as "certainly not a virgin", WB "awoke with a sudden and clear picture: 'My God... I had been raped'" In a subsequent interview, WB further characterized the recovery experience as "complete chaos in my emotions". There are a number of reasons to believe MB's general account of her retrieval experience. First, she had absolutely nothing to gain by feigning the recovery. The individual who raped her was long gone, so there was no potential legal advantage of framing this recollection as a memory recovery. Second, WB contacted the second author barely a week after the experience occurred, thus reducing the possibility that the memory for the recovery would have been significantly forgotten.

Post-retrieval

Although WB clearly perceived herself as having made an important memory discovery from the outset, there is at least the possibility that her memory of the recollection may have evolved with the passage of time. As noted above, originally she was more ambiguous regarding whether she had discovered the original memory or the meaning of the memory, whereas several months later she was generally recalling herself as having discovering the memory itself. It is thus possible that her memory for the discovery experience may have evolved over time, so that she increasingly believed that the discovery involved finding a long lost memory (as opposed to a never-before-found understanding of that memory).

Case 3

TW is a 51-year-old female whose memory discovery occurred at age 24.

Encoding

TW recounted an experience at 9 in which a family friend attempted to fondle her while she was on a vacation. TW's former husband was interviewed and reported that she talked about the abuse several times over the course of their marriage (which ended prior to the recovery). She apparently mentioned the abuse in a relatively matter of fact manner, with little expression of emotion and no reference to any memory difficulties associated with the recollection.

Retention interval

According to TW, prior to the recovery she had no recollection whatsoever about the incident. As TW noted, in between the time she told her mother about the experience and the time she actually recovered it, she believed that "the state of my memory in that period was none ... nonexistent". However, as noted, her husband indicated that she had talked about the abuse a number of times during their marriage, which was a time that she perceived herself to have been amnesic for the abuse.

Retrieval

TW described her initial recollection of the experience as having occurred in her office after an officemate asked her whether she wanted to go to a talk on child molestation. TW recalled the recollection experience quite vividly, noting that it was extremely different from any other memory experience she had. In this case there was a hint that TW's memory for the discovery experience may have become more severe over time. Specifically, one individual who spoke to her about her recollection several years ago, recalls that while she perceived this recollection as somewhat peculiar, he does not remember her ascribing quite as much emotion or significance to it as she does today.

Post-retrieval

TW's memory discovery occurred 26 years prior to our interview. Thus there is certainly the possibility that her construal of the discovery might have evolved over time. Moreover, an individual who heard her original characterization several years before we interviewed her, recalls that she had previously recounted it as a less significant event, which further supports the possibility that the discovery might have increased in significance with time.

Case 4

ND is a 41-year-old female whose memory discovery occurred at age 35.

Encoding

ND reported that when she was in her early twenties she was raped in an elevator of a hospital. She further reported that the case went to court and the alleged perpetrator was found guilty. Because ND's case was actually taken to trial, corroboration was relatively straightforward. In a telephone interview, her lawyer at the time (who is now a judge) verified that the case did in fact go to court, and that the accused was found guilty of rape. Thus we have incontrovertible evidence for one component of this traumatic experience (taking the rape case to court) and extremely compelling evidence for the other component of this trauma (the rape itself) as the individual was found guilty.

Retention interval

ND was positive that she remembered the attack for approximately two years after the rape while she continued working at the same hospital. She then moved to a different state and worked at a different hospital. At some point following her move, she believed that she completely forgot the whole incident including the trial. Indeed, it was her amazement at having forgotten the rape and the ensuing trial that contributed to the remarkable quality of her recovery experience. In this case we have what might be considered strongest evidence that true forgetting had occurred prior to the recovery. When ND entered therapy for victims of sexual abuse, she was given an initial interview to assess her history of abuse. During this interview (as revealed in hospital records made available to the second author), ND described in detail her abuse as a child, but did not mention her rape experience. However, it is possible that she may not have thought about the rape in the same way that she thought about her early childhood abuse, and so she may have failed to mention it at that time.

Retrieval

ND had been in group therapy for victims of child abuse (a memory that she had kept intact all of her life). At one of the therapy sessions, the therapist mentioned that victims of child abuse often continue to be victimized as adults. On her drive home after the session, she thought about the therapist's remark and then all at once she remembered being raped by a stranger at age 22 (13 years prior). ND recounted her recovery experience as follows:

> What she her therapist had said popped into my mind, and then all at once I remembered being a victim when I was like in my early twenties. When I was a nurse at a hospital and it really kind of freaked me out because I remembered that not only had I been a victim but I had to go to court and prosecute the person who had attacked me. And he had been found guilty. And yet I had forgotten all of that.

It is also of interest that the recovery experience is alluded to in her therapy records, further substantiating the validity of her report.

Post-retrieval
ND's memory discovery occurred six years prior to her interview, raising the possibility that her account of this discovery could have changed. However, the fact that she reported the discovery during her therapy sessions supports the view that she perceived herself to have made a discovery at the time.

Case 5

JN is a 31-year-old female who reported a discovery experience soon after she became sexually active at age 18.

Encoding
JN reported that a babysitter fondled her and her older sister when she was age 5. The abuse was corroborated by her mother who indicated that soon after the event took place JN's sister reported it to her.

Retention interval
When asked if there was ever a time in which she had complete prior unawareness of this memory, JN replied, "Yes, Yes, I think there was a time."

Retrieval
JN did not actually recall the precise occasion of her discovery experience although she estimates that it occurred soon after she became sexually active. In particular, she recalled describing her new gained knowledge to her boyfriend noting "I just have a recollection of talking about it with him. I remembered this thing happening but I had never remembered it before." In this case corroboration of the retrieval experience came from the mother who indicated that JN had told her soon after she allegedly recalled the experience, that she had recently remembered being abused by a babysitter and wondered whether or not that had actually happened.

Post-retrieval
JN's discovery occurred 13 years prior to our interview, so, as in many of these other cases, the possibility that her discovery experience recollections evolved is possible. In this case, however, she actually recalls very little of the discovery experience itself, other than that she perceived herself to have discovered a long-forgotten memory of child abuse. The contents of this basic perception were corroborated by the mother who indicated that JN did note having recently remembered the abuse soon after JN reported discovering the memory.

Case 6

CV is a 52-year-old female who recovered her memory at the age of 27.

Encoding

CV described being molested in the bathroom and raped in the bedroom when she was 10 years old. Corroboration of the abuse came from CV's sister who indicated that she had also been molested repeatedly by her father. CV's sister indicated that she had maintained an intact memory of the experience.

Retention interval

During the period that CV believes she had been amnesic for the abuse, she recalled several incidents that, in retrospect, she believes were related to the abuse, but which she did not recognize at the time. Several years prior to her memory discovery experience CV had a conversation with a childhood friend who alluded to the abuse. However, CV recalled completely failing to understand what this friend was describing. CV further reported that several weeks prior to her full discovery experience she had a flashback of sorts while cleaning her bathroom, in which she imagined her father in a lewd manner. However, rather than considering it a recollection, she considered it a bizarre thought: "I felt sickened and shocked that I would think of such a disgusting thing about my stepfather and myself."

Retrieval

Allegedly several weeks later after CV's initial (and dismissed) recollective experience, CV had a subsequent recollective experience (again while cleaning the bathroom) in which "That horrible picture came into my mind but this time it did not go away...a whole reel of pictures started running through my head...I was terrified." This time she reports recognizing the flashback as an actual memory. There was no direct corroboration of her discovery experience, although there was no legal benefit for her to deliberately misconstrue her experience as a discovery.

Post-retrieval

CV was interviewed 25 years after her memory discovery, so once again we need to be wary of the possibility that her recollection of the discovery evolved with time.

Case 7

DJ is a 28-year-old female who reported a memory experience that occurred at the age of 16.

Encoding

DJ estimated that she was abused over 30 times between the ages of 5 and 7 by a next-door neighbor who was the father of a friend. She described the abuse as occurring when she spent the night at her friend's house. The perpetrator allegedly came into her room while she was asleep and took her to his room where "he would perform sexual acts in front of me, or ask me to perform sexual acts to him…it was not normal sex, it wasn't just sexual, it was very kind of sick". The corroboration of the abuse came from DJ's mother who reported that upon learning of the abuse she and the director of the camp at which the alleged perpetrator worked, confronted the man. As she put it, "We brought in the man … presented him with the story, and he said that it was true. He admitted it." DJ's mother further reported that he also admitted molesting other girls. Subsequent to the confession the perpetrator committed suicide.

Retention interval

Following the end of the abuse experiences, DJ believed that she had entirely forgotten the experience. As she put it, "I am absolutely sure that I forgot about it…I remember feeling some intuitive weirdness about like sex…I definitely never linked it to a memory." Her mother indicated that prior to the discovery experience DJ made no mention of the abuse per se; however, she did express some misgivings about the individual.

Retrieval

DJ described her retrieval experience as occurring at age 16 when she attended a dinner party at which the alleged perpetrator was also present. According to DJ, when she saw him the memory came flooding back. "I was very shocked by the memory, I was very overwhelmed I think would be the word. That's a lot to remember…It literally was like a brick wall just hit me." Corroboration of the retrieval experience came from the mother who confirmed that DJ described the memory discovery to her soon after it occurred. She also noted that during the dinner party she noticed that DJ became suddenly very upset.

Post-retrieval

DJ's memory discovery occurred 12 years prior to our interview, again raising the possibility that her recollection could have changed. However, the fact that her mother reports that she maintained largely the same characterization of her discovery throughout those years suggests that, in this case, post-retrieval factors were likely to be modest.

ANALYSIS OF THE CASE-BASED EVIDENCE FOR DISCOVERED MEMORIES

As the foregoing case summaries illustrate, case-based studies, though not without their limitations, can provide valuable evidence for illuminating the encoding, retention interval, retrieval, and post-retrieval components of discovered memories. Below we review and evaluate the evidence in support of the individuals' claims regarding these three phases.

Evidence for the encoding phase

With respect to the encoding phase, all of the cases presented here provide supportive evidence that the alleged incidents of abuse actually took place. Admittedly in each case it is possible to construct alternative accounts of how the memories could have been false; however, in our opinion these alternatives seem considerably less likely than the conclusion that these individuals really were abused. In collectively evaluating the evidence in support of the initial allegations of abuse, it may be useful to consider the evidence as a function of its source. In the following discussion we consider the three general types of corroborative evidence involving the reports of others who (1) were abused by the same perpetrator, (2) had been told about the abuse prior to its discovery, and (3) had knowledge regarding the confession of the perpetrator.

The corroboration of the abuse in Cases 1 and 6 involved the *reports of others who reported being abused by the same perpetrator*. In these cases, it is possible that these individuals generated false memories that implicated individuals who just so happened to have abused other people. However, such an account requires the postulation of a rather remarkable coincidence in both cases. Alternatively, and perhaps more plausibly, the recollections of either the alleged victims in question or the corroborators could have been a product of discussions between the two parties. While we cannot entirely rule out the possibilities that these memories were the product of collusion, in each case there are arguments against this view. In Case 1, JR did not know the corroborating individual until after his recovery, thus it is very difficult to ascribe JR's recollection to the influence of the corroborator. The corroborator of course might have had his memory planted as a function of hearing about JR's accusations; however, as noted, few have so far suggested that adults who report longstanding memories of abuse are likely to be reporting suggested memories. A similar argument holds for Case 6 in which it seems unlikely that CV's discovered memory of a single incident of abuse could have caused her sister to recall an entire history of abuse. It is perhaps more plausible that her sister's experience could have been relayed to CV and caused her recollection of a single abuse episode. However, both individuals claim that they never talked about the sister's abuse prior to CV's memory discovery.

The corroborative evidence for Cases 2, 3, 4, and 5 involved the *reports of others who had been told about the abuse prior to its discovery*. In Cases 2 and 3 the alleged victims told their husbands about the abuse matter of factly without any mention of having forgotten the abuse. Indeed for Case 3 this happened the day after the abuse occurred. Thus, in order to dismiss their recollections we must either question the abuse reports of individuals who originally described never-forgotten experiences of abuse or we must question the husbands longstanding recollections of their wives' reports of abuse. In Case 4 the lawyer of the victim was told about the rape soon after it occurred, and the facts of the case were sufficient to persuade a jury of the guilt of the perpetrator. Thus, in this case the evidence of abuse rests on the previously intact recollection presented by CV soon after the alleged event took place and the recollection of a trial lawyer for the outcome of tried case. Finally in Case 5, JN's mother reported that JN's sister described the abuse done to her and JN soon after it occurred. Thus, to dispute the abuse in this case, we must either challenge the memory of a mother who learned about the abuse of her children, or perhaps more plausibly the memory of a child who has reported abuse immediately after it allegedly occurred. However, though children's memory may be the product of suggestion, we must be very cautious to dismiss such accounts out of hand, particularly when there is no evidence that suggestion played a role in this case.

Finally, in Case 7 the evidence of abuse involved *confessions by the perpetrator*. In Case 7 this confession was communicated to DJ's mother, who in turn described it to us. While the existence of an intermediary provides some possibility for distortion, there seems to be little reason to think that the mother's recollection of such an important fact as a person confessing to the abuse of her daughter would be wholly fabricated.

Evidence surrounding the retention interval phase

Although in each case described above the evidence for the original abuse is (in our view) reasonably compelling, the evidence for forgetting during the retention interval is considerably less strong. As noted in Cases 2 and 3 there is evidence that clearly disconfirms the victim's reports of forgetting, as in both of these cases the victims' husbands indicated that they had referred to the abuse experiences repeatedly during the alleged amnesic periods. In the other cases, there are hints that the memories may have at least been at a reduced degree of accessibility for some period of time. For example, in Case 1, JR's former therapist indicated that prior to the discovery he never made any mention of sexual abuse even though he disclosed many other things. While this is potentially informative, JR's therapist also indicated that he never asked JR about abuse, and it is also possible that JR might have felt reluctant to disclose it. In Case 4, ND did not report her rape experience on her intake interview for childhood sexual abuse. However, once again it is not clear that she would have necessarily thought about this type of experience in the same context as childhood abuse. In Case 7, DJ made reference to the perpetrator as "kind of a jerk, kind of a nerd"; such a description is clearly a long way from identifying him as a child molester, and in this respect does suggest that she did not have full access to her memory of the experience. Nevertheless, the fact that she did refer to him in unambiguously negative terms does suggest that she possessed some knowledge (perhaps only implicit) about having had negative experiences with him.

Evidence surrounding the retrieval phase

In many of these cases individuals' discoveries were reported a significant period of time after the events actually took place. Thus we do need to be potentially concerned that the memories of the discoveries might have evolved with the passage of time. In a number of cases (Cases 1, 2, 4, 5, 7) the individuals told others about their discoveries soon after they occurred. In all of these cases, the individuals originally communicated that they believed they had a significant discovery experience. Although this evidence helps to substantiate that some type of discovery experience did occur in the majority of the cases reported here, we still must be cautious in necessarily assuming that every detail of individual's recounts fully reflected the manner in which the experiences were originally recalled.

Evidence surrounding the post-retrieval phase

In all but one of the cases, the individuals were originally interviewed years after the original discovery of the memory, raising at least the possibility that the individuals' construals of their discoveries could have evolved with time. In two cases there was actually some modest evidence for slight changes in recountings of their discoveries. WB originally seemed less confident that she had absolutely forgotten the experience than she was later, and ND was reported by another as having previously recalled the discovery as being less momentous than the manner in which she described it to us. Although the possibility that individual recounts of their discoveries may have evolved with time seems very real, it also should be kept in mind that, in the majority of cases, there was evidence from other individuals that a discovery had been perceived from the outset.

Conclusion

The above analysis of the cases reviewed indicates that it is at least sometimes possible to ascertain with a reasonable degree of confidence that individuals who perceived themselves to have discovered long-forgotten memories of abuse may be recalling at least the gist of experiences they actually encoded. At the same time, however, we can be far less confident that during the "retention interval" the memories were necessarily as inaccessible as they are reported to have been. We also, in at least some cases, must consider the possibility that individual's construals of their discoveries might have evolved with time. At the very minimum, it seems safe to conclude that individuals who perceive themselves to be in the possession of a discovered memory at the time that they were interviewed, were remembering events which did have some foundation in reality. In the following analysis, we consider the possible mechanisms that could lead individuals to perceive themselves as having discovered long-forgotten memories of abuse that actually occurred.

POSSIBLE MECHANISMS THAT COULD LEAD TO DISCOVERED AUTHENTIC MEMORIES OF ABUSE

Our account of the possible mechanisms that may lead to discovered memories of abuse draws heavily on Schooler's (2000) theory of meta-awareness. Schooler (2000) postulates that experiential consciousness (i.e. the contents of phenomenological experience) can be distinct from meta-awareness (i.e. one being conscious of one's consciousness). Although it might seem that we are necessarily always conscious of our consciousness, a simple example illustrates that this is not so. Imagine that you are reading a very important and difficult paper that you must understand completely. Despite your best intentions, at some point during the reading you realize that for the last several minutes (or more!) you have not been attending to the text but rather have been engaged in a vivid daydream of an upcoming vacation. In such cases we can be vividly conscious of the contents of our daydream yet not be meta-aware of the fact *that* we are daydreaming.

The fact that consciousness can be dissociated from meta-awareness raises the possibility that disjoints between the two may, at least sometimes, have important implications. If meta-awareness is absent from a mundane experience, this is probably of little consequence. If, however, meta-awareness becomes disjointed from the type of highly significant life experience that usually induces reflection, then the subsequent application or reapplication of meta-awareness to that experience may result in a significant sense of discovery. Accordingly, discovered memories are hypothesized to result from a disjointing and subsequent rejoining of consciousness from meta-awareness. This process may involve a combination of factors occurring at the encoding, retention interval, retrieval, and post-retrieval phases. At the encoding phase, disjoints between individuals' conscious experience and their meta-aware understanding may result from a variety of factors including age, stress, dissociation, and the nocturnal nature of the abuse. Even if an experience is initially encoded with a meta-aware understanding, the meta-aware reflection on the experience may dissipate during the retention interphase as individuals retrieve their abuse memories without reflection. At the time of retrieval individuals may experience a profound sense of discovery that results from gaining, or regaining, a new meta-aware understanding of the experience. Finally, during the post-retrieval phase, individuals may revisit the discovery experience itself in the light of meta-awareness, imposing new interpretations on the nature of the discovery experience and what exactly it was that was discovered. In the following discussion we use the consciousness/meta-awareness distinction as a framework within which to explore the encoding, retention interval, retrieval, and post-retrieval processes that may lead to discovered memories. We emphasize this distinction because of its novelty and potential value in clarifying the mechanisms underlying discovered memories.

Encoding mechanisms

At the time of encoding, it is at least in principle possible that individuals could experience traumatic events without explicitly reflecting on their meaning (i.e. without meta-awareness). A variety of factors could contribute to individuals encoding traumatic experiences without meta-awareness.

Stress

It is known that stress has a dramatic influence on physiological processes in the brain, and that the effect can be specific to certain brain structures that are important for memory. Stress is thought to impair hippocampal integration of memories, leading to a lack of an explicit account of the event. Moreover, when stress occurs, the amygdala — a brain structure important for emotional processing — remains unimpaired. A potentially central role of the amygdala in stressful experiences is suggested by LeDoux (1992, 1996), who has demonstrated that the amygdala is critically involved in the learning of fear responses. This idea, coupled with a disruption of the memory consolidation functions of the hippocampus, may be an important contributor in meta-awareness of events. In other words, a failure of the memory of the traumatic experience to be formed under highly stressful situations to be integrated within the frontal cortex and hippocampus might result in a lack of self-awareness of the experience.

Dissociation

Another factor that may prevent a memory from achieving meta-awareness is dissociation. Dissociation is a controversial notion, but is typically defined as a "lack of normal integration of thoughts, feelings, and experiences into the stream of consciousness and memory" (Bernstein & Putnam, 1986, p. 727). During the course of a traumatic event, individuals may dissociate themselves from the ongoing experience — a process that could influence the way in which the experience is encoded and later retrieved. This lack of integration of the event as a whole could prevent the individual from gaining meta-awareness of the event for an extended period of time.

Nocturnal occurrence

Many reported incidents of sexual abuse occur at night, which may contribute to the suspension of meta-awareness during abuse. In fact, the absence of meta-awareness is a key characteristic of nocturnal cognition. Dreams characteristically contain discrepancies and are forgotten upon awakening unless individuals specifically reflect on them soon after awakening (Hobson, 1988). In contrast, lucid dreaming precisely involves becoming self-aware during dreaming and typically works best when the individual is encouraged to regularly meta-aware reflect about the environment during waking hours (LaBerge, 1985). The qualitative difference between normal dreaming and lucid dreaming highlights the lack of meta-awareness that is typically associated with the nocturnal cognition that occurs during dreams.

Lack of schema

Another possible mechanism that could result in the formation of a memory that lacks meta-awareness is lack of schematic knowledge. If the person experiences the abuse at a young age, the person may lack the cognitive faculty to fully understand the nature and extent of the act. In other words, at the time of the event, the victim may not consider the events to constitute sexual abuse. If this were the case, then the individual may have a meta-aware understanding of the experience, as being unpleasant or awkward, but not as sexual abuse. The lack of an adult metaconsciousness of the experience may thus set the stage for a future memory discovery experience in which the individual develops a newfound understanding of what happened.

Retention interval mechanisms

There are a number of factors during the retention interval that could contribute to memories ultimately being characterized as "discovered".

Non-narratively encoded memories

If memories are initially encoded with a lack of meta-awareness, then during the retention interval they may in fact be less accessible because they have not been integrated into the individual's autobiographical life narrative. This lack of initial meta-awareness may then produce memories that are difficult to retrieve volitionally because they lack an explicit tag by which they might be searched. As a result, these memories may be uniquely dependent on environmental cues to be retrieved, and thus may lie dormant during the retention interval until the appropriate matching environmental cue is encountered. However, even when the memories are retrieved by the appropriate environmental cues, their contents still might not make it to meta-awareness.

Changes in context

If an individual lacked meta-awareness during the encoding of an experience, then it is easy to see how these might be forgotten for extended periods of time. However, what can explain the forgetting of experiences in which there probably was meta-awareness during encoding? One possible explanation is that there may be a change of context between the time of the experience and the individual's present state. This change in context may lead to the experience being thought about less and less, until eventually it isn't thought about at all. Both physical and psychological changes of context are crucial. In our seven cases there are numerous examples of individuals who had moved from the original area. For instance, DJ discovered her memory of sexual abuse perpetrated by a neighbor when, after having moved to live in a different state, encountered the perpetrator at a dinner party. This case illustrates one of the postulated hallmarks of traumatic memory — that it is especially cue-dependent (Brewin, Dalgleish & Joseph, 1996).

Directed forgetting

Finally, there is considerable evidence that, with intention, individuals can direct themselves to forget at least some types of memory materials. Thus it is at least possible that directed forgetting processes (Bjork, 1989) may contribute to a reduction in accessibility of the memories during the retention interval.

Avoiding meta-awareness

In addition to postulating possible mechanisms by which abuse memories might actually come to be less available during the retention interval, it also important to identify mechanisms by which the memories might simply "seem" to have been less accessible. In two of the previously reviewed cases, evidence suggests that the individuals misconstrued their prior forgetting. In the cases of TW and WB, ex-husbands reported discussing the event with the victims during a period of time in which the victims thought they had completely forgotten the abuse. In these case they were described as talking about their experiences rather cavalierly. Also importantly, these individuals entirely failed to recall having talked about these experiences. Although we can only speculate about what might have happened here, one plausible account is that the retrieval experiences themselves occurred with an absence of metaconsciousness. The individuals simply did not reflect on the extremely personal experiences that they were describing or on the fact that they were describing them. The absence of metaconscious reflection at the time of retrieval may have contributed to the affectively flat manner in which the memories were described to their husbands, and to their subsequent inability to recall their prior retrievals. Indeed it seems quite plausible that one way in which individuals may manage to cope with traumatic experiences is simply to avoid meta-aware reflections of the experiences when they come to mind. Like mountain climbers who know better than to look down, some individuals with traumatic memories may learn (either deliberately or perhaps through some form of conditioning) to not ponder their recollections when disturbing memories come to mind. In this sense, rather than being repressed, traumatic memories may simply be ignored.

Retrieval mechanisms

At one level of analysis, understanding what happens at the retrieval phase is very straightforward. Some memory cue occurred which caused the individuals to remember and reflect on their prior abuse experience. Indeed it is notable that in all of the cases reviewed there was some significant correspondence between the cue that allegedly prompted the memory and the actual abuse experience (ranging from seeing a movie about sexual abuse to actually seeing the perpetrator). Virtually all theories of memory would suggest that such cues would help to increase the accessibility of prior memories.

Changes in meta-awareness of the event

The cases reviewed here suggest that individuals' retrieval experience did not just involve the recollection of the event itself, but also involved a profound sense of personal discovery with an immediate unpacking and emotional onrush reminiscent of classic insight experiences (Schooler & Melcher, 1995). The perception of profound personal discovery at the time of retrieval may hold an important clue towards understanding discovered memories. In particular, from the vantage of metaconsciousness theory, the discovery experience can be reasonably characterized as the moment in which the individual gains or regains meta-awareness of the experience. If the individuals encoded the experience without meta-awareness originally, then the discovery may involve the first explicit realization of what happened to them. If the memory had previously been explicitly reflected on, then the discovery may involve a re-gaining of meta-awareness of the abuse, after a period of time in which meta-aware reflection of the abuse had been avoided.

Individuals may also impose a new meta-aware understanding of the experience that is qualitatively different from that which originally accompanied the abuse. As WB put it: "In a way, I have managed to repress the *meaning* of what happened all of these years. I may have not completely forgotten the experience...but I have pushed it away, minimized it... It wasn't a real rape." Although WB originally recognized that her discovery might not have been of the memory itself but rather the explicit meaning (or in our terms the metaconscious understanding) of the memory, she later began to believe that she had really forgotten the experience. Thus, the discovery of new metaconscious understanding of the experience may be confused either at the time or later with a discovery of the memory itself, leading individuals to conclude that they had entirely forgotten and then later suddenly remembered abuse. In short, the key element of the perception that one has retrieved a long lost memory of abuse may be the discovery of a new understanding of the meaning of the experience. This new understanding may or may not also involve a new availability of the memory itself.

Onrush of emotions and the forgot-it-all-along effect

In addition to a new (or renewed) meta-awareness of the event, the sheer emotional impact of thinking about the experience may contribute to the profound sense of discovery associated with the retrieval experience. This profound emotional onrush might be caused by a variety of factors. As noted, an increased appreciation of the significance of the event is likely to be one important factor. In addition, if individuals had attempted to suppress the memory for some period of time, then, when it came back, the well-established emotional rebound effect associated with suppressed thoughts (Wegner & Gold, 1995) might imbue the recollection with extra emotion. This emotion might then be used to make a (potentially faulty) inference about their prior knowledge of the experience; i.e. they may underestimate their prior knowledge of the event, a phenomenon previously referred to as the forgot-it-all-along effect (Schooler et al., 1997b). Accordingly individuals may reason, "If I am this shocked and surprised then I must have previously completely forgotten about the experience."

Post-retrieval mechanisms

Although in the cases reviewed here it seems likely that individuals did in fact have a profound discovery experience corresponding to the memories in question, it nevertheless seems plausible that their recollections of that discovery may have evolved with time. This may further contribute to the belief that they had discovered a previously completely forgotten experience. A number of factors could contribute to such changes.

Lack of meta-awareness at the time of retrieval

In the above analysis it was suggested that many discovered memories may involve a new meta-awareness at the time of retrieval of the meaning and significance of the experience. However, it is also possible that, in some cases, an individual's retrieval experience, by virtue of its sheer emotional impact, itself lacks a meta-aware appraisal. In short, individuals may be simply reeling with emotion, not fully aware of what they are experiencing. Later, as they reflect on the experience, they process the retrieval experience itself in the light of meta-awareness. In short they may say to themselves "Wow, what hit me?". The perception of the discovery of a long-forgotten memory may then be constructed as individuals trying in retrospect to make sense of their experience.

Discussion

As individuals continue to recount their recollections of their discovery experience it may become further schematized and streamlined (e.g. Bartlett, 1932), increasingly focusing on the perceived primary element (i.e. the increased availability of the memory) and de-emphasizing other elements (e.g. the discovery of a new understanding of the experience).

Learning about recovered memories

Finally, exposure to materials that describe recovered memories and repression may further contribute to shaping individuals' beliefs about the prior state of their own memories. As they hear about the way in which memories can be entirely buried and then suddenly return in pristine fashion, they may increasingly reinterpret their own recollective experiences in this light.

Caveats

The above analysis illustrates the promise of case-based studies for both documenting discovered memories of authentic abuse and identifying possible mechanisms that might lead to them. At the same time, however, it is important to emphasize the preliminary nature of both the case-based analysis presented here and the mechanisms used to account for them. Additional research using the corroborative approach with larger populations and more systematic sampling techniques are needed to determine the frequency with which the various qualities of the discovered memories identified in the cases described above are observed. How often is it actually possible to provide some independent corroboration of the abuse? How common is it for there to be evidence that individuals overestimated their degree of forgetting? To what degree is the profound sense of self-discovery a common ingredient to discovered memories? How often might it be appropriate to characterize discovered memories within the context of the consciousness/meta-awareness distinction? The evidence presented here cannot adequately answer any of these questions, but it does suggest that the pursuit of such questions is important and timely.

DISCOVERED FABRICATED MEMORIES

With the above case-based analysis of the mechanisms thought to be responsible for discovered authentic memories at hand, we next attempt to apply a similar systematic analysis of the critical encoding, retention interval, retrieval, and post-retrieval variables to discovered false memories. At the outset we must concede that, in contrast to the seemingly authentic cases described earlier, to date we have not personally investigated cases in which the evidence suggests that the memories were false. Nevertheless, there have been many well-documented court cases in which individuals (retractors) have provided sufficient evidence to persuade a judge or jury that abuse memories which the retractors once believed were factual, were actually fictions based on their therapists' suggestions. Of course, as with the memories that we have characterized as authentic, there is rarely any way to indisputably *prove* that a memory as false. We hope that readers will concur with us — and with the judges and juries in the respective cases that we review — that the preponderance of evidence in these cases supports the likelihood that the memories were largely fictitious.

How do we know the memories are fabricated?

Needless to say, trying to demonstrate that some event did not occur is difficult. Yet, there are several factors that can provide support for the conclusion that abuse did not occur. One of these factors is the claim that satanic ritual abuse (SRA) occurred. Memories of SRA are commonly situated in malpractice suits against former mental health providers, and many of these cases serve as examples in our case-based analysis.

However, despite many allegations of SRA, a significant FBI study found no physical evidence substantiating claims of SRA (Lanning, 1992). Lanning reports that there is little or no corroborative evidence of organized satanic cults. Absence of supporting data for these events, despite extensive searching, suggest that memories of SRA are probably not based on reality. Another factor shedding doubt on the veracity of a memory is the likelihood that events from a certain age can be remembered. Typically, people are unable to remember events that happened prior to their third or at the earliest second birthday (Usher & Neisser, 1993); yet, many fabricated memories concern alleged abuse prior to the lifting of infantile amnesia and sometimes since birth. Also, any lack of physical or medical evidence in situations where it would be expected can also serve as evidence for false memories. For example, in one case in which, under the guidance of a church counselor, a woman came to believe that her father had raped her, got her pregnant and performed a coat-hanger abortion, medical evidence suggested that she was a virgin and that her father had had a vasectomy (Rutherford v. Strand et al., 1996). When available, this type of physical evidence provides further doubts about the credibility of the discovered memory.

The following cases of discovered fabricated memories are generously taken from the legal arena. The main reason for this bias is two-fold. First, legal cases retain a lot of documented evidence that can be consulted and evaluated, providing a kind of corroboration. Second, when following a thorough review of all of the available evidence where a court rules affirmatively in a malpractice case concerning a former patient against a therapist for using suggestive techniques that induced false memories, it strengthens our confidence that the discovered memories were fabricated rather than authentic. We next review seven cases, which are taken from a sample of malpractice suits claiming injury to misdiagnosis and false memory implantation. As with the seemingly authentic discovered memories, in each case we review the relevant encoding, retention interval, retrieval, and post-retrieval factors that are known about each case. Although this basic division of the memory process similarly applies to fabricated memories, its application is somewhat different. In the case of false discovered memories, there is typically no evidence for the encoding of the experience at the time it is alleged; rather the evidence for encoding is seen in the context of therapy where the seeds of the memory are first planted. Following this initial "planting" the retention interval corresponds to the period where the therapist encourages memory recovery with hypnosis, visualization, and other techniques, resulting in the development of the memory. The retrieval phase involves the time at which the patient finally comes to accept the therapist's suggestions as real memories. Finally, at least in the cases that we are reviewing here, the post-retrieval phase involves a growing skepticism of the memory, leading ultimately to a complete rejection of the memory, and resentment towards the therapist for planting it.

Case 1

Elizabeth Carlson's memory discovery experience occurred at age 35. She was 59 at the time of the malpractice trial against her former psychiatrist (Carlson v. Humenansky, 1996).

Encoding

Carlson was referred to a psychiatrist while being treated for severe depression. The psychiatrist, Humenansky, immediately suggested that her problem was not depression, but probably multiple personality disorder (MPD). She further suggested that MPD was associated with forgotten childhood sexual abuse, so she was probably abused. Carlson noted that when her therapist told her that she wasn't responsible for her current depression, but that uncontrollable past events were to blame, she felt a sense of relief concerning her situation.

Retention interval

Since Carlson didn't have any "memories" yet, her therapist suggested several techniques. In particular, Humenansky used hypnosis and sodium amytal to help Carlson remember the childhood events. During the trial, Richard Ofshe, an expert on cults and the suggestive techniques that they use, detailed specific coercive and suggestive statements made by Humenansky during a sodium amytal interview she had conducted with Carlson. Guided imagery was also conducted in a similar suggestive manner, with Carlson being instructed to imagine scenes of abuse by different people even though she had no such memories. Carlson was given books to read, such as Bass and Davis's *The Courage to Heal* (1988) and books about MPD cases, and was instructed that if anything felt uncomfortable to her while she read them, it was an indication that similar things had happened to her. All of these measures were used in the hope of memory recovery, in conjunction with administration of strong medications such as several benzodiazepines, Ativan, Prozac, and various other drugs.

Retrieval

Carlson eventually entered group therapy with other MPD patients. As a result of the treatment, Carlson says she developed a false belief that she was part of an intergenerational satanic cult, participating in satanic rituals, and she eventually became suicidal. Carlson had become convinced that she had created multiple personalities to deal with supposed sexual assaults by her parents, relatives, and neighbors. Carlson's mental condition had deteriorated, rather than improved.

Post-retrieval

Carlson began to doubt her memories when she got a new prescription that made her feel better, causing her to flush all her other pills down the toilet. During group therapy, the participants began to notice the similarity in their abuse memories, and how they resembled events in the books they had been given to read. Other patients even admitted that they had made up alters to fit in with the group. Carlson confronted Humenansky concerning this revelation, and soon the therapist dropped all of her MPD patients. The jury found Humenansky negligent in failing to meet recognized medical standards and that her diagnosis, care, and treatment were direct causes of harm to Carlson. Carlson and her family were awarded $2.5 million in damages.

Case 2

Patricia Burgus's memory discovery experience occurred at age 30. She was 41 when she received a settlement in a medical malpractice suit against her psychiatrist (Burgus v. Braun et al., 1997).

Encoding

Patricia Burgus entered therapy for post-partum depression, but was soon diagnosed with MPD and placed in the dissociative disorders unit of Bennett Braun at Rush-Presbyterian Hospital in Chicago. Braun then told Burgus that it was likely she was involved in a cult that participated in satanic ritual abuse, since this was typical of patients with MPD. Braun's beliefs, regardless of Burgus's lack of memories, are highlighted by his extensive publications documenting his view that MPD is caused by repressed memories of trauma (e.g. Braun, 1986), and his role as a founding member of the International Society for the Study of Multiple Personality and Dissociation. Furthermore, he failed to advise Burgus that the diagnosis of MPD was controversial and didn't obtain informed consent, instead eventually telling her that the memories being uncovered represented real memories of actual historical events. Burgus noted the use of authoritative suggestions that implied that she had to remember in order to get better.

Retention interval

Burgus claims that hypnosis and other treatments, such as drug therapy, were used in an effort to help her to remember. During testimony at a disciplinary hearing of Braun, Burgus noted, "we were put on massive experimental medicines, we were hypnotized, we were brainwashed". Burgus's sons were also hospitalized because they were told that they may be genetically predisposed to MPD. Under high doses of medication and hypnotism, Burgus now says that reality and fantasy blended together. In the complaint against Rush-Presbyterian, Burgus states that Braun prescribed Inderal, Halcion, Xanax, sedatives and hypnotic psychotropic drugs at experimental, untested, and medically inappropriate dosage levels. Additionally, Burgus was occasionally kept in leather restraints during therapeutic sessions.

Retrieval
Burgus recovered memories of being part of a satanic cult, including cannibalism, being sexually abused by numerous men, and abusing her own two sons. She eventually became convinced that she had over 300 alternative personalities as a result of repeated and extensive traumatic childhood abuse. To exemplify the pervasiveness of the belief in this memory, her husband brought to the therapist some hamburger meat served at a picnic to run tests on to determine if its origin was human.

Post-retrieval
Burgus often questioned the validity of her memories, but she was repeatedly told that she was the only one to express doubt. Finally, when she got out of the hospital, Burgus couldn't find any proof of her memories and began to get even more suspicious. Her case against Braun was settled in the amount of $10.6 million, and Braun's medical license has since been revoked.

Case 3

Lynn Carl's memory discovery experience occurred approximately when she was 40 years old. She was 46 at the time of the trial (Carl v. Peterson et al., 1997).

Encoding
Lynn Carl initially entered therapy for depression. She was soon diagnosed with MPD, and was hospitalized for two years at Spring Shadows Glen in the dissociative disorders unit.[2] The treating mental health workers indicated

---

[2] In October of 1997 a federal grand jury indicted a psychiatric hospital administrator and four mental-health practitioners in Houston on counts of conspiracy and mail fraud, charging therapists with having intentionally misdiagnosed MPD for money (U.S. v. Peterson et al., 1997). This was the first time criminal charges had arisen from false memory allegations. The indictment alleged that the former employees of Spring Shadows Glen Hospital gained millions in fraudulent insurance payments by eliciting statements of satanic ritual abuse and cult activities and other false experiences and memories from patients. This case declared a mistrial in February 1999 due to jury problems, and the judge stated that there is not to be a retrial because of the toll on witnesses. The hospital's controversial dissociative disorders unit was closed in March 1993 after state investigators cited the unit for excessive use of physical restraints on patients, and censorship of patient mail and phone calls.

to Carl that they believed she had experienced satanic ritual abuse as a child. When Carl told her therapists that she didn't believe any such events had happened, she was told that her memories had been repressed in order to deal with the satanic ritual abuse. During the trial it was evident that Keraga, one of the treating therapists, failed to obtain informed consent and failed to disclose to Carl that memories recovered through hypnosis might not be reliable. Carl was also authoritatively told that she had to remember in order to become better, and that unless she continued recovering memories about the abuse, she would remain in denial and her children wouldn't get well.

Retention interval
In order to help Carl to remember the supposed SRA, hypnosis was extensively used during her therapeutic sessions. Additionally, physical restraints were periodically used, and contact with anybody from outside the unit (including mail) was prohibited

Retrieval
Carl became convinced that she had developed more than 500 personalities because of repressed memories of involvement in a satanic cult. This included murder, cannibalism, sexual abuse and incest, and eventually the belief that she abused her own children. Earlier, she was forced to report herself to the police as a child abuser even though she had no detailed memory of abusing her own children. As a result of this confession, the children were removed from her custody. Moreover, despite seeing no improvement in Carl, Keraga continued with the treatment. One of Carl's therapists testified that she didn't know if the specific memories that Carl recovered in therapy were true, but said she believed the gist of them.

Post-retrieval
After two years of therapy Carl left the hospital and was cut off from her family. She later underwent therapy in Florida and then Baltimore, and began to realize the memories she had were false. She eventually won a $5.8 million judgment for medical negligence during psychotherapy that allegedly produced false memories of SRA.

Case 4

Diana Halbrooks was 36 years old at the time of her discovery experience and was 47 at the time of the trial (Halbrooks v. Moore, 1995).

Encoding
Halbrooks sought treatment for recurring depression and familial conflicts. She began attending group counseling sessions with Moore, a

licensed professional counselor and ordained minister. To Halbrooks' surprise, Moore suggested that she suffered from MPD and started her with group therapy with other MPD patients. Halbrooks noted that when she began attending a Saturday morning group, none of the group members, including herself, was reporting parental sexual abuse.

Retention interval
In her testimony, Halbrooks alleged that Moore exerted an ever-increasing control over her and caused her to disassociate from her family and have an unnatural and unhealthy dependence on him. After reading several MPD books and within a year of group treatment, a large percentage of the group members believed they suffered from parental sexual abuse. Similarly, initially only one group member believed she was the victim of SRA, but by the time Halbrooks left the group three years later, a large number of group members had such beliefs

Retrieval
Halbrooks discovered false memories of being a victim of sexual abuse, child abuse, and incest from several family members. Moore had also convinced her that she suffered from MPD. Interestingly, Halbrooks testified that she attributed her visions and memories of abuse to hearing other group members talk each week about their abusive experiences.

Post-retrieval
Halbrooks began to doubt her memories after leaving therapy. The jury found Moore guilty of negligence and that his actions were the proximate cause of damage to Halbrooks. She was awarded $105,000 and the defendant was found 60% liable.

Case 5

Nicole Althaus was 16 years old at the time of her discovery experience. At the time of the trial she was only 19 (Althaus v. Cohen, 1994).

Encoding
Althaus entered therapy when she became depressed because her mother was seriously ill. She initially confided in a teacher, who suspected that her depression stemmed from something other than her mother's illness. Althaus initially denied having memories of abuse events, and the teacher indicated that she probably repressed them. Althaus began seeing a psychiatrist, Cohen, who diagnosed her as suffering from post-traumatic stress disorder brought on by sexual abuse, despite having no memory of the alleged abuse.

Retention interval

During the course of therapy, Cohen refused input from the parents or any other outside sources concerning her suspicions. After reading several books about abusive experiences, Althaus began having nightmares about being abused herself. These dreams were interpreted by her therapist as being snippets of real memories.

Retrieval:

Althaus claimed that she had become convinced that her father had sexually abused her, and eventually believed that she had been raped and tortured and had given birth to three children, all of whom were murdered. Other reports from Althaus suggest that her grandmother flew about on a broom, that she was tortured with medieval thumbscrews, and that she was raped in view of diners in a crowded restaurant. As Althaus's charges became progressively more outlandish, the stories were never challenged. Although Cohen said that she never believed the wildest tales of orgies, murder and torture, she said that it was her job to treat Althaus, not investigate her. As a result of Althaus's allegations of sexual molestation and ritual abuse, her parents were arrested on more than one occasion. Even though Althaus brought criminal charges against her parents, the court noted that the psychiatrist knew that at least some of the girl's allegations were not true, but she essentially validated unwittingly false testimony during and before the criminal proceedings. In fact, Cohen repeatedly stated that she was not required to make any determinations about the credibility of Althaus's allegations.

Post-retrieval

The criminal charges against the parents were withdrawn after Althaus underwent an independent psychiatric evaluation. The court-appointed psychiatrist testified that she suffered from borderline personality disorder and that the abuse allegations were a product of the disorder, which rendered Althaus unable to distinguish fact from fantasy. In the malpractice trial, the court ruled that a duty was owed to the accused parents as well as the defendant therapist's patient. The jury awarded Althaus and her parents $272,232 in compensatory damages against the psychiatrist for failure to properly diagnose and encouraging her to believe in fictitious events.

Case 6

Mary Shanley's discovery experience occurred when she was 39 years old and she was 45 around the time of the trial (Shanley v. Peterson et al., 1996; Shanley v. Braun et al., 1997).

Encoding

Shanley entered therapy because she was suffering from increased anxiety, depression, and panic attacks after undergoing a total hysterectomy and being attacked by a parent in her classroom. She was soon diagnosed with MPD and told by Braun, her psychiatrist, that she had to uncover repressed memories of early childhood trauma because dissociative disorders are usually caused by SRA (Braun is the same psychiatrist who treated the patient in Case 2, in which his unsubstantiated beliefs about repressed memories of trauma were in question). At one time an "expert" in satanic cults was brought in (a Chicago police officer who acted as a private consultant), who was able through the use of an international cult-awareness network computer to verify that not only was she in fact a five-generation Satanist, but that she was satanic cult royalty. She was sent to a hospital in Houston for deprogramming, and eventually her 9-year-old son was sent to the same hospital with an MPD diagnosis. During the entire ordeal, Shanley expressed doubts concerning her memories, initially denying having any knowledge of the alleged abusive and satanic events. In Braun's notes of therapeutic sessions he noted that "she was struggling with the acceptance of the diagnosis of MPD and dissociation, having a high level of denial". Moreover, Shanley was isolated from outside influences since her therapists didn't allow contact with anyone outside of the unit, and threatened her if she attempted to leave the hospital.

Retention interval

Shanley started to have dreams in which abusive events occurred. In an attempt to help Shanley recover memories, she was informed that her dreams of abuse were indicative of real memories and that she should believe them. Shanley testified that she was given such high amounts of salt when her blood pressure became too low, that her body retained the fluid. She was told that this was a body memory of a pregnancy when she was in the cult. Shanley commented that several times her already high levels of medication were increased in an attempt to elicit more memories and in an effort to decrease switching between her alleged alter personalities. Physical restraints were used during abreactive therapy sessions when therapists tried to bring forth her alter personalities. She testified that she was placed in restraints more than 100 times during her hospitalization, sometimes for as long as 20 hours at a time. In the insurance fraud criminal trial against the hospital that treated Shanley (see footnote 2), a claims reviewer for an insurance company testified that, at the time of the review, she was concerned that Shanley had been hospitalized for more than a year with little improvement. Shanley actually remained in the hospital for more than two years.

Retrieval
Shanley claims that she had 10,000 alters. One of the treating psychiatrists allegedly was able to communicate with Shanley through the use of "finger signals", and diagnosed her as MPD "polyfragmented". Braun's notes in a discharge summary contend that Shanley had memories of her brother being put in a cage with a dog and having to kill the dog, being taken home with a nurse after cult meetings, being conditioned through electrical shock and other tortures, drinking blood from a cow, being put in a cold bin, and being stripped of all of her clothing, to name a few.

Post-retrieval
Eventually Shanley was released from the hospital, and, in the absence of the suggestive influence of her therapists, came to realize that her memories weren't memories after all. Her case was settled out of court under confidential terms.

Case 7

Nadean Cool's age at the time of her discovery experience was 34. She was 44 at the time of trial (Cool v. Olson, 1997).

Encoding
Plagued with problems of depression after a traumatic event experienced by a family member, Cool started therapy with Olson, which spanned over a six-year period. To her surprise, she was diagnosed as having MPD and was told that she probably couldn't remember some horrible satanic childhood events. Cool stated that she trusted her psychiatrist completely, to the point that she believed whatever he told her, especially the comment that she needed to remember events in order to get better.

Retention interval
During treatment, Olson put Cool under hypnosis. She was told to separate parts of her ego, such as her anger side, and was regressed back to childhood. Cool testified that before Olson hypnotized her for the first time, he never warned her of the risks involved or that false memories might occur. He also insisted that if she denied the memories evoked under hypnosis she would never get better. When Cool asked after hypnotic sessions why she had not remembered such child abuse, Olson convinced her that under hypnosis you become someone else and only that person remembers these things. Additionally, Olson performed an exorcism on her to rid her of demonic spirits. He also prescribed a regimen of drugs, some addictive, but far beyond what is acceptable, leading to hallucinations. It also appears that the psychiatrist used fear to convince Cool

that her family and members of a satanic cult wanted to kill her, further alienating her from outside sources.

Retrieval
Cool believed that she had more than 120 personalities, including a duck, angels that talked to God and Satan, and was the bride of Satan. She believed that she had been a member of a satanic cult, had killed babies, and had eaten human flesh. Cool also came to believe that she had knifed babies in the heart and passed them around for other cult members to eat. To become Satan's bride, Olson told Cool that she had to be raped by 60 or 70 men and have sex with animals. He said the only way Cool would get better was to describe such acts to him in detail. Her psychiatrist believed that the personalities were brought on by sexual and physical abuse she suffered when she was young. As her mental condition deteriorated and she became more hopeless, Cool attempted suicide several times during her therapy.

Post-retrieval
Finally, Cool told Olson that she was discontinuing treatment because she felt like dying all the time and couldn't see how she'd ever get better. "When I understood what it was really like was when the compound in Waco burned down and all those people followed that man to their deaths and Jim Jones' followers killed themselves," Cool noted, comparing her experience to the brainwashing of cult members. Cool received $2.4 million in an out-of-court settlement with the psychiatrist.

ANALYSIS OF THE CASE-BASED EVIDENCE FOR FABRICATED MEMORIES

The preceding case summaries highlight many components that are potentially crucial during the encoding, retention interval, retrieval, and post-retrieval stages of fabricated memories. Below we review and evaluate the evidence in support of the individuals' claims regarding these four phases.

Evidence surrounding the encoding phase
There appear to be two general trends that occur during the encoding phase. Firstly, there is usually some form of a suggestion of past abuse that the patient is unaware of, and this suggestion usually stems from the conclusion that the patient has multiple personality disorder. In Case 1, even though Carlson entered therapy with complaints of depression, she

was diagnosed with MPD and told that MPD was associated with for-gotten childhood sexual abuse. Similarly, Burgus in Case 2 was diagnosed with MPD and told that she was likely involved in a cult that participated in satanic ritual abuse since that was typical of patients with MPD, despite Burgus's initial complaint of post-partum depression. Carl's therapists in Case 3 emphasized that even though she entered therapy for depression with no memories of childhood abuse, she really had multiple personal-ities and that her memories had been repressed to deal with the horrible events. In Case 6, Shanley's experience was similar, which isn't all that surprising because one of her treating psychiatrists was one of Carl's. Shanley was diagnosed with MPD, despite complaints of anxiety and depression, and was told that she had to uncover repressed memories of early childhood trauma because MPD is usually caused by satanic ritual abuse. A similar scenario occurred in with Cool, Case 7. Cool entered therapy because she felt guilty about a traumatic event experienced by a family member, but soon found out that she had MPD and had to remem-ber sexually abusive events in order to get better. Althaus in Case 5 became depressed over a family member's illness, but was informed by several mental health practitioners that she really was suffering from repressed memories of abuse and post-traumatic stress disorder. In all of these examples, each of the patients had entered therapy in search of relief from depression, anxiety, or guilt, but were instead diagnosed with MPD and blatantly told about memories of abuse that were repressed (despite having no such memories).

Secondly, in response to the initial suggestions of abuse and diagnosis of MPD, many of the patients expressed doubt over the therapist's asser-tion. Carl in Case 3 stated that she argued with the therapists that she didn't believe what she was being told, and that these alleged satanic abusive events had never occurred. Likewise, in Case 4, Halbrooks was placed in group therapy for parental sexual abuse, even though she denied having any memories. Althaus in Case 5 initially denied having any memories of childhood abuse despite her therapist's persistence that she was abused. In the remaining four cases, all of the patients also denied having any form of memory for the alleged traumatic childhood events, causing them to initially express doubt. However, many of them also noted that they placed an extraordinary amount of belief and trust in the practitioner.

Evidence surrounding the retention interval phase

In all of the cases the evidence for the retention interval is very compelling. After the initial suggestion of abuse by the therapist, in each case various techniques were used to help the patient to remember the unrecallable memories. In every case there were reports of suggestive techniques (i.e. memory recovery techniques) being used by the therapists. These methods ranged from hypnosis to guided imagery and from dream interpretation to drug therapy. In an attempt to foster memory recovery, a plethora of techniques were used with Carlson in Case 1. Both hypnosis and sodium amytal were used in conjunction with suggestive statements offered by the therapist. Additionally, Carlson imagined various abusive acts committed by numerous people, despite having no real memories. Books outlining abusive acts were offered as an exercise in memory recovery in that Carlson was told that if anything she was reading made her feel uncomfortable, then similar things had happened to her. Hypnosis and experimental levels of various medications were administered to Burgus in Case 2, who noted that under this regimen she began to confuse reality and fantasy. The predominant technique in Case 3 was also the use of extensive hypnosis. The recovery of memory for Halbrooks, Case 4, seemed to rely on the mixture of group therapy and the fact that all of the group members were reading the same books on childhood sexual abuse and SRA. The confluence of reading material and dream interpretation also appears to be the predominant technique used with Althaus in Case 5. Dream interpretation was also important in Shanley's experience (Case 6), along with the use of massive amounts of drugs and physical restraints. Finally, in Case 7 the mixture of hypnosis and drugs led to Cool's hallucinations, which were then interpreted as real memories. The use of hypnosis in these therapeutic situations was often not accompanied with any warnings about the risks involved or that the memories might be the result of imagination. In contrast, the memories that appeared under hypnosis were blatantly portrayed as factual events.

Evidence surrounding the retrieval phase

In all of the cases, the retrieval of the alleged fabricated memories did not occur immediately after therapy began. The course of memory fabrication appears to require both the use of suggestive techniques and an extended period of time. It seems that the amount of time that had passed before the individuals in our seven cases came to believe that the memories were real ranged from a couple of months to a year. Cases 1 through 7 all recovered memories of abuse that they did not have prior to entering therapy. Some of these recovered memories appear to have felt like very real memories, accompanied by vivid images and bodily sensations, while others appear to rely more on the firm belief that these horrible events had happened in the absence of this vivid conscious experience. Cases 1, 2, 3, 6, and 7 had all believed that they were all part of different intergenerational satanic cults, involving baby breeding, blood drinking, cannibalism, murder, and orgies. Whether or not these beliefs were accompanied with false vivid recollections is unclear; however, it is clear that these beliefs dramatically altered their lives. Similarly, the woman in Case 5 claimed that she had given birth to three children and had murdered all of them (despite being only 16 years old), that she was raped in front of people in a crowded restaurant, and even that her grandmother flew around on a broom. In each of these instances the memories or beliefs were not present when the patient initially entered therapy, but only came into existence after the suggestive techniques were used for an prolonged period of time.

Despite the outlandishness of some of the claims, many of the therapists didn't doubt the veracity of their patient's memories, or didn't find it necessary to question them. Take, for example, this court statement by the therapist in Case 1, "I've never had somebody recover a memory that was wrong. I don't believe in false memories." In Case 3 one of the therapists testified that she believed the gist of the memories that Carl recovered in therapy, but didn't know if the specifics were accurate. It appears that this wasn't important for treatment. Althaus's practitioner (Case 5) claimed that it wasn't her job to investigate the veracity of her memories, only to treat her. However, this same therapist testified in court concerning the alleged parental sexual abuse, despite disallowing any input from the parents during the course of therapy. Cool, who thought she had over 120 personalities including angels and the bride of Satan, attests that her therapist uncritically accepted whatever came out of her mouth. This noncritical acceptance, and blatant belief that everything must be uncovered before the patient can get better, probably was a major contributor to many of these cases of fabricated memories.

Evidence surrounding the post-retrieval phase

Documenting post-retrieval factors is also important in gaining a finer understanding of false memories. Although the specifics are not clear in some of our cases, there do appear to be several factors that can account for the retraction of previously held memories and beliefs. First, several of the patients began to seriously doubt their memories when they were able to leave the therapists' influence. This appears especially to be the situation in Cases 2, 3, 6, and 7. Other patients started to question their memories after they stopped taking the massive amounts of medication that had previously kept them in a suggestive state, such as Case 1, while others began to wonder why everyone in their group had similar memories, such as Case 4. Finally, when Althaus in Case 5 had to be independently evaluated by a psychiatrist in the child abuse case against her parents, she came to realize that she was misdiagnosed with MPD and that what she was reporting as memories weren't really memories after all. What this analysis suggests is that when the patients are taken out of the situation in which they are cut off from outside influences, given massive amounts of drugs, and extensively hypnotized, then they are able to think clearly again and seriously examine their claims.

Conclusion

The above analysis of the seven cases indicates that at least sometimes it is possible to ascertain with a reasonable degree of confidence that individuals who perceived themselves to have retrieved long-forgotten memories of abuse may be recalling suggested events and histories that were the product of questionable techniques. In the following analysis, we consider the possible mechanisms that could lead individuals to perceive themselves as having discovered long-forgotten memories of abuse that didn't actually occur.

POSSIBLE MECHANISMS THAT COULD LEAD TO DISCOVERED FABRICATED MEMORIES OF ABUSE

Next we will discuss the encoding, retention, retrieval, and post-retrieval factors that may have contributed to the discovery of the fabricated memories. Supplementary evidence from empirical studies of retractors will also be addressed when appropriate.

The encoding phase

As noted in all of the cases, the patients arrived in therapy with no memory of ever having been abused and no evidence that they had in fact been abused. Nevertheless a variety of conditions occurring during the process of therapy seem likely to have led to the encoding of memories that never actually occurred.

Therapist suggestion

The initial idea that people have hidden histories of childhood abuse is often suggested by the therapist, most often by therapists who have a strong belief that adult maladjustment and psychopathology are the result of childhood abuse and other trauma (e.g. Blume, 1990; Briere, 1992; McCann & Pearlman, 1990). In certain circumstances a variety of techniques, known collectively as memory work, are used to help patients recover, explore, and integrate traumatic memories (McCann & Pearlman, 1990). Although not every therapist adheres to this assertion, there are many documented cases in which therapists have blatantly told patients, in the absence of any memory, that they were abused as a child and they need to remember what happened (Ofshe & Watters, 1994; de Rivera, 1997; Lief & Fetkewicz, 1995). This is especially notable in the cases reviewed above, such as Althaus, Burgus, and Carl. In a study of 40 retractors, 93% of the respondents recovered memories during therapy, and 89% of these stated that their therapist offered a direct suggestion that they were victims of sexual abuse prior to any recovered memories, despite the fact that they entered therapy for family or marital problems, depression, eating disorders, and anxiety-related issues (Lief & Fetkewicz, 1995). In another analysis of retractors, many patients were told that they had the symptoms of someone who had been sexually abused, even though they had no such memory (de Rivera, 1997).

In medical malpractice cases against therapists, it is often the case that the therapists had an underlying belief that repressed memories of childhood trauma, and sometimes SRA, were the catalyst for current adult problems. This belief appears to be the rule rather than the exception in all of our cases of retractors. For example, Dr Braun, a defendant in two of the cases, has published extensively on his view that MPD is caused by repressed memories of trauma (Braun, 1986), and played a key role in defining the modern approach to MPD.

Suggestions from authority figure

The encoding of false memories appears to rely on the suggestive influences coming from a respected authority figure. When a person enters therapy it is because the patient trusts and respects the therapist's expertise in the hope of being cured. For instance, one retractor stated, "I had doubts all the time, but I was told that this was my denial, my not wanting to get well. I believed the therapist. After all, who was I to question someone who was supposed to know everything? I looked at him as a god who could do no wrong" (Lief & Fetkewicz, 1995, p. 424). Additionally, Lief and Fetkewicz (1995) found that when retractors were asked what most influenced the development of their memories, the most common response was the therapist. In our case of Burgus, she explained that she was told that until she hit rock bottom and remembered everything, she would never get better. And, in the case of Carl, her therapist told her that unless she continued recovering memories about the abuse, she would remain in denial and wouldn't get better.

Indeed, Herman (1992) bluntly states that "the patient enters therapy in need of help and care. By virtue of this fact, she voluntarily submits herself to an unequal relationship in which the therapist has superior status and power" (p. 134). The former patient in Case 7 stated, "This type of therapy does the same thing to you. You believe it; you do what you're told. It's like a guru-type of relationship you had with this physician and you trust him completely, and I did." It is important to note that the use of authority has been established as a key component in heightening interrogative suggestibility (Gudjonsson, 1992) and false confessions (Kassin, 1997a), suggesting that the similarity among these types of situations might be a viable avenue for future research.

Another factor that may contribute to memory fabrication that is related to the authoritarian nature of the relationship is when patients are deprived of contact with the outside world, either by becoming an inpatient or cutting off contact with family members who do not believe the memories. As an example, Shanley in Case 6 was not allowed contact with anybody outside of the dissociation unit as part of her treatment. She was also told that there would be serious consequences if she attempted to leave her voluntary confinement.

Uncertainty

People want to know why they are experiencing mental and emotional disturbances. This search for meaning makes people more susceptible to outside influences in the effort to construct a narrative to explain their current problems. These judgments of reality depend on the person's belief system, and if the therapist repeatedly asserts that the patient was sexually abused, this belief becomes instilled in the patient and the search begins. People start to hypothesize what happened for a sense of closure and relief, and the recovery of memories of abuse offers a solution to this uncertainty about the source of the patient's problems. As an example, when Carlson's therapist told her that her problems with unhappiness stemmed from MPD, her life made sense to her for the first time. She had been unemployed for four years and had been hospitalized five times for depression. The blame didn't fall on her, but on her alternate personalities, and this offered a sense of relief.

Reinterpretation of past events

People may have always had continuous recall of other non-abusive but unpleasant childhood experiences and reinterpret them as abusive if it has been suggested to them that they were abused. Memories of past experiences are distorted to make them congruent with present beliefs and attitudes (Dawes, 1989). In an effort to recover memories, other unpleasant experiences may be recalled under the guise of abuse, when in fact it may have been an innocent spanking or necessary enema. This appears to be true with one of de Rivera's (1997) cases, whose father spanked her and asked her to pull her pants down, and her mother gave her an enema at age 5. These events were reinterpreted as abusive when memory recovery became the goal of therapy. When another patient exerted effort in an attempt to recover memories, she paid more attention to her dreams and strange sensations she had experienced since childhood (de Rivera, 1997). However, as noted by Lynn, Stafford, Malinoski and Pintar (1997) this patient's strange sensations are most likely attributable to sleep paralysis, but they were reinterpreted as memories of abuse since that was her predominant belief and attitude.

Books

Along with explicit and implicit suggestions of abuse, if a patient has a suspected history of childhood abuse she is often provided with books about incest, repression, MPD, or SRA. A widely known example is Bass and Davis's (1988) *The Courage to Heal*. In the absence of any true memory, these books provide schemas of childhood abuse that patients may later use in reconstructing their past. In Lief and Fetkewicz's (1995) analysis of retractors, 75% had read *The Courage to Heal* and 80% reported reading other self-help literature. In particular, one retractor noted that her therapist had her read several books and take notes: "He provided reading materials, books, articles on MPD, PTSD, Satanism" (de Rivera, 1997, p. 428). Humenansky gave Carlson *Sybil* to read, and told her that anything in it that startled or offended her was probably something that happened to her that was a repressed memory; she also read *The Courage to Heal* and *The Three Faces of Eve*. Carlson says that she was also given videotapes, and that if she felt any physical discomfort while watching them it was a sign that those things had happened to her. Humenansky based much of her practice on *The Courage to Heal* and *Sybil*, and said that she was also influenced by watching the authors on television talk shows. Halbrooks in Case 4 says that most of her satanic memories came from materials she had read, saw, and discussed.

The media

A final factor that may play an important role in the encoding of false memories is that many false beliefs about MPD and SRA are propagated by the media. Talk shows have featured individuals who claim to have forgotten horrific childhood events, and have remembered the episodes through hypnosis or through the diagnosis of MPD. Yet, no mention is made that the validity of MPD has recently been called into question; most specifically the underlying claim that MPD is the result of repressed childhood abuse (Hacking, 1995). With such a positive and reinforcing response and a community of believing — almost a celebration — it is easy to see why some people have the desire to remember such events and lack the critical defenses to prohibit such false memories. Like reading material, the media coverage of MPD and SRA provides people with schemas of what should happen in these circumstances, providing material for future patients to use to incorporate into their own memories. For instance, Halbrooks (Case 4) realized that something was amiss when she found that her memories were similar to those of other people in her survivor group — all the memories of SRA followed a similar pattern. This observation suggests that people have the schematic information to use in discovering fabricated memories.

The retention interval phase

In addition to encoding factors, there are several factors that encourage the growth of the memory during the retention interval. Memory work, unfortunately, contains many elements that are very suggestive, sometimes yielding memories that are grossly distorted or false outright (e.g. Kihlstrom, 1997; Lindsay & Read, 1994; Loftus & Ketcham, 1992). So, in an attempt to help patients get better, therapists may unknowingly (or knowingly) incorporate techniques that have been shown to generate inaccurate and blatantly false memories. It is clear that these techniques increase the risk of distorted or false memory, because they create, and capitalize on, the conditions for interrogative suggestibility to occur in therapy (Shobe & Kihlstrom, in press).

In one study of retractors, it was found that 78% of the sample experienced deep relaxation, 75% age regression, 73% guided imagery, 70% dream interpretation, and 68% hypnosis techniques in therapy (Lief & Fetkewicz, 1995). These techniques often suspend reality orientation and lower critical judgment and deserve further consideration than is currently allowed in our discussion.

Hypnosis

A prominent view of trauma therapists is that hypnotic techniques help patients access repressed and dissociated memories (Dolan, 1991; McCann & Pearlman, 1990). A trance state is induced, and then several techniques may be used to help patients to remember. A common approach is to use age regression in which the client is told that she is getting younger and younger, back to the time of the trauma. At that point the person becomes the child once again and talks about what she sees. Or, screen techniques require the patient to project the traumatic images or thoughts onto an imaginary screen. The images and thoughts do not have to be accurate portrayals of the traumatic event that is remembered; they can be whatever the patient chooses (Price, 1986).

The social context of hypnosis increases the suggestibility of the hypnotized person. To demonstrate, when subjects were given pre-hypnotic suggestions that being hypnotized would help them to remember past lives, the type of lives remembered was dramatically influenced (Spanos,

Menary, Gabora, DuBreuil, & Dewhirst, 1991). The social context contained within the hypnotic setting suggests to people that they should adopt a lax standard for distinguishing between reality and fantasy, making retrieval of false memories more likely. To highlight this concern, several professional institutions have issued guidelines about hypnosis and suggestibility such as the American Society of Clinical Hypnosis, the American Psychological Association, and the American Medical Association. The suggestive effects of hypnosis on memory have been discussed elsewhere (Lindsay & Read, 1994; Orne, Whitehouse, Orne & Dinges, 1996).

Indeed, it is hard to find a case of false memory, through retractors and legal cases, in which hypnosis was *not* used. In Case 7, Cool's psychiatrist put her under hypnosis, during which she revealed 126 separate personalities that were allegedly brought on by childhood sexual abuse. The use of hypnosis in malpractice cases is the rule rather than the exception — hypnosis was used in every single case, leading people to develop alternative personalities and remember SRA. In Carlson's case, she said that the psychiatrist used hypnosis and a "truth serum" to help to recover previously unimagined memories of abuse by her family members as part of satanic cults. One retractor noted, "my therapist insisted that hypnotically induced memories were true memories" (Lief & Fetkewicz, 1995, p. 427). Another retractor stated that "after arguing for two or three months with the therapists that I had no memories, I guess I broke. Then he got me to do hypnosis. I left thinking I had been satanically abused, hung up, raped, hot wax poured on me" (Lief & Fetkewicz, p. 425).

Medication
In therapy, medication is often given to treat depression and other problems. However, when large doses are given, patients become more receptive to suggestive techniques. This appears to be true in many of our cases. Burgus states that reality and fantasy blended together as she received high doses of medication along with hypnosis. A recent complaint against Dr Braun by the Illinois Department of Professional Regulation states that Burgus received Inderal, Halcion, Xanax, sedatives and hypnotic psychotropic drugs from Dr Braun, at doses at experimental, untested, and medically inappropriate levels. The Board also noted in their complaint that Dr Braun prescribed these medications knowing that they would increase the patient's vulnerability to suggestion. Similarly, Shanley alleges that at one time her already high levels of medication were increased further to produce more memories of her involvement in the satanic cult. Carlson in Case 1 also received strong medications such as Valium, Halcion, and Xanax (benzodiazepines), Ativan for anxiety, Pamclor, Desyrcl, Prozac for depression, and Restoril for insomnia. Under

the influence of these drugs, it isn't surprising that Carlson remembered bizarre and implausible events.

Repetition

The use of suggestive techniques increases familiarity and confidence, and creates source confusion. The more a fictitious image or fragment is used, the more likely it will be accepted either by the process of repetition or through source-monitoring difficulties. So, when patients are repeatedly trying to uncover images or memories, whatever is uncovered will seem familiar and valid. Similar to Dywan's (1995) illusion of familiarity, during hypnosis when a person attempts to retrieve information, the items remembered are generated more vividly and with greater fluency and are more likely to induce the feeling of familiarity. Familiarity is an important component in determining the status of a memory (Mandler, 1980), and if a false sense of familiarity is capitalized upon, then the resulting decision may be inaccurate (Park, Shobe & Kihlstrom, 2001).

Visualization

Many of the techniques used in memory recovery rely on visualization and imagination. A prominent technique is guided imagery, which begins with the patient picking a focal point and allowing himself to imagine what would have happened next (McCann & Pearlman, 1990). The truth about whatever the patient remembers while imagining usually waits until later. This exercise may provide the impetus for feelings of familiarly associated with the projected images and thoughts, making it later difficult to decide the validity of the memory. In a compelling laboratory demonstration, the mere act of imagining a childhood event that didn't occur increased subjects' confidence that it did indeed occur (Garry, Manning, Loftus & Sherman, 1996). Another problem with visualization techniques is that each revisualization of a suspected event increases the perceptual detail that accompanies it, diminishing the ability for source monitoring (Johnson, 1988).

Take, for example, Case 1, in which Carlson did visualization exercises at the urging of her therapist, imaging scenes of abuse by various people. Carlson says that after using this technique she came to remember being molested by 50 relatives. Another technique used was guided imagery, in which Carlson was talked through an imaginary scene in order to uncover buried memories. It is through this exercise that Carlson remembered cannibalism.

Dreams

Dream content is sometimes interpreted to reflect repressed childhood events (Williams, 1987). It has been suggested, by a well-read author, that repressed memories often surface through fragments or symbols, suggesting that dreams can be a gateway to repressed memories (Fredrickson, 1992). Despite this assertion, it has been demonstrated that the veridicality of flashbacks and dreams even in people who have documented trauma is suspect (Brenneis, 1997; Frankel, 1994). A therapeutic situation in which memory recovery is the central focus can be detrimental as well. The dream content of a group of college students in group therapy was determined by the person's pre-sleep experience (Berger, Hunter & Lane, 1971). The material that was aroused during the therapy sessions was represented and worked over in the dreams, such that the content of the dreams was related to the material discussed in the preceding group session. So, if a therapist suggests that a patient was abused, this suggestion may become the basis for future dream content, even if it is false, strengthening the memory. Finally, dream content is mistaken for real memories.

Several cases of retractors in malpractice suits exemplify this concern. Shanley reports that her psychiatrist informed her that dreams of abuse are real memories and that she should believe them. Additionally, after it was suggested to Althaus that she was abused, she began to have nightmares about being abused, especially after she was given several books with detailed descriptions of abuse cases. The therapists then took these dreams as a sign that her recollections of abuse were returning. After the dreams began, during an interview with police Althaus said that she had been abused. Yet, during the trial when her attorney asked her if it had ever happened, Althaus responded, "No, I was more or less reporting what was in my dreams."

The retrieval phase

Vague memories and source-monitoring failures
When fabricated memories are first "uncovered", they are usually vague and fuzzy, but this usually doesn't deter the therapist from accepting them as valid and providing encouragement for new memories. Indeed, some sources promoting memory retrieval techniques claim that memories uncovered will be vague, sketchy, and hazy, even after many workings and, moreover, that these qualities signify the authenticity of the memory (Bass & Davis, 1988). One patient in de Rivera (1997) had no clear memories, but had sensations, feelings, and fuzzy dreams that were interpreted as veridical memories signifying that abuse had occurred. In Shanley's court testimony in the criminal case of Spring Shadows Glen, she said that when she expressed doubts about her satanic abuse memories her therapists would threaten her if she tried to leave.

Additionally, it appears that false memories arise from a blending of information that was both experienced and imagined, further making source monitoring difficult. This blending can have detrimental effects when therapists take the memory at face value. When Burgus's sons in Case 2 were hospitalized for three years under Braun's care, they were encouraged to develop alter personalities and remember episodes of abuse, receiving stickers when they told "yucky secrets". Interestingly, during court testimony, Dr Braun gave one of 5-year-old John's memories as proof of satanic activities — sticking a knife in a man's abdomen and how the intestines popped out and smelled terrible. This story could only come from direct experience, Braun said. Burgus says that she informed Braun that her son had seen a Star Wars movie in which something similar happens, in which Luke Skywalker cuts open the beast he was riding, all the guts spill out and he comments on how rancid it smells. Braun didn't think to consider that John's memory was taken from the movie.

Reinforcement

Another factor in the final acceptance, or retrieval of fabricated memories is reinforcement, whether it is through explicit or implicit feedback. This reinforcement of memory recovery supports a confirmation bias as well. Many retractors were rewarded with attention and care when memories were recovered, especially the more traumatic the memories (Lief & Fetkewicz, 1995). Rewards and encouragement were given in response to recovered memories. "The sick thing about this was that I was getting a lot of attention ... and so I continued the process", states a former patient in de Rivera (1997, p. 284). This reinforcement of recovered memories creates a high demand for patients to remember. However, there is evidence that high demand to remember events that are implausible actually increases the probability that they will be "remembered" (Green, Lynn & Malinoski, 1998). In these experiments, subjects initially reported their earliest memory, and then were told to visualize, focus, and concentrate to remember earlier memories. Subjects in the condition with a high demand to remember reported their earliest memory at 2.8 years, down from 3.7 years. The lowest memory age was 1.6 years. Subjects in the low demand condition went down to only 3.45 years. In other words, a high demand to remember lowered the earliest memory reported to an age where it seems unlikely that the memory was valid.

Group therapy

Often when a person has a suspected history of childhood abuse, she joins a support group at the suggestion of her therapist. The goal of this group therapy is to help the patient to remember and recover, even if she has no firm memory of abuse. In this situation material from other members in the group can become blended into the memories recovered by the patient, especially when there is peer pressure from the others to remember, only to be reinforced and accepted when memories are recovered. In Cases 2 and 4 the former patients eventually entered group therapy with other MPD patients and noted the influence of group therapy on their memory recovery.

Non-critical acceptance of memories
Finally, false memories of SRA supported by the diagnosis of MPD would not be able to propagate without the unabashed acceptance by therapists. This relates to the difference between historical truth and narrative truth (e.g. Spence, 1984), and while it can be debated whether or not it is the clinician's responsibility to determine if uncovered memories are veridical, when so much devastation results from these memories it is hard to see why they are not concerned with their accuracy. As Peterson, a defendant in Case 3, noted during trial, "They bring the content to therapy. The therapist does not." Or, "memories like these can't be implanted. You have to experience it," and "It came out of her mouth". Statements such as these signify the role of the therapist in validating the fabricated memories. As another example, a retractor noted, "I had many, many doubts, but my therapist didn't respond well to my doubts. She seemed more interested, more responsive, and more sympathetic if I suspected abuse...finally I gave in..." (Lief & Fetkewicz, 1995, p. 423).

Interestingly, most of the literature on memory work does not address or explore the issue of alternative explanations. Of course, the therapist's task is not determine if the historical truth is accurate, but rather if the narrative truth makes sense. However, Burgus noted that her psychiatrist told her that the memories being uncovered represented real memories of actual historical events and that she was the only one questioning the validity of the memories. Burgus was never advised about the possibility that the memories may be due to the suggestive techniques she experienced, nor was she ever told about the debate within the mental health community about the MPD diagnosis. And, in Carl's case, her therapist testified that she didn't know if the specific memories Carl recovered in therapy were true, but said she believed the gist of them. Moreover, therapists never warned her that the memories she recovered through hypnosis and other forms of psychotherapy might be unreliable.

Similarly, in the case of the young patient Althaus, the Althauses contend that Cohen failed to consider that the allegations were being made up or were false, and that her inaccurate diagnosis caused Nicole to hold these false beliefs. No alternative explanation of Althaus's psychological state was ever examined or investigated, and eventually the psychiatrist was found liable of negligent treatment for the increasingly bizarre allegations made by Althaus. Non-critical beliefs such as these on the part of the treating mental health worker lay the groundwork for the creation of fabricated memories.

Additionally, in many of the documented false memory cases, no informed consent was given to patients about the use of memory recovery techniques such as hypnosis, and the controversial nature of the MPD diagnosis. In several cases the defendant therapist failed to inform the patient that the techniques used were unsupported by any reliable scientific evidence or that the diagnoses were controversial (Cases 2, 3, 6, 7). The non-critical acceptance of recovered memories was also the focus of a complaint filed against Bennett Braun, a treating psychiatrist in two of our cases. The negligence cause of action included the implantation or encouragement of false memories of childhood abuse through the use of suggestive techniques. This indictment also seemed to suggest that the therapist knew of the suggestive nature of his techniques, but didn't stop to consider the validity of what was being reported or express concern to his patient.

The post-retrieval phase

None of the cases in our case based analysis would be available if those involved had never begun to doubt their memories and retract their claims. The process of retraction that occurs during the post-retrieval phase is just as important to our analysis as the creation of the false memories. However, the available evidence for this end of the process is not as extant as the evidence for the suggestive influences used to form the false memories. How does a person become to doubt his or her own memories? Carlson stated that she came to realize the absurdity of the memories after she stopped taking some of her medication, and during group sessions she started to note certain things. All of the participants had similar abuse memories, and those memories seemed awfully similar to the stories in the books they read. Eventually, one woman admitted to making up an alter, and that got the ball rolling. Carlson phoned Humenansky to make an appointment, and at that point Humenansky forbade all further contact between the two. And in another case, Burgus states, "I started to check out certain things that we had now based our lives on, these horror stories. I couldn't find any proof of anything."

Several cases from de Rivera's (1997) analysis of retractors highlight important factors in the retraction process. One former patient's husband weaned her off medications and made her stop going to group meetings. Another's new therapist taught her to deal with current problems and doubted her belief in abuse. Finally, while hospitalized and after she stopped taking medication, another former patient with the help of a friend realized that flashbacks of giving birth at 13 were flashbacks of actual birth of her daughter. This undermined her entire belief system. It appears that when the suggestive influences are withdrawn, people are able to examine their memories critically.

Caveats

This review of possible mechanisms derived from a qualitative analysis of seemingly false memory cases suggests a host of encoding, retention interval, retrieval, and post-retrieval factors that provide the fertile ground in which discovered false memories may be planted, raised, and harvested. Despite the promising nature of this analysis, we again must emphasize the preliminary nature of this analysis and the need for caution in interpreting the cases and mechanisms suggested. As a number of authors have articulated, there are inherent challenges in the analysis of retractor cases in general, and against specific articles particularly due to methodological problems, including representatives, sample size, interviewing technique and, objectiveness (e.g. Coons, 1997; de Rivera, 1997; Gudjonsson, 1997; Kassin, 1997b). Future expansions of case-based evidence for false memories might profitably compare cases of discovered memories on the basis of whether or not corroboration of the memories can be found. If certain conditions are found to be more likely associated with memories that are corroborated, and other conditions associated with memories that tend to be uncorroborated, then this would provide important additional insights into the factors that may particularly lead to false memories. Indeed, one very strong prediction that emerges from the above analysis is that memories that are discovered outside of the context of therapy should on average be more likely to be potentially corroborated than those that are discovered within the context of aggressive memory recovery therapy. It is also important to determine whether corroboration can ever be found for the abuse memories of individuals who ultimately retract their memories. Although we think it is reasonable to assume that the former abuse memories of retractors, for which no corroboration exists, are often likely to be false, it cannot be assumed that a memory was necessarily false just because it was retracted. Indeed, it seems quite plausible that many of the same mechanisms such as suggestions and pressure from authority figures that can lead to the formation of false memories of abuse, might also lead to the retraction of real memories of abuse.

CONCLUSIONS

This review of the case-based approach to the study of authentic and fabricated discovered memories highlights the utility of the approach in gaining a finer understanding of the encoding, retention interval, retrieval, and post-retrieval mechanisms that may contribute to such memories. Undoubtedly some readers steeped in the experimental tradition, and (probably others as well) have serious misgivings about aspects of the case analysis described here. How do we compare case studies involving retrospective reports of experiences that often occurred many years prior to controlled experimental studies? How do we determine the standards of evidence in qualitative cases? How do we deal with issues of replication and accessibility of data? How do we separate the scientific issues under question from the legal, political, and ethical issues that surround this controversy? These are just some of the reasonable concerns that individuals might voice about the approach presented here.

As experimental psychologists, we are extremely sympathetic to the above concerns and indeed have grappled with them seriously ourselves. Ultimately, we believe the issue of how exactly to fit case-based analyses into the science of psychology is a question which remains to be resolved. Clearly, some headway on this matter can be made by conducting more extensive studies, with larger populations, an explicit sampling procedure, and coders who rate the strength of the corroboration blind to any additional information associated with the case. However, even with such measures, many of the limitations to the case study approach will remain. Nevertheless, it must be emphasized that the case study approach, despite its many imperfections, addresses issues that are especially elusive from the perspective of a strict experimental approach. Experimental investigations of the processes that might lead to discovered authentic memories are fundamentally limited by the time scale of the process, the trauma of the experience, and the ecological settings in which such memories are formed and retrieved. Experimental investigations of discovered false memories are constrained by ethical limitations in the degree of coercion that can be applied and the types of experiences that can be suggested. (Not to mention the huge amount of time necessary to mimic the amount of effort often expended in therapy before recovered memories are "found".) In short, despite their imperfections, case studies are strongest precisely where experimental studies are weakest, as they provide a natural opportunity to study the recollection of memories that (at least sometimes) can be shown to be associated with highly traumatic experiences and/or highly suggestive therapeutic practices.

Although both the experimental and the case-based approaches have severe limitations, ultimately the combination of the two approaches offers great promise. There are many ways in which at least some of the hypotheses suggested by case-based studies might profitably be explored in the lab. For example, if, as the case-based analysis suggests, discovered memories of trauma can result from dissociations between consciousness and meta-awareness, then similar dissociations might also be seen in the laboratory. Similarly, if individuals can confuse the discovery of a new understanding of an experience, with the discovery of the memory itself, then similar discovery misattributions should be producible in the laboratory (see Schooler, Dougal & Johnson, 2000). The implications of laboratory studies might also be profitably applied in case studies. For example, recent investigation by Wegner, Dunn and Schooler (2000) suggest that the act of trying not to think about highly unlikely experiences actually increases individuals' subsequent estimation that those experiences actually occurred. Such findings suggest that cases in which individuals reported having received suggestions of abuse, and then subsequently tried not to think about it, might be associated with memories that are especially difficult to corroborate. By using the two approaches in tandem, the field may be able to move beyond the polarizing questions of whether recovered memories are authentic v. false, or whether laboratory v. case-based studies are the more appropriate forms of evidence in this controversy. Instead, drawing on the unique strengths of each approach we may begin to understand how individuals can come to discover memories of abuse that are sometimes grounded in fact and at other times only fiction.

CASES

Althaus v. Cohen (1994). Court of Common Pleas, Allegheny Co., PA, No. GD92020893.

Burgus v. Braun, Rush-Presbyterian (1997). Circuit Court, Cook County, IL, Case Nos 91L08493/93L14050.

Carl v. Peterson, Spring Shadows Glen Psychiatric Hospital et al. (1997). U.S. District Court, Southern District of Texas, Houston Division, Case No. H-95–661.

Carlson v. Humenansky (1996). Dist Ct. 2nd District, MN, No. CX-93–7260.

Cool v. Olson (1997). Circuit Ct., Outagamie Co., Wisc. No. 94CV707.

Halbrooks v. Moore (1995). District Court, Dallas Co., TX No. 92–11849.

Rutherford v. Strand et al. (1996). Circuit Ct., Green Co. MO, No. 1960C2745.

Shanley v. Peterson, et al. (1996) U.S. District Court, Houston Div. Texas, No. H-94–4162.

Shanley v. Braun et al. (1997). U.S. District Court Ill. No. 95C6589.

U.S. v. Peterson et al., (1997). No. H-97–237, S.D. Texas, Houston Division.

REFERENCES

Bartlett, F. C. (1932) *Remembering*. Cambridge: Cambridge University Press.

Bass, E. & Davis, L. (1988) *The Courage to Heal: A Guide for Women Survivors of Child Sexual Abuse*. New York: Harper & Row.

Berger, L., Hunter, I. & Lane, R. (1971) The effect of stress on dreams. *Psychological Issues*, **7**, 1–213.

Bernstein, E. & Putnam, T. (1986). Development, reliability, and validity of a dissociation scale. *Journal of Nervous and Mental Disorders*, **174**, 727–735.

Bjork, R. A. (1989). Retrieval inhibition as an adaptive mechanism in human memory. In H.L. Roediger & F.I.M. Craik (Eds), *Varieties of Memory and Consciousness: Essays in Honour of Endel Tulving* (pp. 309–330). Hillsdale, NJ: Lawrence Erlbaum.

Blume, E. S. (1990). *Secret Survivors: Uncovering Incest and its Aftereffects in Women.* New York: Ballantine.

Braun, B. G. (Ed.) (1986). *Treatment of Multiple Personality Disorder.* Washington, DC: American Psychiatric Press.

Brenneis, C. B. (1997). *Recovered Memories of Trauma: Transferring the Present to the Past.* Madison, CT: International Universities Press.

Brewin, C. R., Dalgleish, T. & Joseph, S. (1996). A dual representation theory of posttraumatic stress disorder. *Psychological Review*, **103**, 670–686.

Briere, J. (1992). *Child Abuse Trauma: Theory and Treatment of the Lasting Effects.* Newbury Park, CA: Sage.

Coons, P. M. (1997) Distinguishing between pseudomemories and repression of traumatic events. *Psychological Inquiry*, **8**, 293–295.

Costello, R. B. et al. (Eds) (1991). *Webster's College Dictionary.* New York: Random House, Inc.

Courtois, C. (1988). *Healing the Incest Wound: Adult Survivors in Therapy.* New York: W. W. Norton & Co.

de Rivera, J. (1997). The construction of false memory syndrome: The experience of retractors. *Psychological Inquiry*, **8**, 271–292.

Dawes, R. M. (1989). Experience and the validity of clinical judgment: The illusory correlation. *Behavioral Sciences and the Law*, **7**, 457–467.

Dolan, Y.M. (1991). *Resolving Sexual Abuse: Solution-Focused Therapy and Ericksonian Hypnosis for Adult Survivors.* New York: W. W. Norton & Co.

Dywan, J. (1995). The illusion of familiarity: An alternative to the report-criterion account of hypnotic recall. *International Journal of Clinical and Experimental Hypnosis*, **43**, 194–211.

Frankel, F. (1994). The concept of flashbacks in historical perspective. *International Journal of Clinical and Experimental Hypnosis*, **42**, 321–336.

Fredrickson, R. (1992). *Repressed Memories: A Journey to Recovery from Sexual Abuse.* New York: Simon & Schuster.

Garry, M., Manning, C. G., Loftus, E. F. & Sherman, S. J. (1996). Imagination inflation: Imagining a childhood event inflates confidence that it occurred. *Psychonomic Bulletin and Review*, **3**, 208–214.

Green, J. P., Lynn, S. J. & Malinoski, P. (1998). Hypnotic pseudomemories, pre-hypnotic warnings, and the malleability of suggested memories. *Applied Cognitive Psychology*, **12**, 431–444.

Gudjonsson, G. H. (1992). *The Psychology of Interrogations, Confessions, and Testimony.* Chichester, UK: Wiley.

Gudjonsson, G. H. (1997). False memory syndrome and the retractors: Methodological and theoretical issues. *Psychological Inquiry*, **8**, 296–299.

Hacking, I. (1995). *Rewriting the Soul: Multiple Personality and the Sciences of Memory.* Princeton, NJ: Princeton University Press.

Harvey, M. R. & Herman, J. L. (1994). Amnesia, partial amnesia, and delayed recall among adult survivors of childhood trauma. *Consciousness and Cognition*, **3**, 295–306.

Herman, J. L. (1992). *Trauma and Recovery* (2nd edn). New York: Basic Books.

Hobson, J. A. (1988) *The The Dreaming Brain*. New York:. Basic Books

Holmes, D. (1990). The evidence for repression: An examination of sixty years of research. In J. Singer (Ed.), *Repression and Dissociation: Implications for Personality Theory, Psychotherapy, and Health* (pp. 85–1–2). Chicago, IL: The Uuniversity of Chicago Press.

Hyman, I. E. & Pentland, J. (1996). The role of mental imagery in the creation of false childhood memories. *Journal of Memory and Language, 35*, 101–117.

Johnson, M. K. (1988). Reality monitoring: An experimental phenomenological approach. *Journal of Experimental Psychology: General, 117*, 390–394.

Joslyn S., Carlin, L. & Loftus, E. F. (1998). Remembering and forgetting childhood sexual abuse, *Memory, 5, 701–724.*

Kassin, S. M. (1997a). The psychology of confession evidence. *American Psychologist, 52*, 221–233.

Kassin, S. M. (1997b). False memories turned against the self. *Psychological Inquiry, 8*, 300–302.

Kihlstrom, J. F. (1996). Suffering from reminiscences: Exhumed memory, implicit memory, and the return of the repressed. In M.A. Conway (Ed.), *Recovered Memories and False Memories* (pp. 100–117). Oxford: Oxford University Press.

Kihlstrom, J. F. (1997). Memory, abuse, and science. *American Psychologist, 52*, 99–995.

Kihlstrom, J. F. (1998). Exhumed memory. In S. J. Lynn & K. M. McConkey (Eds), *Truth in Memory* (pp. 3–31). New York: Guilford.

Lanning, K. V. (1992). *Investigator's Guide to Allegations of "Ritual" Child Abuse.* Behavioral Science Unit, National Center for the Analysis of Violent Crime, Federal Bureau of Investigation, Quantico, Virginia.

LaBerge, S. (1985). *Lucid Dreaming*. New York: Putnam Publishing Group.

LeDoux, J. E. (1992). Emotion as memory: Anatomical systems underlying indelible neural traces. In Sven-Ake Christianson (Ed.), *The Handbook of Emotion and Memory: Research and Theory* (pp. 269–288). Hillsdale, NJ: Lawrence Erlbaum Associates, Inc.

LeDoux, J. (1996). *The Emotional Brain: The Mysterious Underpinnings of Emotional Life*. New York: Simon & Schuster.

Lief, H. I. & Fetkewicz, J. (1995). Retractors of false memories: the evolution of pseudomemories. *The Journal of Psychiatry and Law, 23*, 411–435.

Lindsay, D.S. & Read, J. D. (1994). Psychotherapy and memories of childhood sexual abuse: A cognitive perspective. *Applied Cognitive Psychology*, 281–338.

Loftus, E. F. (1994). The repressed memory controversy. *American Psychologist, 49*, 443–445.

Loftus, E. F. & Ketchum, K. (1992). *The Myth of Repressed Memories: False Memories and Allegations of Abuse*. New York: St Martins Press.

Lynn, S. J., Stafford, J., Malinoski, P. & Pintar, J. (1997). Memory in the hall of mirrors: The experience of "retractors" in psychotherapy. *Psychological Inquiry, 4*, 307–312.

Mandler, G. (1980). Recognizing: The judgment of prior occurrence. *Psychological Review, 87*, 252–271.

McCann, I. L. & Pearlman, L. A. (1990). *Psychological Trauma and the Adult Survivor: Theory, Therapy, and Transformation*. New York: Brunner/Mazel Publishers.

Ofshe, R. & Watters, E. (1994). *Making Monsters: False memories, Psychotherapy, and Sexual Hysteria*. New York: Scribner's.

Orne, M., Whitehouse, W., Orne, E. & Dinges, D. (1996). "Memories" of anomalous and traumatic autobiographical experiences: Validation and consolidation of fantasy through hypnosis. *Psychological Inquiry, 7*, 168–172.

Park, L., Shobe, K., & Kihlstrom, J. (2001). Associative and categorical relations in the associative memory illusion. *Manuscript submitted for publication.*

Price, R. (1986). Hypnotic age regression and the reparenting of self. *Transactional Analysis Journal,* **16,** 120–127.

Schooler, J. (1994). Seeking the core: Issues and evidence surrounding recovered accounts of sexual trauma. *Consciousness and Cognition,* **3,** 452–469.

Schooler, J. W. (2000). Discovered memories and the "delayed discovery doctrine": A cognitive case based analysis. In S.Taub (Ed.), *Recovered Memories of Child Sexual Abuse: Psychological, Legal, and Social Perspectives on a Mental Health Controversy.* Springfield, IL: Charles C. Thomas.

Schooler, J. W. (in press). Discovering memories in the light of meta-awareness. *The Journal of Aggression, Maltreatment and Trauma.*

Schooler, J. W. & Melcher, J. (1995). The ineffability of insight. In S. M. Smith, T. B. Ward & R. A. Finke (Eds), *The Creative Cognition Approach* (pp. 97–133). Cambridge, MA: MIT Press.

Schooler, J. W. & Dougal, S. (in press). Why creativity is not like the proverbial typing monkey. *Psychological Inquiry.*

Schooler, J. W. & Eich E. E. (in press). Memory for emotional events. In E. Tulving & F. I. M. Craik (Eds), *Oxford Handbook of Memory.* New York: Oxford University Press.

Schooler, J. W., Ambadar, Z. & Bendiksen, M. A. (1997a). A cognitive corroborative case study approach for investigating discovered memories of sexual abuse. In J. D. Read & D. S. Lindsay (Eds), *Recollections of Trauma: Scientific Research and Clinical Practices* (pp. 379–388). New York, NY: Plenum.

Schooler, J. W., Bendiksen, M. & Ambadar, Z. (1997b). Taking the middle line: Can we accommodate both fabricated and recovered memories of sexual abuse? In M. Conway (Ed.), *False and Recovered Memories* (pp. 251–292). Oxford, UK: Oxford University Press

Shobe, K. K. & Kihlstrom, J. F. (1997). Is traumatic memory special? *Current Directions in Psychological Science,* **6,** 70–74.

Shobe, K. K. & Kihlstrom, J. F. (in press). Interrogative suggestibility and "memory work". In M. Eisen, G. Goodman & J. Quas (Eds), *Memory and Suggestibility in the Forensic Interview.* Mayway, NJ: Erlbaum.

Spanos, N. P., Menary, E., Gabora, N. J., DuBreuil, S.C. & Dewhirst, B. (1991). Secondary identity enactments during hypnotic past-life regression: A sociocognitive perspective. *Journal of Personality and Social Psychology,* **61,** 308–320.

Spence, D. P. (1984). *Narrative Truth and Historical Truth.* New York: Norton.

Usher, J. A. & Neisser, U. (1993). Childhood amnesia and the beginnings of memory for four early life events. *Journal of Experimental Psychology: General,* **122,** 155–165.

Wegner, D. M. & Gold, D. B. (1995). Fanning old flames: Emotional and cognitive effects of suppressing thoughts of a past relationship. *Journal of Personality and Social Psychology,* **5,** 782–792.

Williams, M. (1987). Reconstruction of early seduction and its aftereffects. *Journal of the American Psychoanalytic Association,* **35.** 145–163.

Williams, L. M. (1994). Recall of childhood trauma: A prospective study of women's memories of child sexual abuse. *Journal of Consulting and Clinical Psychology,* **62,** 1167–1176.

Winograd, E. & Neisser, U. (Eds) (1992). *Affect and Accuracy in Recall: Studies of "Flashbulb Memories".* Cambridge: Cambridge University Press.

7

IS IT POSSIBLE TO DISCRIMINATE TRUE FROM FALSE MEMORIES?

Graham M. Davies

In 1989, Holly, an outwardly cheerful and well-adjusted college student, but who nonetheless was receiving therapy, began to experience a series of disturbing flashbacks. They appeared to be long-forgotten memories of her childhood and featured her father perpetrating sexual assaults upon her. At first, the memories were fleeting and fragmentary, lacking a time and place, but later memories were more detailed. One early memory was described as follows:

> *I am in my room at Diamond Bar. There is a sheet over me. My father is sitting by the side of the bed. I remember the pink lamp on the light in my room. His hand is rubbing my upper thigh on the inside I was feeling frozen and I couldn't move' She could see her own face and her hair halfway pulled up...some hair in a half ponytail. Holly could see her father's face.*
>
> (From Johnston, 1997, p.83)

Holly confronted her father, Gary Ramona, with her revelations, which he strongly and consistently denied. His wife Stephanie sided with Holly and a divorce ensued. In an effort to clear his name, Mr Ramona took Holly's therapist to court, alleging that the memories had been implanted

Recovered Memories: Seeking the Middle Ground. Edited by Graham M. Davies and Tim Dalgleish. © 2001 John Wiley & Sons Ltd.

through incompetent therapeutic practices. The jury found the therapist guilty of malpractice and awarded Mr Ramona damages. Stephanie and Holly continue to believe in the essential truthfulness of Holly's memories (Johnston, 1997).

The Ramona trial came at a turning point in the debate over the credibility of recovered memories in the United States. Just as the Franklin case (see MacLean, 1993, for a full description) marked the initial acceptance of recovered memories as evidence of sufficient credibility to lead to a conviction for murder and a life sentence for the accused, so the Ramona trial marked the emergence of widespread scepticism towards such evidence. At both trials, psychologists appeared as expert witnesses for each side, reflecting the academic debate between, on the one hand, many clinical psychologists who accept the essential veracity of recovered memories and, on the other, numerous cognitive psychologists who support research demonstrating that it is possible through suggestion to induce beliefs in persons which are confidently held, but wholly false (see Lindsay & Read, Chapter 5 in this volume). Such clashes of opinion served to sharpen and polarise the debate.

Can the truth or falsity of recovered memories be established in an objective way? On occasion, such memories may be strikingly corroborated by other evidence or the admissions of the accused (see Shobe & Schooler, Chapter 6 in this volume). In other instances, the memories can be shown to be demonstrably false, in that the events and actions they describe are wholly at variance with established fact or science. However, in most cases involving recovered memories of child sexual abuse, such as the Ramona case, evidence sufficient to resolve the issue is lacking and much depends upon the relative credibility of accounts provided by the defendant and his or her alleged victim. Does psychology offer any prospect of developing ways of evaluating the truth of such statements derived from recovered, or indeed continuous, memories?

Psychologists have long been interested in developing objective measures to discriminate between witnesses telling lies and those telling the truth. A variety of behavioural indices has been proposed, including type and frequency of non-verbal gestures or facial expressions and the use of physiological measures such as respiration and perspiration, epitomised in the polygraph or lie detector. While some of these measures show promise of reliably distinguishing liars from truth tellers under experimental conditions, none has proved sufficiently robust to be used with any consistency in a court of law (see Vrij, 2000, for a review). As yet, there is no Pinocchio test (Ceci & Bruck, 1995). Whatever their validity, such measures are of limited value in assessing the truth or otherwise of recovered memories. In the vast majority of such cases there is no suggestion that the complainant has deliberately fabricated an allegation and is maintaining it as an act of malice. With recovered memories, the complainant genuinely believes and accepts the validity of such memories as a part of their lives.

For these reasons, much of the conventional lie-detection literature is of limited applicability to issues surrounding the validity of recovered memories. Of course, an accused who denies an allegation may seek to undertake some form of test, typically a polygraph test, to buttress their denials. Gary Ramona pursued this course in an attempt to rebut Holly Ramona's testimony and was assessed as telling the truth (Johnston, 1997). However, on the basis of her own self-belief, it seems likely that had Holly taken such a test, she too would have passed, leaving the matter firmly with the judge and jury. There are, however, other measures which potentially offer a more satisfactory method of resolving disputes, which are not dependent upon assessing the non-verbal behaviour which allegedly accompanies deception. These involve an analysis of the content of what the witness says in an effort to detect features which are believed to characterise truthful as opposed to fabricated or fantasy-based testimony. Such an approach to truth determination has a long tradition in countries where the inquisitorial system of justice encourages a wider range of expert evidence: evidence which would be rejected in Britain and the United States as trespassing on the ultimate issue of the defendant's guilt or innocence which is entrusted to the jury. In this chapter, two such procedures—content-based credibility analysis and reality monitoring—are described and evaluated and their potential for evaluating credibility by the courts is considered.

CONTENT-BASED CREDIBILITY ANALYSIS

In 1955, the German Supreme Court made a ruling which required that the statements of all children who made allegations of sexual abuse should be assessed for credibility by a suitably qualified psychologist prior to the trial. The original ruling was prompted by the work of Udo Undeutsch, who argued that statements based on real memories differed quantitatively and qualitatively from those derived from coached accounts or fantasy: the Undeutsch Hypothesis (Undeutsch, 1989). Various criteria were suggested by Undeutsch which he believed characterised true, as opposed to false recollections. These were subsequently collated and refined by Kohnken, Steller and others and integrated into a formal system of interview and assessment, termed Statement Validity Assessment (Kohnken & Steller, 1988; Steller & Kohnken, 1989; Raskin & Esplin, 1992).

Statement Validity Assessment (SVA) involves three major stages. The first consists of a *Semi-structured Interview* with the child where he or she provides first a free account of the allegation which is then expanded upon through open-ended questioning. This is recorded verbatim and transcribed, together with any notes on the behaviour and demeanour of the witness. The second stage involves scrutiny of the content of the interview for the presence of various criteria which are believed to characterise truthful as opposed to fabricated statements. This second stage is known as *Criteria-based Content Analysis* or *CBCA*. In the final phase, the outcome of the CBCA analysis is assessed alongside the *Validity Check-list*—a list covering such issues as the child's intelligence, suggestibility, report consistency and sexual history, which can provide an additional source of evidence on credibility. The psychologist then makes a report to the court, drawing upon all three sources of information (Kohnken, in press).

While practitioners emphasise the importance of rigorous training in all stages of SVA and the importance of drawing upon information from all three phases of the investigation, it has been CBCA criteria which has excited the most research interest to date. A list of criteria employed in the SVA system, derived from Raskin and Esplin (1992), is shown in Table 7.1.

Table 7.1: Criteria-based content analysis

General Characteristics

(1) *Logical Structure*   Is the statement coherent? Is the content logical? Do the different segments fit together? (*Note*: Peculiar or unique details or unexpected complications do not diminish logical structure.)

(2) *Unstructured Production*   Are descriptions unconstrained? Is the report somewhat unorganised? Are there digressions or spontaneous shifts of focus? Are some elements distributed throughout? (*Note*: This criterion requires that the account is logically consistent.)

(3) *Quantity of Details*   Are these specific descriptions of place or time? Are persons, objects, and events specifically described? (*Note*: Repetitions do not count.)

Specific Contents

(4) *Contextual Embedding*   Are events placed in spatial and temporal context? Is the action connected to other incidental events, such as routine daily occurrences?

(5) *Interactions*   Are there reports of actions and reactions or conversations composed of a minimum of three elements involving at least the accused and the witness?

(6) *Reproduction of Speech*   Is speech or conversation during the incident reported in its original form? (*Note*: Unfamiliar terms or quotes are especially strong indicators, even when attributed to only one participant.)

(7) *Unexpected Complications*   Was there an unplanned interruption or an unexpected complication or difficulty during the sexual incident?

Table 7.1 continued

(8) *Unusual Details* Are there details of persons, objects, or events that are unusual, yet meaningful in this context? *(Note*: Unusual details must be realistic.)

(9) *Superfluous Details* Are peripheral details described in connection with the alleged sexual events that are not essential and do not contribute directly to the specific allegation? *(Note*: If a passage satisfies any of the specific criteria (4)–(18), it probably is not superfluous.)

(10) *Accurately Reported Details Misunderstood* Did the child correctly describe an object or event but interpret it incorrectly?

(11) *Related External Associations* Is there reference to a sexually toned event or conversation of a sexual nature that is related in some way to the incident but is not part of the alleged sexual offences?

(12) *Subjective Experience* Did the child describe feelings or thoughts experienced at the time of the incident? *(Note*: This criterion is not satisfied when the witness responds to a direct question, unless the answer goes beyond the question.)

(13) *Attribution of Accused's Mental State* Is there reference to the alleged perpetrator's feelings or thoughts during the incident? *(Note*: Descriptions of overt behaviour do not qualify.)

Motivation-Related Contents

(14) *Spontaneous Corrections or Additions* Were corrections offered or information added to material previously provided in the statement? *(Note*: Responses to direct questions do not qualify.)

(15) *Admitting Lack of Memory or Knowledge* Did the child indicate lack of memory or knowledge of an aspect of the incident? *(Note*: In response to a direct question, the answer must go beyond "I don't know" or "I can't remember".)

(16) *Raising Doubts About One's Own Testimony* Did the child express concern that some part of the statement seems incorrect or unbelievable? *(Note*: Merely asserting that one is telling the truth does not qualify.)

(17) *Self-Deprecation* Did the child describe some aspect of his/her behaviour related to the sexual incident as wrong or inappropriate?

(18) *Pardoning the Accused* Did the child make excuses for or fail to blame the alleged perpetrator, minimise the seriousness of the acts, or fail to add to the allegation when the opportunity occurred?

Reprinted from Raskin & Esplin (1992), with permission from Elsevier Science.

The criteria are grouped into three categories. The first relates to the *General Characteristics* of the Statement. True accounts should be reducible to a coherent and consistent account (*Logical Structure*), even though the facts tumble out in no particular order (*Unstructured Production*), but the account should contain a significant amount of detail relating to the actors and the acts (*Quantity of Detail*).

The second category relates to the *Specific Contents* of the Statement. Statements concerning real events are expected to be anchored to a particular time and place: "It happened after Uncle Ben took me to the football match at Christmas" (*Contextual Embedding*). Accounts should show a clear sequence of development involving actions and reactions by the child and the adult (*Interactions*) and may include fragments of remembered conversation (*Reproduction of Speech*). The presence of *Unusual Details* or *Unexpected Complications* ("he stopped when the telephone rang") are thought to be particularly diagnostic. Credibility is increased if there are references to *Superfluous Details* (e.g. the weather at the time of the incident) or if there is narrative development through *Related External Associations*. Sometimes, naïveté may lead a child to describe a sexual act incorrectly: for instance, an orgasm may be described as a sneeze (*Accurately Reported Details Misunderstood*). References to the witness's own feelings (*Subjective Experience*) or to the presumed feelings of the perpetrator (*Attribution of the Accused's Mental State*) are also thought to increase credibility.

The third category, *Motivation-Related Contents*, refers to a number of criteria said to be frequently present in the accounts of persons telling the truth, but which are unlikely to occur to people providing coached or fabricated narratives. Thus, the presence in authentic narratives of *Spontaneous Corrections or Additions, Admitting Lack of Memory or Knowledge, Self-Deprecation* and *Raising Doubts About One's Own Testimony*, even *Pardoning the Accused* may be contrasted with a glib, assured and stereotyped account, more typical of fabrications.

Two types of study have been conducted in an attempt to validate the assumptions of CBCA. In *experimental studies*, volunteers are requested to give an account of a personal event in their own words and the content of this account is contrasted with a second, which is a fabrication, usually on the instructions of the experimenter. In *field studies*, the content of interview transcripts with persons who have genuinely experienced an event are contrasted with transcripts derived from interviews involving false or malicious accounts of similar experiences. Both types of study possess advantages and disadvantages. Experimental studies provide clear control of variables, but ethical considerations quite properly constrain the range of experiences covered in the real and fabricated accounts. The transcripts employed in field studies ensure that the content of the memories is of forensic relevance, but frequently there are real difficulties in establishing the truth or falsity of accounts beyond doubt. Both types of research are pursued in the hope of establishing *convergent validity*: common principles and findings which are found from both styles of research.

Experimental studies

There have now been a substantial number of experimental studies of CBCA and this review will be restricted to those most relevant to the recovered memories controversy (see Vrij, 2000; Pezdek & Taylor, in press, for comprehensive reviews). Steller, Wellerhaus and Wolf (1988), asked children aged 6–7 and 10–11 years to provide either a true or fabricated account of an emotionally charged incident, such as a fight with another child or an attack by a dog. In all, the frequency of 13 of the 18 CBCA criteria employed were significantly higher in the true, as opposed to fabricated accounts. A classification based on total scores successfully identified 78% of the true accounts and 62% of the false, where 50% represented chance. These figures were significantly higher than those achieved by independent observers using intuitive judgements (68% and 50% respectively). Both CBCA and intuition produced a truth bias: a tendency to perceive more stories as truthful than was in fact the case.

Steller et al. did not report on the impact of age of child on their findings. Akehurst, Kohnken and Hofer (1998b), had children aged 7–8 or 10–11 years and adults have their photographs taken by a professional photographer and later give an account of this to an interviewer. Parallel groups saw a video of the proceedings or read a verbal description of it and were then asked to provide accounts as though they themselves had been photographed. Decisions based on the presence of CBCA criteria correctly classified 73% of first-hand accounts and 67% of the fabricated accounts based on reading a description. However, the difference in number of criteria between first-hand accounts and those based on video-tapes failed to reach statistical significance. No interactions were found between criteria present and age, indicating that CBCA was equally effective for both adults and children in this study.

Akehurst et al.s (1998b) findings suggest that CBCA might be useful in some circumstances as an aid to differentiating truthful from fabricated accounts of adults as well as children, a critical consideration in the case of recovered memories of abuse. Clearly some of the criteria are tailored to the developmental status of children (e.g. *Accurately Reported Details Misunderstood*), but in principle, the Undeutsch hypothesis should be applicable to all witnesses, irrespective of age. Vrij (2000) reviews some 13 experimental studies which have explored CBCA in an adult context. Nearly all report positive findings in terms of differentiating truthful from fabricated accounts, despite the use of incidents with comparatively low levels of witness stress. An exception is a study reported by Ruby and Brigham (1997) who failed to find any advantage for CBCA-trained raters in discriminating truthful from fabricated accounts of a negative, emotional personal experience. However, the raters received only 45 minutes training in the procedure and took less than three minutes to evaluate each transcript, training times not considered adequate by experienced practitioners (see below).

Field studies

Raskin and Esplin (1991) conducted the first systematic field study, which contrasted 20 transcripts of interviews with children in confirmed cases of sexual abuse with the same number of transcripts from interviews derived from doubtful cases. Assessment of the two sets of transcripts by a single researcher trained in CBCA produced perfect differentiation: there was no overlap at all between the distributions of total scores of the confirmed and doubtful cases. Significant differences were also found for 13 of the 18 individual criteria, with all others in the expected direction. However, serious criticisms have been levelled at the methodology of this study. Wells and Loftus (1991) questioned whether there was a selection bias operating in both groups. The doubtful group contained many more younger children than the confirmed group, which may have influenced the quality and quantity of information provided. The criteria used for selection of the doubtful group increased this concern: they included the accused successfully passing a polygraph test, persistent denial by the accused or a failure to prosecute. All of these could in turn be linked to a weak and ineffectual allegation by a child, the converse being true for the confirmed cases. Thus, a self-fulfilling prophecy could have operated in the choice of cases and the very emphatic results might not be representative of child abuse cases as a whole.

Concerns over establishing the ground truth of allegations has been a persistent issue in all subsequent field studies. (Horowitz et al., 1995). The best-controlled study to date is probably that of Lamb et al. (1997). They gained access to a database of 1,187 interviews conducted by Israeli interviewers with child complainants of sexual abuse, aged between 4 and 13 years. A total of 98 cases were selected for study, on the basis of actual physical contact between a known accused and the child and an element of corroboration being present. The cases were also rated for plausibility, using such measures as the presence of medical evidence or admissions by suspects. The transcripts were then assessed for the presence of CBCA criteria, using a minimum of two trained, independent raters. Total CBCA score did predict rated plausibility, however the strength of the relationship was much weaker than in the Raskin and Esplin (1991) study. Moreover, scores on, at most, six individual CBCA criteria were significantly linked to plausibility ratings.

If Raskin and Esplin's study can be said to represent a best-case scenario, it can be argued that Lamb et al.'s (1997) study represents a worst case . First, only 13 of the 98 cases were rated as quite (or very) unlikely, hence the capacity of CBCA to differentiate effectively within a representative range of transcripts of the kind encountered in normal practice may have been underestimated. Second, in contrast to Raskin and Esplin, only 14 of the possible 18 criteria were used to score the transcripts . Third, criteria were scored as either present or absent, rather than the three-point scale (present; absent; strongly present) recommended by German practitioners and used by Raskin and Esplin, which may have reduced the sensitivity of the procedure.

Most field studies of CBCA have used statements from children. More directly relevant to recovered memories is a study of adult memories by Parker and Brown (2000).They selected 43 transcripts of police interviews with rape complainants, of which 16 were classified as true, 12 as false and 15 as indeterminate. As with the child studies, the ground truth of the statements is difficult to establish beyond doubt, though the authors did employ reasonably robust decision rules. The transcripts had come from interviews conducted by officers trained in the use of the Cognitive Interview, which emphasises free narrative and open-ended questioning (Fisher & Geiselman, 1992). All were assessed independently for the presence of CBCA criteria by police officers trained in its application. Unusually, they also assessed the cases on the background measures incorporated in the Validity Checklist, which covers such matters as the consistency of statements and susceptibility to suggestion. The Checklist was scored separately and then incorporated into an overall assessment. Overall, the use of SVA identified all 16 of the true statements and 11 of the 12 false statements (one was classified as indeterminate). The use of CBCA criteria alone enabled 14 of the 16 true cases to be identified and 11 of the 12 false cases. True statements averaged over 10 reality criteria per transcript, while the false scored only 4. SVA-trained officers consistently outperformed experienced investigative officers not trained in the use of SVA in the detection of true and false statements. Parker and Brown conclude that the technique may have a significant role in the evaluation of rape case evidence.

Critique and overview

Overall, it is apparent from both laboratory and field studies of CBCA that the effectiveness of the technique may be described as promising rather than convincing. Results from research on children's accounts raise serious concerns over the reliability and consistency in the application of at least some of the criteria. Some criteria, such as *Logical Structure* and *Quantity of Details* appear to be present in virtually all of the selected accounts and cannot be used to differentiate between true and false accounts, whereas other criteria, such as *Pardoning the Accused* are rarely reported (Lamb et al., 1997). Some criteria appear to be difficult to apply with any consistency (Horowitz et al., 1997). It is evident that extensive training is required of assessors to provide consistent results. Kohnken (in press) recommends a minimum of five days training and there is evidence that crash courses in CBCA can be counter-productive (Akehurst, Bull & Vrij, 1998a).

There are also concerns about the link reported in several studies, both experimental (Santtila, Roppola, Runtti & Neimi, 2000) and field (Davies, Westcott & Horan, 1999; Lamb et al., 1997) between age and the quantity of CBCA criteria elicited. While SVA requires that the age of the witness be taken into account in reaching decisions on credibility, there is at present no formal decision rules for doing this. Finally, while it is gratifying that many studies have reported that overall CBCA scores independently predict account plausibility, a significant overall result may be less useful as a pointer to decisions in individual cases. There is no accepted minimum figure for the quantity of criteria that must be present for an account to be judged as true. Given the significant impact of age and the mental development of the witness, it is hard to see how a single, universal figure could be endorsed. In their study of adult statements, Parker and Brown (2000) specified that the presence of 5 or less criteria placed a statement in the doubtful category; but for some professionals, 5 would be sufficient to classify a child's statement as true (Yuille, 1988). German experts do not recommend a minimum figure, instead preferring to make individual judgements which take account of age and the presence of certain criteria which are believed to be particularly diagnostic (Kohnken, in press). Clearly, while there is support for the fundamental precepts of the Undeutsch hypothesis, much further research is required to place the idea into a properly validated forensic test for children's statements. Applying such a system to the recovered memories of adults presents additional difficulties.

While the encouraging results from Akehurst et al. (1998b) and Parker and Brown (2000) illustrate that CBCA is applicable in principle to discriminating false from veridical memories in adults, no studies to date have examined systematically the criteria present in recovered memories, as opposed to deliberately fabricated and truthful statements. Such a limitation is not present for a second approach to identifying veridical statements, i.e. the reality monitoring hypothesis of Marcia Johnson.

REALITY MONITORING

Johnson's approach to cognition emerged from her laboratory studies of recall and, in particular, her opposition to strength theories of memory which reduce all experiences to a single homogeneous trace (Johnson &

Raye, 1981). According to Johnson, memories embody different sources of information which reflect the nature of the original experience (*external sources*) as well as relics of the cognitive operations triggered by the original event (*internal sources*). Among the external sources which contribute to the memory are *perceptual information* (information relating to the sensory channels stimulated by the experience), *contextual information* (indications of the time and place at which an event occurred) and *affective information* (something of the emotional reaction which the event provoked). Imagined events, by contrast, will contain many more *cognitive operations* — evidence of mental processes triggered by the event in question, i.e. links to related events, reflections, elaborations and interpretations. Johnson argues that memories of events which are experienced at first hand will contain far more information from external than internal sources. Real events by their nature will induce automatic and non-effortful processing, with an absence of search and decision-making processes. Imagined events, by contrast, will contain a preponderance of internal references, reflecting the cognitive operations that have gone into elaborating the mental construct.

According to Johnson (1988), it is precisely the different qualities of memories of imagined and real events which enable us routinely to discriminate between true memories and thoughts, dreams and fantasies—a process which she refers to as *reality monitoring*. Thus, a person's memory of a first date will contain perceptual (the appearance of their partner, their scent and perhaps, with luck, some tactile information), contextual (time and place), and affective (feelings and reactions, positive or negative) information. However, a verbal description of a date, read in a book or recounted by a friend, may lead to some perceptual, affective and contextual information being encoded, but cognitive operations will be much more evident: comparisons with one's own experiences, for instance, or reflections on implications.

A number of studies from Johnson's lab have supported this analysis. For instance, participants were invited to think of a recent routine event such as going to the library or dentist and also an imagined event: a fantasy or dream. Ratings of the content of their memories for these two classes of event by the participants revealed that perceptual, temporal and contextual information was more often present for actual events, though affective information was also reported for the imagined events, perhaps reflecting the choice of dreams or fantasies as material. When participants were invited to perform the same exercise for childhood memories and fantasies, overall ratings of perceptual and contextual detail were much lower and the differences between the two types of memory were much less marked (Johnson, Foley, Suengas & Raye, 1988). It is tempting to see the loss of differentiation over time as being due to reminiscence: repeated retelling of childhood stories might serve to increase the reconstructive elements of the narrative (Johnson, 1988). This might suggest an immediate limitation on the applicability of the technique to recovered memories, given their alleged origin in the past. However, recovered memories by their very definition, have not been subject to reminiscence. Further, there is evidence that imagined events show a disproportionately greater loss of external cues over time compared to memories for real events (Suengas & Johnson, 1988).

Johnson (1988) noted that reality monitoring could in principle be applied to true and false statements, but speculated that perhaps the differences in information would be less marked because of the changes induced by the social conventions of story telling (imposition of structure; elimination of irrelevant detail, etc.). A number of other researchers have sought to develop Johnson's Memory Characteristics Questionnaire (MCQ) as a tool for analysing the content of witness statements with a view to developing reality monitoring as a technique for detecting truthfulness. Once again, both laboratory experiments and field studies have been used to explore these issues.

Experimental studies

Alonzo-Quecuty was among the first researchers to apply reality monitoring to eyewitness testimony. Hernandez-Fernaud and Alonzo-Quecuty (1997), for instance, asked adults to view a video of a car theft for which, subsequently, they provided either true or false accounts. True statements were assessed as containing significantly more contextual and sensory information than the false accounts, but there was no difference in the number of references to cognitive operations.

Sporer (1997) published the first fully developed version of the MCQ for validating witness statements: the Judgements of Memory Characteristics Questionnaire (JMCQ). Participants were scored on a range of items relating to eight separate subscales which in turn were derived from the original MCQ. Sporer requested adult volunteers to recount 40 wholly true and 40 wholly false experiences to camera. He then used multiple-discriminant analysis to demonstrate that the JMCQ was effective in differentiating between 75% of the true statements and 68% of the invented accounts. Some subscales (emotions; realism) were particularly diagnostic but, once again, there was no appreciable difference as regard cognitive operations. Santilla, Roppola and Niemi (1999) used an adapted version of the JMCQ to assess samples of true and false stories generated by children aged 7–14 years. Once again, discriminant analysis showed effective differentiation between true and invented statements. On this occasion, true statements contained more sensory and temporal information but less affective information and once more, there was no difference in references to cognitive operations. As with CBCA, the incidence of reality criteria was correlated with increasing age and verbal ability, suggesting that the system was most effective with elaborated narratives.

Sporer (1998) developed a more advanced version of the JMCQ which he termed the Aberdeen Report Judgement Scales (ARJS). The ARJS was successful in discriminating between narratives furnished by adult army officer trainees who had, or had not, taken part in a night training exercise. However, the system was less successful when the trainees concerned were given 24 hours notice to prepare their accounts. The main structure of the ARJS is shown in Table 7.2.

Field studies

Roberts, Lamb, Zale and Randall (1998) used their own adaptation of the MCQ in the only study to date to assess the content of confirmed and unconfirmed accounts provided by children of sexual abuse. Accounts which were confirmed by perpetrator confessions or medical and physical evidence produced significantly higher ratings overall than cases which lacked such confirmation, with the presence of actions

Table 7.2: Grouping of Aberdeen Report Judgement Scales Criteria.

Global Criteria
(1) Realism and coherence (cf. logical consistency)
(2) Clarity and vividness

Quantity and precision of details
(3) Quantity and precision of details (cf. contextual embedding):
    (3a) Core and peripheral details and precision of details
    (3b) Spatial information
    (3c) Time information
    (3d) Sensory impressions

Internal Processes
(4) Emotions and feelings
(5) Cognitive operations:
    (5a) Thoughts and cognitive processes
    (5b) Memory processes and rehearsal

Social Aspects
(6) Verbal and non-verbal interactions
(7) Extraordinary details
(8) Absence of social desirability

Autobiographical Memory
(9) Personal significance and implications

Reprinted, with permission, from Sporer (1998).

or perceptual information proving particularly diagnostic. However, as with the CBCA studies, the status of the unconfirmed cases remains problematic (it is interesting, for instance, that 5 of the 16 unconfirmed cases scored higher than the average for the confirmed).

CRITIQUE AND OVERVIEW

These studies suggest that while the reality monitoring approach offers some promise of differentiating between true and false accounts, considerable development work is required to turn the system from a research tool into a reliable clinical test. Considerable training is required to score protocols with any degree of consistency. Sporer (1997) reports that satisfactory reliability could only be achieved after prolonged training, but even after training, his raters still produced significant differences in absolute ratings on six of the eight subscales of the JMCQ. With the exception of Sporer's work, there are no other published studies on the reliability or factor structure of the existing tests: researchers tend to produce their own version and add or subtract scales as they think fit.

How does reality monitoring as a technique compare for accuracy with CBCA? As Vrij (2000) has pointed out, reality monitoring shares many of the same assumptions as CBCA, particularly in relation to the *General Characteristics* and *Specific Contents* criteria. The *Time Information* and *Spatial Information* scales of JMCQ are clearly linked to the concept of *Contextual Embedding* used in CBCA. Sporer (1997) intercorrelated judgements across transcripts for the two sets of criteria and found 26 out of 88 correlations were significant, indicating a degree of overlap. In these circumstances, it is not too surprising that when the two schemes are compared, there appears to be little difference in their predictive power, whether in identifying true and false accounts collected under experimental conditions (Sporer, 1997; Santtila et al., 1999) or actual allegations of abuse by children (Roberts et al., 1998).

Despite these similarities between the two approaches, there are also important differences. Reality monitoring has its roots in cognitive experimental research with adults. CBCA was developed as a clinical forensic technique specifically for evaluating the statements of children in the context of allegations of abuse. Development of reality monitoring is at a much earlier stage, and as yet it lacks procedures such as CBCA's Validity Checklist for formally taking into account wider factors beyond content, such as age or event plausibility. Reality monitoring, on the other hand, does contain criteria which are associated with both truth and fabrication, which makes it potentially a more balanced and reliable procedure than CBCA which contains only indicators of truthfulness

(Vrij, 2000). Not surprisingly, there have been calls for the development of a hybrid system incorporating the best features of both. There is certainly evidence that the diagnosticity of the two sets of criteria operating in tandem is somewhat greater than each on its own. Sporer (1997) reported an overall accuracy rate of 79% in his experimental study when findings from both systems were pooled. However, before urging the application of such a hybrid scheme for evaluating recovered memories, the differences as well as the similarities between recovered and continuous memories need to be explored.

TRUTH, LIES AND RECOVERED MEMORIES

In this review so far, all the studies cited have contrasted true accounts with deliberate lies. However, with a recovered memory, the person involved does not deliberately set out to deceive. Almost by definition, what characterises even patently false recovered memories is a belief on the part of witnesses in the authenticity of the experience they describe (see Skinner, Chapter 3, in this volume). Ceci and Bruck (1995) have suggested that systems such as CBCA are unlikely to detect differences between authentic and false recovered memories, because as far as the witness is concerned, the event actually occurred and thus such memories will have all the qualities of conventional continuous memories. Clearly, it is important for researchers to address the issue of how, if at all, true and false recovered memories differ from conventional memories and deliberate fabrications respectively. Researchers have recently begun to address this issue.

One established method of inducing a false memory, pioneered by Elizabeth Loftus, is to expose witnesses to an event and then, in subsequent questioning, make reference to a non-existent object. A substantial minority of participants—perhaps 30%—will later testify that they saw the suggested object as part of the original event: the post-event misinformation effect (Loftus, 1977). In a series of studies, Schooler, Loftus and colleagues asked witnesses who responded positively to the presence of the suggested objects to provide descriptions of them and compared these with descriptions provided by controls who actually saw the objects concerned (Schooler, Clark & Loftus, 1988; Schooler, Gerhard & Loftus, 1986). Schooler and colleagues found that, relative to witnesses describing a suggested object, those reporting an actual object were more likely to mention sensory detail and less likely to include references to their own cognitive processes—findings which they related explicitly to Johnson and Raye's Reality Monitoring framework. Pickel (1999) extended this work by including a third condition where participants were briefed to deliberately lie about having seen the target object. In Pickel's study, all participants were unwitting witnesses to a staged robbery of the target object, a calculator. However, only one group actually saw the calculator lying on the desk, the remainder were either given suggestions that they had seen the calculator or were told to pretend that they had. When, subsequently, all participants were asked to describe the calculator, witnesses who had actually seen the object included greater sensory detail and made fewer references to cognitive processes, confirming the earlier results of Schooler et al. By contrast, the deceptive group produced a different profile, with the highest number of sensory details; references to cognitive processes fell between the other two groups.

Taken together, these results suggest that accounts of real events might differ in systematic ways from those which are the product of suggestion, though there is a yawning gulf between recall of an isolated object and the extended narratives which typify recovered memories. Two recent studies have explored more elaborate suggestions. Porter, Yuille and Lehman (1999) contacted the parents of a group of students and asked them to identify some traumatic events experienced by their children, such as a serious animal attack. The students were then repeatedly interviewed about one of these events, together with a plausible but false event that the interviewer implied had been mentioned by their parents, a procedure known to induce false recollections in participants (Loftus & Pickrell, 1995). At the end of the process, some 26% of the participants had recovered a complete memory for the false event with a further 30% recalling some aspect of it. The content of these false memories was compared in turn with that for the genuine memory. In addition, participants were asked to fabricate an account of an event from their childhood. The narratives from all three conditions were then assessed by a mix of rating scales, including items drawn from Reality Monitoring and CBCA. On this occasion, there was no difference between the three types of narrative in either sensory information or references to mental experiences, but suggested memories were assessed as less vivid than either true or fabricated accounts and to be held with less confidence. Interestingly, there was no difference in the amount of detail in true and suggested memories, but fabricated accounts contained significantly more. The authors note that many of the suggested incidents which participants came to believe were highly serious and stressful (e.g. falling down and being taken to hospital for stitching), although no childhood sexual memories were included for obvious ethical reasons.

A second study did not deliberately induce false memories, but rather, ingeniously capitalised on an urban myth. Ost, Vrij, Costall and Bull (in press) solicited volunteers in a shopping complex in the immediate aftermath of the death of Princess Diana and asked them if they had seen film on television of the fatal crash occurring (no such record is known to exist). Some 20 out of the first 45 people approached claimed to have seen the film and these were invited to complete the MCQ with reference to their (false) memory of the event. Those people who denied seeing the film were encouraged to imagine what such a film might have been like and to complete the MCQ on that basis. Individual MCQ subscales did not distinguish between those who believed they had seen the film and those who had simply imagined what it might be like. On this occasion, however, there was no true memory of the crash to which to compare the false and fabricated memories. However, when these two groups were compared to a third who simply filled in the MCQ on the basis of their own memories of hearing of the tragedy, similarities and differences in profile did emerge: participants who claimed to have seen the film scored more highly on the cognitive operations subscale, but did not differ on the sensory content.

Clearly, research is at an early stage, but existing results do not preclude the possibility that suggested false memories may have different characteristics to true memories. Studies to date have not produced consistent findings: the increase sensory content shown in the suggested object studies was not replicated in the continuous narratives elicited by Porter et al. (1991) and Ost et al. (in press). Evidence of enhanced cognitive operations found by Schooler et al. was confirmed in the Ost study, but not by Porter. There is clearly a need for further work, particularly for studies which analyse narratives whose content contains material typically found in recovered memories of abuse. A study by Dalenberg (1996) shows one way forward. She compared the statements of a group of women with a known history of sexual abuse, but who had recovered further memories in later life, with a comparable group of retractors: women who had at first claimed a recovered memory and then concluded that their memories were false. The number of women in the study was small and her analysis was consequently limited, but there is no reason in principle why the same comparison could not be repeated using a much larger sample and standardised versions of CBCA or JMCQ. Only when studies of this kind are conducted will it be possible to talk of building a content profile typical of true or false recovered memories.

CONCLUDING COMMENTS

This review of the literature has considered research on the content of memory narratives, particularly as it relates to CBCA and reality monitoring criteria. While considerable development and refinement is required for both systems, they show promise of being able in principle to distinguish between samples of truthful and fabricated accounts at well above chance level. There is no indication that one system is necessarily superior to the other. On the contrary, many of their criteria overlap and it might be possible to produce a hybrid system which embraces the most reliable features of both techniques.

However, success in this endeavour would not necessarily mean that content analysis would necessarily assist in validating recovered memories. As has been noted, false recovered memories are not normally deliberate deceptions of the kind that CBCA and the JMCQ were developed to detect, but by definition, the holder of such memories believes them to be true. A survey of the existing research which has contrasted the characteristics of memories induced by suggestion on the one hand, with real and fabricated memories on the other, suggests that differences may exist, but are smaller and less consistent than those between real and fabricated memories. However, research is at an early stage and has yet to capture many of the features which characterise recovered memories in and out of therapy.

For instance, studies have only considered false memories induced by verbal suggestion. It is alleged that false memories can result from scrutiny of visual material such as films or photographs (Pendergrast, 1996). The laboratory study of Akehurst, Kohnken and Hofer reviewed earlier found that CBCA criteria correctly distinguished between truthful and fabricated accounts, but failed to distinguish between participant accounts and those who had viewed a videotape. Similar difficulties in discriminating between experiences at first- and second-hand have been reported by Alonzo-Quecuty (1996) using reality monitoring criteria. Perhaps the addition of criteria covering smell and taste might assist in differentiating such experiences.

Researchers have not begun to consider many of the variables which colour the content of real-world recovered memories of child and adult sexual assault, but do not figure in laboratory-induced false memories. There are, as yet, no studies which have explored the impact of representative delays on the content of what is reported and no studies of the impact of the number of times a story has been related. Vrij (2000) has speculated that repeated retelling is likely to alter the balance in favour of structural and cognitive elements at the expense of perceptual information. As Porter et al. (1999) have emphasised, no existing research has examined the effect of social factors on the content of suggested and real narratives, yet these are a feature of many memories recovered in therapy. Most importantly, the nature of the memories themselves may alter the characteristics and content of a recovered memory of abuse. In survey research conducted by Tromp, Koss, Figueredo and Tharan (1995), women who reported being raped rated the experience as less clear and vivid, less well remembered and less thought or talked about, compared to other intense, unpleasant experiences (see also Koss, Figueredo, Bell, Tharan & Tromp, 1999).

This represents a formidable research agenda, but is a measure of how far the objective study of the credibility of recovered memories has to advance before a system can be considered viable. It will be a formidable task to produce an instrument capable of differentiating reliably between individual true and false accounts, as opposed to discriminating within a large batch of statements at a statistically satisfactory level. Only in the Raskin and Esplin (1991) and Parker and Brown (2000) studies was credible differentiation at the level of individual statements achieved. In the meantime, therapists and the courts should view with extreme caution experts who claim to be able to divine truth or falsity from the internal qualities of a recovered memory narrative alone. There may come a time when content analysis reaches a level of sophistication where it can play an important role in determining the truth value of such statements, but it will be too late for Gary or Holly Ramona and other victims of the memory wars.

REFERENCES

Akehurst, K., Kohnken, G. & Hofer, E. (1995, August). *The reliability of Content-Based Criteria Analysis in judgements of the credibility of adult and child witness statements*. Paper presented at the 5th European Conference of Psychology and Law, Budapest, Hungary.

Akehurst, L., Bull, R. & Vrij, A. (1998a, September). *Training British police officers, social workers and students to detect deception in children using Content-Based Criteria Analysis*. Paper presented at the 8th European Conference of Psychology and Law, Krakow, Poland.

Akehurst, L., Kohnken, G. & Hofer, E. (1998b, August). *Content credibility of accounts derived from live and video presentations*. Paper presented at the International Congress of Applied Psychology, San Francisco, CA.

Alonzo-Quecuty, M. L. (1996). Detecting fact and fallacy in child and adult witness accounts. In G. Davies, S. Lloyd-Bostock, M. McMurran & C. Wilson (Eds), *Psychology, Law and Criminal Justice: International Developments in Law and Practice* (pp. 74–80). Berlin: De Gruyter.

Ceci, S. J. & Bruck, M. (1995). *Jeopardy in the Courtroom: A Scientific Analysis of Children's Testimony*. Washington, DC: American Psychological Association.

Dalenberg, C. J. (1996, June). *The prediction of accurate recollections of trauma*. Paper presented at the NATO Advanced Study Institute on Recollections of Trauma, Port Bourgenay, France.

Davies, G. M. Westcott, H. L. & Horan, N. (1999). The impact of questioning style on the content of investigative interviews with suspected child sexual abuse victims. *Psychology, Crime and Law, 6*, 81–97.

Fisher, R. P. & Geiselman, E. (1992). *Memory Enhancing Techniques for Investigative Interviewing*. Springfield, IL: C. C. Thomas.

Hernandez-Fernaud, E. & Alonzo-Quecuty, M. L. (1997). The cognitive interview and lie detection: A new magnifying glass for Sherlock Holmes? *Applied Cognitive Psychology*, **11**, 55–68.

Horowitz, S. W., Lamb, M. E., Esplin, P. W., Boychuk, T. D., Reiter-Lavery, L. & Krispin, O. (1995). Establishing ground truth in studies of child sexual abuse. *Expert Evidence*, **4**, 42–51.

Horowitz, S. W., Lamb, M. E., Esplin, P. W., Boychuk, T. D., Krispin, O. & Reiter-Levery, L. (1997). Reliability of criteria-based content analysis of child witness statements. *Legal and Criminological Psychology*, **2**, 11–21.

Johnson, M. K. (1988). Reality monitoring: An experimental, phenomenological approach. *Journal of Experimental Psychology: General*, **117**, 390–394.

Johnson, M. K., Foley, M. A., Suengas, A. G. & Raye, C. L. (1988). Phenomenal characteristics of memories for perceived and imagined autobiographical events. *Journal of Experimental Psychology: General*, **117**, 371–376.

Johnson, M. K. & Raye, C. L. (1981). Reality monitoring. *Psychological Review*, **88**, 67–85.

Johnston, M. (1997). *Spectral Evidence*. Boulder, CO: Westview Press.

Kohnken, G. (in press). A German perspective on children's testimony. In H. Westcott, G. Davies & R. Bull (Eds), *Children's Testimony: Psychological Research and Forensic Practice*. Chichester, UK: Wiley.

Kohnken, G. & Steller, M. (1988), The evaluation of the credibility of child witness statements in the German procedural system. In G. Davies & J. Drinkwater (Eds), *The Child Witness: Do the Courts Abuse Cildren?* (Issues in Criminological and Legal Psychology, no. 13). (pp. 37–45). Leicester: British Psychological Society.

Koss, M. P., Figueredo, A. J., Bell, I., Tharan, M. & Tromp, S. (1999). Traumatic memory characteristics: A cross-validated mediational model of response to rape among employed women. In L. M. Williams & V. L. Banyard (Eds), *Trauma and Memory* (pp. 273–290). Thousand Oaks, CA: Sage.

Lamb, M. E., Sternberg, K. J., Esplin, P. W., Hershkowitz, I., Orbach Y. & Hovav, M. (1997). Criterion-based content analysis: a field validation study. *Child Abuse and Neglect*, **21**, 255–264.

Loftus, E. F. (1977). *Eyewitness Testimony*. Cambridge, MA: Harvard University Press.

Loftus, E. F. & Pickrell, J. E. (1995). The formation of false memories. *Psychiatric Annals*, **25**, 720–725.

MacLean, H. N. (1993). *Once Upon a Time*. New York: Harper-Collins.

Ost, J., Vrij, A., Costall, A. & Bull, R. (in press). Crashing memories and reality monitoring: Distinguishing between perceptions, imaginings and false memories. *Applied Cognitive Psychology*.

Parker, A. D. & Brown, J. (2000). Detection of deception: Statement Validity Analysis as a means of determining truthfulness or falsity of rape allegations. *Legal and Criminological Psychology*, **5**, 237–259.

Pendergrast, M. (1996). *Victims of Memory*. London: Harper-Collins.

Pezdek, K. & Taylor, J. (in press). Discriminating between accounts of true and false events. In D. F. Bjorklund (Ed.), *Research and Theory in False-Memory Creation in Children and Adults*. Mahwah, NJ: Erlbaum.

Pickel, K. L. (1999). Distinguishing eyewitness descriptions of perceived objects from descriptions of imagined objects. *Applied Cognitive Psychology*, **14**, 399–414.

Porter, S., Yuille, J. C. & Lehman, D. R. (1999). The nature of real, implanted, and fabricated memories for emotional childhood events: Implications for the recovered memory debate. *Law and Human Behavior*, **23**, 517–537.

Raskin, D. C. & Esplin, P. W. (1991). Assessment of children's statements in sexual abuse. In J. Doris (Ed.), *The Suggestibility of Children's Recollections* (pp. 153–165). Washington, DC: American Psychological Association.

Raskin, D. C. & Esplin, P. W. (1992). Statement Validity Assessment: Interview procedures and content analysis of children's statements of sexual abuse. *Behavioral Assessment*, **13**, 265–291.

Roberts, K. P., Lamb, M. E., Zale J. L. & Randall, D. W. (1998, March). *Qualitative differences in children's accounts of confirmed and unconfirmed incidents of sexual abuse.* Paper presented at the biennial meeting of the American Psychology-Law Society, Redondo Beach, NC.

Ruby, C. L. & Brigham, J. C. (1998). The usefulness of the criteria-based content analysis technique in distinguishing between truthful and fabricated allegations. *Psychology, Public Policy and Law*, **3**, 705–737.

Santtila, P., Roppola, H. & Niemi, P. (1999). Assessing the truthfulness of witness statements made by children (aged 7–8,10–11, and 13–14) employing scales derived from Johnson and Raye's model of reality monitoring. *Expert Evidence*, **6**, 273–289.

Santtila, P., Roppola, H., Runtti M. & Neimi, P. (2000). Assessment of child witness statements using Criteria-Based Content Analysis (CBCA): The effect of age, verbal ability and interviewers emotional style. *Psychology, Crime and Law*, **6**, 159–179.

Schooler, J. W., Clark, C. A. & Loftus, E. F. (1988). Knowing when memory is real. In M. M. Gruneberg, P. E. Morris & R. N. Sykes (Eds), *Practical Aspects of Memory: Current Research and Issues, Vol. 1: Memory in Everyday Life* (pp. 83–88). Chichester, UK: Wiley.

Schooler, J. W., Gerhard D. & Loftus, E. F. (1986). Qualities of the unreal. *Journal of Experimental Psychology: Learning, Memory and Cognition*, **12**, 171–178.

Sporer, S. L. (1996). The less travelled road to the truth: Verbal cues in deception detection in accounts of fabricated and experienced events. *Applied Cognitive Psychology*, **11**, 373–397.

Sporer, S. L. (1998, March). *Detecting deception with the Aberdeen Report Judgement Scales (ARJS): Theoretical development, reliability and validity.* Paper presented at the Biennial Meeting of the American Psychology-Law Society, Redondo Beach, CA, USA.

Steller, M. & Kohnken, G. (1989). Criteria-based statement analysis. In D. C. Raskin (Ed.), *Psychological Methods in Criminal Investigation and Evidence* (pp. 217–245). New York: Springer.

Steller, M., Wellerhaus, P. & Wolf, T. (1988, June). *Empirical validation of criteria-based content analysis.* Paper presented at the NATO Advanced Study Institute on Credibility Analysis, Maratea, Italy.

Suengas, A. G. & Johnson, M. K. (1988). Qualitative effects of rehearsal on memories for perceived and imagined complex events. *Journal of Experimental Psychology: General*, **117**, 377–389.

Tromp, S., Koss, M. P., Figueredo, A. J. & Tharan, M. (1995). Are rape memories different? A comparison of rape, other unpleasant, and pleasant memories among employed women. *Journal of Traumatic Stress*, **8**, 607–627.

Undeutsch, U. (1989). The development of statement reality analysis. In J. C. Yuille (Ed.), *Credibility Assessment* (pp. 101–121). Dordrecht, The Netherlands: Kluwer.

Vrij, A. (2000). *Detecting Lies and Deceit: The Psychology of Lying and the Implications for Professional Practice.* Chichester, UK: Wiley.

Wells, G. L. & Loftus, E. F. (1991). Commentary: Is this child fabricating? Reactions to a new assessment technique. In J. Doris (Ed.), *The Suggestibility of Children's Recollections* (pp. 168–171). Washington, DC: American Psychological Association.

Yuille, J. C. (1988). The systematic assessment of children's testimony. *Canadian Psychology, **29**, 247–262.*

PART III

CLINICAL ASPECTS

8

THERAPEUTIC TECHNIQUES, THERAPEUTIC CONTEXTS AND MEMORY

D. A. Bekerian and M. H. O'Neill

Memory theories, and memory theorists, have often been used in the debate over recovered memories and false memories (see Conway, 1997, pp. 150–191; Loftus, 1979; Weiskrantz, 1995). Other chapters in this volume have already considered the empirical literature and the theoretical explanations that have been applied to evidential settings (see Lindsay & Read, Chapter 5 in this volume). This chapter will focus on techniques that might be employed within a therapeutic context, and the general question of how such techniques might influence the way people report and ultimately remember and interpret their past.

The chapter considers therapeutic techniques in terms of cognitive theories, without any assumptions regarding psycho-dynamic mechanisms, such as repression. It is assumed that explanations used to account for empirical data on memory are adequate to anticipate the effects that might be observed in non-experimental contexts, such as the therapeutic environment (e.g. Lindsay & Read, 1994; Morton, 1994; McCloskey & Zaragoza, 1985; Wood, Bekerian & Foa, 1999). Clearly, there are important differences between behaviours demonstrated in the laboratory and those demonstrated in the therapeutic context (e.g. Bekerian & Goodrich, 1999).

Recovered Memories: Seeking the Middle Ground. Edited by Graham M. Davies and Tim Dalgleish. © 2001 John Wiley & Sons Ltd.

However, there are sufficient similarities, and many of the points that are raised here will be reminiscent of those that have been addressed in other chapters, particularly those dealing with memory in forensic contexts (again see Lindsay & Read, Chapter 5).

There are also important issues that are beyond the scope of this chapter; for example, we assert that there is no homogeneous class of recovered memories, rather than get drawn into a discussion of the nature of recovered memories. The heterogeneity in recovered memories of abuse is apparent when one considers the different types of memories that are associated with recovery (see Goodrich & Bekerian, 1999). Somatic or body memories are reported, as are behavioural memories; factual and episodic remembering also occur, with the latter varying in the degree of phenomenal awareness (see also Andrews, Chapter 9 in this volume). Harvey and Herman (1994) clearly documented that clients show different phenomenal awareness of the past when recovering traumatic memories; and that recovery itself is a complex process which varies across different clients.

Similarly we avoid discussion of whether memories that are recovered in therapy are true or false. There is evidence for at least one case where a recovered memory was true, and one case where a recovered memory was false (see Bekerian & Goodrich, 1999; Goodrich & Bekerian, 1999). In principle, recovered memories can be true or false, and, in some majority of cases, true and false. For example, Hyman and his colleagues have amply demonstrated that false memories can contain components of real autobiographical experiences (e.g. Hyman & Pentland, 1996). Consequently, we maintain that little is to be gained by considering whether recovered memories are true or false in any absolute sense.

The major argument put forward here is that certain therapeutic techniques potentially render the client and therapist[1] "vulnerable" to the effects of re-interpretation and reporting inaccuracies. This does not mean that such techniques should be avoided, or that restrictions should be placed on the manner in which techniques are used. The arguments are therefore not whether the techniques represent good practice (see Courtois, 1997). Rather, the intent is to highlight the potential consequences of using certain therapeutic techniques, and consider the impact such consequences might have for clients and therapists. A similar approach has been adopted by others discussing recovered memories (e.g. Saywitz & Moan-Hardie, 1994). Arguably, this moderate position will prove to be most productive in amassing information that can inform the question of recovered memories of sexual abuse (*ACP*, 1994).

---

[1] The term therapist is used, although the issues apply to any practitioner who works therapeutically with clients, e.g. counsellors, practitioners, therapists.

Vulnerability within therapeutic settings will refer to potential distortions in reporting, remembering and interpretation that are introduced by the therapist; the client (as in auto-suggestibility, e.g. Reyna & Titcomb, 1997); or both (Denes, 1997). On the one hand, there are factors that exist regardless of the particular techniques employed. On the other, there are factors that are introduced by virtue of using specific techniques. Here, we highlight one very general factor that will affect all clients, in any therapy, before considering more specific therapeutic techniques. Some directions for future discussions are then suggested.

One factor present across all types of therapies is the therapeutic relationship itself. Regardless of the specific therapeutic approach that is adopted, or techniques that are used, the therapeutic relationship is the source of highly potent dynamics. Crucially, the therapeutic setting is associated with an individual's desire to change something, whatever the specific reason.[2] Indeed, most therapeutic doctrines assume that the client enters therapy to change.

The therapist is regarded as the facilitator of this change. There is no endorsement that this role is absolutely productive or desirable; rather, it is merely a statement of fact. The therapist is the agent within the therapeutic setting who assists the client to identify his or her difficulties and affect ways of changing them. In some cases, the therapist may deliberately assume this role, as a means of therapeutic intervention; in others (and perhaps more regularly) the therapist is given this role by the client (as with processes of transference). In any event, the therapist is no more equal to a client than a lawyer would be to a client in matters of law (see Denes, 1997).

This relationship between the client and the therapist thus comes with certain responsibilities for the therapist. The most obvious one is that the therapist can be regarded as an authority figure, for example a parent surrogate (see Denes, 1997). The therapist has enormous influence on the manner in which a client experiences and re-experiences events that are recalled either during or outside of sessions, and the way in which the client interprets symbolic behaviours or recreations (e.g. dreams). As noted by Kempler (1975), therapists sample from the therapeutic environment and attend to those features of their client's behaviour that are most relevant to them. The potential always exists for the therapist to direct the client towards issues that have more significance for the therapist than they do for the client. This is so obvious that most authors — regardless of their respective cultures or positions on recovered memories — highlight the responsibility which must be accepted by the therapist on this matter (e.g. Courtois, 1997; Lindsay & Read, 1994).

---

[2] This situation refers to clients who voluntarily engage in therapy.

When therapists consistently fail to be aware of their own personal issues, they and their clients are more susceptible to a variety of factors. The most familiar factor identified in the memory literature is misleading post-event information, where inaccurate information about an event is suggested to the person after the fact (cf. Loftus, 1979). The empirical literature on misleading suggestions in experimental contexts argues that some individuals will respond in accordance to what they think is expected of them by the experimenter, or authority figure (e.g. McCloskey & Zaragoza, 1985). For example, some people will report what they think the experimenter wishes them to remember, rather than what they actually remember. They may remember a detail differently from what is being suggested by the experimenter and conform to the inaccuracy in order to comply or "be a good experimental subject". Alternatively, people may fail to remember a detail, and be uncertain; yet, they may report an inaccuracy suggested by the experimenter, again to comply.

These descriptions complement discussions of the processes of unhealthy confluence in the therapeutic setting (O'Leary, 1997). The client endeavours to be consistent with the therapist, accepting the therapist's interpretations, opinions, and beliefs as truth. This is a powerful factor that must never be underestimated in the therapeutic setting, particularly as some confluence is regarded as essential in developing a relationship between therapist and client (again see O'Leary, 1997).

The experimental evidence has also pointed to the possibility of source confusion errors, wherein the source of the information is wrongly attributed to a past event (e.g. Johnson, Nolde & de Leonardis, 1996). People may have a memory for a detail, but fail to know the particular episode in which they experienced it. When told by the experimenter that the detail occurred in a specific event, people may "remember" the detail as having occurred, in spite of the fact that it occurred in another event. Alternatively, people may misattribute the source of the information to their own personal experiences, instead of associating it with an external, or outside source. Some detail that was suggested by the experimenter can be wrongly remembered as having been experienced personally (e.g. Wood & Bekerian, 1999).

It is similarly possible that suggestions, reactions and interpretations from the therapist become assimilated into the client's memory. This assimilation can occur at the level of episodic memories, where specific details or entire events might become incorporated (see Hyman & Pentland, 1996). For example, Hyman and Pentland (1996) report on a series of experiments designed to simulate false suggestions under naturalistic conditions. In these experiments, the experimenter falsely suggests to an individual that he or she had experienced a traumatic event as a child. The person is told that the event has been confirmed by another family member, e.g. an older brother. The person is then asked to recall this event over a series of sessions. Some people come to believe that they experienced the trauma, sometimes reporting more details over time. Assimilation of external, false information is more readily accomplished when the details and events are consistent with the individual's personal experiences. This can result in the person having salient phenomenological experiences of events that never occurred.

Most recently, Johnson et al. have provided evidence that source accuracy for specific events is impaired, when the materials are stressful and emotionally disturbing (emotionally disturbing statements). While the finding needs to be replicated with more ecologically relevant materials, the implications of the data are far-reaching for the therapeutic setting. There is also some evidence that chronic, heightened anxiety or emotional arousal may also render people more susceptible to source confusion errors. For example, Wood and Bekerian (1999) have suggested that clients suffering from post-traumatic stress disorders (PTSD) show poorer source recognition for words that are rated as stressful and negative. Such findings argue that the circumstances for source confusion errors might be greater if clients were to experience heightened emotional arousal over prolonged periods of time.

It is important to note that any information expressed or reported in therapy can have an impact on higher-level structures of self (see Conway, 1997), and abstract, global concepts regarding world beliefs and self (e.g. Teasdale & Barnard, 1993). Many cognitive theories have asserted that people are motivated to maintain coherent, consistent views of the world, and themselves. McCarthy and Warrington (1990, p. 296) argue that people develop psychological structures for personal memories so as "...to maintain a constantly changing and updated record of salient public and private events" (see also Barsalou, 1988; Conway & Bekerian, 1987). Others suggest that personal experiences are structured and organised, so that "temporally distributed experience(s) [get grouped] into thematically-related 'streams'" (Robinson, 1993, p. 223). For example, Wagenaar (1993) suggests that those events that violate self-notions or beliefs are well remembered and phenomenally salient for the very reason that they are difficult to integrate into one's held notion of self. In this way, a person's identity is ordered and coherent, rather than chaotic[3] (e.g. Sampson, 1983). The assumption of a coherent self is also dominant in cognitive theories of emotion that model the effects of post-traumatic stress disorders (e.g. Power & Dalgleish, 1997).

Higher-level beliefs about self (e.g. Teasdale & Barnard, 1993) and themes in one's own life (see Conway, 1997, for a discussion of life-themes)

---

[3] It should be noted that this applies to Western cultures.

are regularly affected by what goes on between the client and the therapist. This may or may not be a goal of the therapy; either way, if clients were led to believe consistently in a particular interpretation or reconstruction of past events, they are likely to modify and accommodate the new information into their life-story, or life-stories. Most people will strive for some consistency, which they can understand and ultimately manipulate. The therapist has influence over how the client constructs, modifies and up-dates his or her life narrative. It is essential, therefore, that personal attitudes, opinions and beliefs held by the therapist about a client's life-themes or patterns are identified as such, and distinguished from "fact".

Most guidelines and codes of practice strongly advise against therapists introducing information in order to bias a client towards a particular course of action either within or outside the therapeutic setting (e.g. British Psychological Society, 1995; Courtois, 1997). For example, most therapists may believe that difficulties experienced in the present are related to earlier experiences, often those that have occurred during childhood. However, therapists who insist on the client recovering memories of childhood experiences are not looking after the best interests of the client or themselves. Similarly, most conscientious practitioners are aware of the dangers of encouraging clients to vindicate any past acts, and discourage the client from engaging in vendettas. As stated by Courtois (1997, p.223):

> *Therapists must assist clients to understand the radical difference between exploring...(or even becoming convinced about the reality of something in the absence of concrete evidence) in therapy and using it as a basis for serious...actions outside the therapy setting, especially in the legal arena.*

Any practitioners who fail to fulfil this responsibility render the clients, and themselves, equally vulnerable, regardless of their therapeutic training. A therapist's own motives, perceptions and biases should be monitored not only during the session but also during any subsequent supervisions (for example, through the examination of any counter-transference issues).

As already noted by others (e.g. Courtois, 1997), the clinical or psycho-therapeutic community do not acknowledge the existence of any formal recovered memory therapies. Nonetheless, there are many practitioners who work in an integrative way, and combine techniques that are taken from more than one approach, e.g. Gestalt techniques combined with Cognitive Behavioural techniques (see Feltham & Horton, 1999). Rather than focus on any particular therapeutic frameworks or approaches, we examine techniques that might be adopted by a range of different practitioners.

There are certain techniques that draw attention to the client's non-verbal behaviours. For example, a client may have the sensation of itchiness on the soles of her feet after taking her shoes and socks off. The therapist may ask the client to question what message her feet are giving. Such dialogic techniques (Goodrich & Bekerian, 1999) essentially enable the therapist and the client to interpret a non-verbal behaviour (e.g. body sensations). The facts are, of course, that there may be many reasons for the client experiencing itchy feet (e.g. carpet is made of wool, client is allergic to wool). The one that is singled out is that which fits both the therapists and the client's perceptions at the moment. For example, Goodrich and Bekerian (1999) illustrate how implicit, body memories might be misinterpreted. They suggest that the causal events leading to body or implicit memories are notoriously difficult to identify, particularly when the traumatic events occur prior to a child's verbalisation. As the point of departure, they expand on the case of KB, who was reported in Howe, Courage and Peterson (1994). KB experienced a highly traumatic event involving a fish bone stuck in her throat, as a young, pre-verbal child (see Howe et al., 1994). Howe et al. document that KB showed behavioural aversions to specific details associated with the traumatic event (e.g. she disliked having the doctor look down her throat). However, she failed to have any explicit, episodic memory for the event. Goodrich and Bekerian suggest that this body memory could be consistent with a number of interpretations, e.g. sexual abuse. Should the therapist be inclined to interpret the non-verbal behaviour in a particular way, KB might be convinced that she had been sexually abused, but could not remember the event(s). This highlights the point that the therapist must exercise a certain amount of subjectivity with non-verbal behaviours, and this means that biases can be introduced.

Similarly, the client may be asked to act out symbolic behaviour (e.g. engage in and enact out fantasies, or adopt role-plays). For example, Gestalt techniques for dream working ask the person to assume each part of the dream, speaking as if the dream were occurring in the present. It is assumed that each part of the dream represents a part of the individual, one that is projected out into the dream character (Bekerian & Goodrich, 1999). Working in a Gestalt manner, clients would be asked to assume the role of each dream character and reflect on how they are like that character. This encourages clients to "re-own" the parts of themselves. Such re-enactments can be powerful and provide the opportunity for substantial emotional growth, and change. At the same time, because re-enactment requires the use of creativity and "play", the individual is susceptible to all the risks known when imagination is used.

As a rule, errors in reporting and re-experiencing are possible whenever a technique relies on the person reconstructing the event through imagery or fantasy. This is an intriguing point, since interview techniques that are commonly used in the forensic setting encourage imagery and context reinstatement, e.g. the cognitive interview technique, or the guided memory technique (see Lindsay & Read, Chapter 5 in this volume). For example, the guided memory technique asks people to imagine going through the event in a methodical fashion, focusing on perceptual details, actions and emotions. The person is encouraged to form images at various stages, and encouraged to speak in the present tense, "I see the door of the room and it's brown". These techniques have been empirically demonstrated to enhance the recall of correct information. It is also the case that errors can increase, and that confabulations can be introduced.

Bartlett (1932) noted the potential problems that techniques like mental imagery might introduce, such as gap filling (see also Bekerian, Dennett, Hill & Hitchcock, 1992). Any rehearsal, particularly in the therapeutic context, of otherwise imaginary events can lead people into believing that such events were actually experienced (Johnson et al., 1996).

It is not a problem that many of these techniques are considered vital elements of the therapeutic process (Bonano, 1990). It is essential that clients are encouraged to communicate through as many means of expression as possible, non-verbally, symbolically, explicitly, metaphorically, narratively. What is equally essential is that the therapist is aware of potential biases that can be introduced whenever behaviour is interpreted.

There are certain techniques which, if used, are likely to generate some raised eyebrows and suspicion, even from the most moderate of advocates. These are techniques that induce trance-like states. Dissociative states ("it's as if it's happening to someone else")—states where the person has out of the body experiences, or induced hypnosis, be they induced through trauma or through therapy—render the person susceptible to suggestion, and mental passivity (e.g. Herman & Schatzow, 1997). These conditions are ripe for any unintentional biases to be introduced, either by the client, the therapist, or collusively between client and therapist. Again, the issue is not whether to use such techniques, but rather what the possible consequences are when used, and whether these consequences are desirable. Provided both the therapist and client are aware of the potential difficulties, the technique may be potentially useful, when used by practitioners who have had adequate experience and training, and are supervised.

FUTURE QUESTIONS

It is essential that future research pay close attention to the nature of the relationship between therapist and client. Given that whatever changes occurring in therapy are the consequence of the interactions between the therapist and client, it is important to determine the relative contribution of each to the final, agreed version of the past. Data that have provided information regarding the client's behaviours are essential (see Andrews, Chapter 9 in this volume). However, it now becomes quite critical to document the contribution of the therapist, and illustrate how both the therapist and the client are subject to similar processes that operate in the context of dialogue, such as conversational maxims. Only detailed discourse analyses of the therapeutic sessions will ensure that the therapist–client dyad and the role it plays in the recovery of memories are better understood.

Perhaps most critically, therapist must consider how they might protect themselves and their clients from increased vulnerability. There has been heated debate regarding the accreditation of practitioners, counsellors, and psychotherapists. There are the extreme positions: those who believe that regulation of all practitioners should be strictly enforced and supported by guidelines and codes of practice; and, those who react vehemently to restrictions on the nature and quality of techniques that might be used in the therapeutic setting (see also Robertson, Chapter 10 in this volume).

The moderate position is to suggest that both the therapist and client require some sort of safety net. Therapy and counselling venture into nebulous territories, the past, the unconscious. Powerful emotional reactions will be experienced, and, importantly, the person will need to be able to integrate these emotions in the context of their everyday life. Courtois (1997) considers that both trauma and non-trauma treatments explore the importance of the client's safety, in terms of ego defences, personal resources, stabilisation of mood and personality.

Joining a particular organisation, one that is empowered with the ability to accredit the credentials and abilities of a therapist, will not guarantee that the therapist will provide either a personal safety net or one for the client. However, membership does provide both parties the opportunity to engage in independent counsel regarding any mismanagement or impropriety on either side. There is a danger that practitioners will not work with people bringing memories of sexual abuse due to the possibility of litigation. Independent accrediting organisations can provide at least some initial testing ground, with the interests of both the therapist and the client being considered impartially.

Finally, of all the potential areas for future discussion, the issue of the truth is the one of which we have the least understanding. In terms of people's lives, and people's relationships, the truth is crucial. There have been many attempts to define criteria that would enable people to distinguish true from non-factual accounts (see Bekerian & Dennett, 1992, for a review). However, these criteria-assessment approaches have yet to be formally demonstrated as reliable across a range of interviewers and clients. As such, practitioners must concede to the fact that they may never know the validity of a client's memories, and should actively reject the role of arbitrator of the truth. Whatever the particular approach or training, the therapeutic community can protect its profession, and clients and their families, provided everyone is prepared to live with a bit of uncertainty.

REFERENCES

ACP (1994). Recovery of memories of child sexual abuse (special issue). *Applied Cognitive Psychology*, **8**, No. 4.

Barsalou, L. W. (1988). The content and organisation of autobiographical memories. In Neisser & E. Winograd (Eds), *Remembering Reconsidered: Ecological and Traditional Approaches to the Study of Memory*. New York: CUP.

Bartlett, F. (1932). *Remembering*. Cambridge, England: Cambridge University Press.

Bekerian, D. A. & Dennett, J. D. (1992). The truth in statement validity assessment. In F. Losel, D. Bender & T. Bleisener (Eds), *Psychology and Law: Facing the Nineties*, (2 vols) Amsterdam: Swets & Zeitlinger.

Bekerian, D. A., Dennett, J. L., Hill, K. & Hitchcock, R. (1992). Effects of detailed imagery on simulated witness recall. In F. Losel, D. Bender & T. Bleisener (Eds), *Psychology and Law: Facing the Nineties*, (2 vols). Amsterdam: Swets & Zeitlinger.

Bekerian, D. A. & Goodrich, S. J. (1999). Forensic applications of theories of cognition and emotion. In T. Dalgleish & M. Power (Eds), *Handbook of Cognition and Emotion*. Chichester: Wiley.

Bonano, G. (1990). Remembering and psychotherapy. *Psychotherapy*, **27**, 175–186.

British Psychological Society (1995). *Recovered Memories: The Report of the Working Party of the British Psychological Society*.

Conway, M.A. (1997). Past and present: Recovered memories and false memories. In Conway, M. A. (Ed.) (1997). *Recovered Memories and False Memories*. Oxford: Oxford University Press.

Conway, M. & Bekerian, D. A. (1987). Organisation in autobiographical memory. *Memory and Cognition*, **15**, 119–132.

Courtois, C. A. (1997). Delayed memories of child sexual abuse: critique of the controversy and clinical guidelines. In M. A. Conway (Ed.), *Recovered Memories and False Memories* (pp. 206–229). Oxford: Oxford University Press.

Denes, M. (1997). Paradoxes in the therapeutic relationship. *The Gestalt Journal*, **20** (2), 75–93.

Feltham, A. & Horton, I. (Eds) (1999). *Handbook of Counselling and Psychotherapy*. New York: Sage.

Goodrich, S. J. & Bekerian, D. A. (1999). Recovered memories of sexual abuse: Theoretical versus practical issues. In A. Feltham & I.Horton (Eds), *Handbook of Counselling and Psychotherapy*. New York: Sage.

Harvey, M. R. & Herman, J. L. (1994). Amnesia, partial amnesia and delayed recall among adult survivors of childhood trauma. *Consciousness and Cognition*, **3** (3/4), 295.

Herman, J. L. & Schatzow, E. (1997). Recovery and verification of memories of childhood sexual trauma. *Psychoanalytic Psychology*, **4**, 1–14.

Howe, M. L., Courage, M. L. & Peterson, C. (1994). How can I remember when "I" wasn't there? Long-term retention of traumatic experiences and emergence of the cognitive self. *Consciousness and Cognition*, **4**, 327–355.

Hyman, I. E. & Pentland, J. (1996). The role of mental imagery in the creation of false childhood memories. *Journal of Memory and Language*, **35**, 101–117.

Johnson, M., Nolde, S. F. & de Leonardis, D. M. (1996). Emotional focus and source monitoring. *Journal of Memory and Language*, **35**, 135–156.

Kempler, W. (1975). *Gestalt and Family Therapy*. New York: Sage.

Lindsay, D. S. & Read, J. D. (1994). Psychotherapy and memories of childhood sexual abuse: A cognitive perspective. *Applied Cognitive Psychology*, **8**, 281–338.

Loftus, E. F. (1979). *Eyewitness Testimony*. Cambridge, MA: Harvard University Press.

McCarthy, R. & Warrington, E. (1990). *Cognitive-Neuro Psychology: A Clinical Introduction*. San Diago, CA: Academic Press.

McCloskey, M. & Zaragoza, M. (1985). Misleading post-event information and memories for events: Arguments and evidence against Memory Impairment hypothesis. *Journal of Experimental Psychology: General*, **114**, 1–16.

Morton, J. (1994). Cognitive perspectives of memory recovery. *Applied Cognitive Psychology*, **8**, 389–398.

O'Leary, E. (1997). *Gestalt Therapy: Theory, Practice and Research*. London: Chapman & Hall.

Power, M. J. & Dalgleish, T. (1997). *Cognition and Emotion: From Order to Disorder*. Hove: Psychology Press.

Reyna, V. F. & Titcomb, A. L. (1997). Constraints on the suggestibility of Eyewitness Testimony: A "Fuzzy Trace" analysis. In D. Payne & F. Conrad (Eds), *Intersections in Basic and Applied Memory Research*. Mahwah, NJ: Erlbaum.

Robinson, J. A. (1993). First experience memories: Contexts and functions in personal histories. In M. Conway, D. Rubin, H. Spinnler & W. Wagenaar (Eds), *Theoretical Perspectives on Autobiographical Memory* (pp. 223–240). Dordrecht, The Netherlands: Kluwer.

Sampson, E. (1983). The de-centralisation of identity. *American Psychologist*, **40**, 1203–1211.

Saywitz, K. J. & Moan-Hardie, S. (1994). Reducing the potential for distortion of child-hood memories. *Consciousness and Cognition*, **3**, 408–425.

Teasdale, J. & Barnard, P. (1993). *Affect, Cognition and Change*. Hove: Erlbaum,

Wagenaar, W. (1993). Remembering my worst sins: How autobiographical memory serves the updating of the conceptual self. In M. Conway, D. Rubin, Spinnler, H. & Wagenaar (Eds), *Theoretical Perspectives on Autobiographical Memory*. Dordrecht, The Netherlands: Kluwer.

Weiskrantz, L. (1995). Comments on the report of the working party of the British Psychological Society on "Recovered Memories". *The Therapist*, **2**, 4.

Wood, J., Bekerian, D. & Foa, E. (1999). *Counterfactual Reasoning in Rape Trauma Victims*. (Manuscript submitted for publication.)

Wood, J. & Bekerian, D. A. (1999). *Recognition Memory and Source Monitoring in PTSD*. (Manuscript submitted for publication.)

9

RECOVERED MEMORIES IN THERAPY: CLINICIANS' BELIEFS AND PRACTICES

Bernice Andrews

Despite growing evidence that a sizeable proportion of recovered memories of traumatic experiences are likely to occur outside therapy (Andrews et al., 1995; Elliott, 1997; Feldman-Summers & Pope, 1994), the central focus of public and academic debate has been on the role of therapy in their production. Anecdotal reports abound in the general literature of overzealous unqualified practitioners using risky techniques to produce false memories. However, the problem becomes more complex when account is taken of surveys of qualified practitioners. While large proportions of respondents in some surveys report using memory retrieval techniques (Poole, Lindsay, Memon & Bull, 1995; Polusny & Follette, 1996), surveys also show that the majority of qualified therapists endorse the belief that recovered memories can be false or inaccurate in some respects (Andrews et al., 1995; Poole et al., 1995; Polusny & Follette, 1996; Palm & Gibson, 1998). The question arises of how to reconcile these incompatible practices and beliefs. Speculating from their own findings, based on 145 US and 57 UK psychologists, Poole et al. (1995) arrived at two explanations. One was that therapists use memory recovery techniques in open-minded and cautious ways and there is thus little if any tension between beliefs and practices. They suggested that an alternative explanation was more likely in the majority of cases, namely that therapists are in transition: the enthusiastic use of techniques may be giving way to concerns about the risks involved in using them.

One difficulty in evaluating these ideas arises from the type of evidence from which they are derived. Some commentators have questioned the extent to which survey questionnaires reflect therapists' true beliefs and practices (Olio, 1996; Pope, 1997). My own investigations with colleagues in the area of recovered memories has involved a large-scale question-naire survey of therapists followed by an in-depth interview study (Andrews et al., 1995; 1999). Data from both investigations are discussed and further analysed in this chapter in an attempt to shed light on what lies behind therapists' beliefs, and the apparent tension between beliefs and practices.

THERAPISTS' BELIEFS ABOUT RECOVERED MEMORIES: SURVEY DATA

In our original survey (Andrews et al., 1995) questionnaires were sent to all British Psychological Society (BPS) practitioner members of the Division of Clinical Psychology, the Division of Counselling Psychology, the Health Psychology Group and the Psychotherapy Section. The overall response rate was 27% (n=1,083), which is similar to rates reported in other surveys of this kind (see Andrews et al., 1995). The sample was almost completely representative in terms of age and sex of all members mailed, and also representative in terms of membership of the relevant BPS divisions and groups.

The 19-item questionnaire was developed as part of the investigations conducted by the BPS Working Party on Recovered Memories (Morton et al., 1995). Respondents were informed of the investigations of the Working Party and of our interest in memories of early sexual abuse. They were instructed that the target group we were interested in comprised adult clients (over 18) with non-psychotic and non-organic disorders. Respondents were asked to answer the questionnaire in full if they saw any clients in the target group. If they did not they were nevertheless asked to answer some demographic and background questions and return the ques-tionnaire. Of the 1,083 members who responded, 810 had clients in the target group, and the results are based on their responses. Questions included therapeutic approach (there were no questions about memory retrieval techniques, apart from the general use of hypnotic regression), experience of clients with recovered memories, and general beliefs about the accuracy and falsity of recovered memories. The three survey items about recovered memory beliefs were:

1. To what extent do you think that recovered memories of CSA events from total amnesia can be taken as essentially accurate? (never/sometimes/usually/always)

2. Do you think it is possible that a person could falsely 'remember' that he or she had been repeatedly sexually abused as a child if no abuse had actually taken place? (yes/no)

3. Have you ever believed this to be the case in your own practice? (never/once/more than once)

The second question was modified from an item from Poole et al.'s survey: "Do you think it is possible that a person could come to believe that she was sexually abused as a child if no abuse had actually occurred (i.e. illusory memories or beliefs about childhood sexual abuse)?"

Although the use of hypnotic regression was relatively uncommon in this sample (10% had used it), overall, 60% of our respondents reported they had at some time (in the past year or previously) at least one client who had some type of recovered memory (that is, for any traumatic event either within or outside therapy), and 47% had at least one client with a recovered memory involving childhood sexual abuse (CSA). What, then, were respondents' general and particular beliefs concerning such memories? Table 9.1 shows that most respondents believed that, in general, recovered memories were essentially accurate at least sometimes, although only a very small minority believed they were always so. The majority also believed, in general, that false memories were possible, and 15% thought this had been the case in their own practice (Table 9.1). This proportion was increased to 20% among respondents who reported having had clients recover memories in therapy with them.

Factors associated with respondents' beliefs

To get a better understanding of what might be fuelling therapists' beliefs, we conducted regression analyses with responses to the belief questions as the dependent variables in separate analyses (see Andrews et al., 1995,

Table 9.1: Respondents' beliefs about recovered memories

Belief in accuracy of recovered memories:			
3% (never)	53% (sometimes)	38% (usually)	6% (always)
Belief in possibility of false memories:			
67% (yes)	33% (no)		
False memories in own practice:			
85% (never)	11% (sometimes)	4% (more than once)	

for fuller details). Included as independent variables were age and sex of the respondents, their therapeutic approach (psychodynamic, cognitive-behavioural, client-centred/humanist, systems and feminist), therapeutic practice (focus on early experiences and use of hypnotic regression), number of clients with CSA seen in the past year, and whether or not the respondent had ever had a client with a recovered memory. Taking all factors into account, the significant independent indicators of belief in accuracy of recovered memories were having had a patient recover a memory in therapy, and to a lesser extent, a focus on early experiences in therapy. Significant indicators of reduced belief in accuracy were being a man, being older, and having a cognitive-behavioural approach to therapy. The significant predictors of a belief in the possibility of false memories were almost exactly the reverse of those for belief in the accuracy of recovered memories: being a man, being older, and having a cognitive-behavioural approach to therapy increased the likelihood of believing that false memories were possible. Having a client recover a memory in therapy decreased the likelihood. There was no significant interaction between age and sex: although women were less likely than men of a similar age to believe that false memories were possible, like men, the older they were, the more likely they were to endorse such a belief.

At this stage in the research we could only speculate about the causal direction of the strong relationship between a general belief in the essential accuracy of recovered memories and the experience of having a client with a recovered memory. It was possible that those sympathetic to the idea of recovered memories were more open to the possibility and were facilitating such recovery in their clients through the use of memory recovery techniques. On the other hand, the experience of having witnessed a client recover a memory, may have led to greater conviction of the general validity of such memories (Andrews et al., 1995).

A further influence on the therapists' responses to the questions on belief may well have involved the way the survey questions were asked. The proportion in our study who believed that false memories were possible was lower than that found in Poole et al.'s study — 67% compared to 91%. One reason for this apparent difference may have been due to the slight variation in the question: in the Poole et al. survey respondents were asked whether it was possible that a person could falsely come to believe that he or she was sexually abused; in our survey respondents were asked whether it was possible for a person to falsely remember *repeated* sexual abuse. A suggestion of how this difference in wording might have affected the response came from additional remarks written on the questionnaire by some respondents. They noted that they thought it might be possible to falsely remember one such event, but not repeated events. This observation is an interesting contrast to the notion that the case for the validity of recovered memories is stronger for single traumas, as experimental evidence suggests that single events are more likely to be forgotten than repeated events (Lindsay & Read, 1995). However, based on clinical observation, Terr (1994) has argued that single traumas tend to be well remembered, whereas repeated inescapable traumas are more likely to lead to the development of cognitive strategies that enable them to be forgotten.

Overall it was clear that a proportion of our respondents had problems with the questions. Around 10% did not answer the question on false memory and 15% did not answer one or other of the questions about the falsity or accuracy of recovered memories. Among all respondents who did and did not answer the questions a number added comments on the questionnaire qualifying their response. A recurring theme for many was that they did not feel qualified to answer the questions as they had not sufficient experience of clients with recovered memories, others wrote that their answer would depend on the context and that they needed more response options. What was apparent was that many therapists, whether they answered or not, did not feel confident in their response.

BELIEFS: THE INTERVIEW STUDY

Our general impression from the survey was that many of the therapists had opinions and experiences that were not being fully or accurately represented by their survey responses. The obvious frustration with the survey item options shown by some respondents, coupled with their often lengthy comments, prompted us to conduct a more detailed investigation. Although the survey was confidential, respondents were asked to identify themselves if they were willing to take part in future research. Of the 291 who reported having at least one client who recovered a traumatic memory in therapy in the previous year, 208 (71%) identified themselves for further research. In the time available (the study was funded for one year), 108 valid interviews were conducted. The mean age of the respondents was 48 (SD=9.5), and 61% were women. The representativeness of the interviewed sample was investigated by comparing responses to the 19 original survey questions between (1) those with valid interviews, (2) those self-identified but not interviewed, and (3) those who did not identify themselves for further research. Significant relevant group differences involved case load, and belief in the accuracy of recovered memories (there was no significant group difference in the belief that memories could be false). In post-hoc comparisons the interviewed group had higher case loads than those who did not identify themselves, and the self-identified groups (both interviewed and non-interviewed) reported a greater belief in the accuracy of recovered memories than those who did not identify themselves.

Interviews took place around 18 months on average after the survey. Therapists were instructed to calculate in advance the total number of recovered memory clients seen since April 1993 (the year before the questionnaire survey). They were further instructed to consult their clinical notes in advance on up to three such clients for more detailed questioning. This procedure generated 236 detailed client cases.

GENERAL BELIEFS: COMPARISON BETWEEN SURVEY AND INTERVIEW RESPONSES

Prior to questions about individual clients, the therapists were asked the same questions about their beliefs as they had been asked in the survey. They were reminded of their previous responses and asked if that would be their response again. Instead of the yes/no response option to the question of whether false memories were possible, they were given an additional choice: they could answer 'not possible', 'unlikely' or 'likely'. In the context of the interview they were also given the opportunity to comment on their responses.

We first considered whether therapists' beliefs had changed in the 18 months or so since they responded to the original survey. This was to investigate the proposal that therapists are becoming increasingly aware of the need for caution in the area of recovered memory (Poole et al., 1995). If this was the case, then there should be a significant reduction in beliefs about the essential accuracy of the content of recovered memories of CSA. However, change in this direction was not apparent. Among the 97 therapists for which there was complete data at both time points, the proportions reporting that recovered memories were sometimes, usually or always essentially accurate were 27%, 63% and 10% respectively in the original survey, and 27%, 64% and 9% in the subsequent interview (none had reported at either time point that they were never accurate). Only 14 had changed their responses and they were fairly equally divided between being more certain of accuracy (n=6) and less certain (n=8).

As outlined above, the response options were changed on the question about whether false memories were possible. This was to explore in further detail whether the therapist's responses to questions about belief were a function of the way the question was originally put. We had a suspicion that the response options in the original survey were not sufficiently sensitive. This suspicion was based on the finding that while only 10% of this sample of therapists with recovered memory cases reported such memories were *always* essentially accurate nearly half (47%) also reported that false memories of repeated CSA were not possible. Once given the extra options in the interview, only 15% reported that they believed false memories of childhood sexual abuse were not possible, with 73% believing that they were possible but unlikely, and 12% believing that they were likely. Overall, only 5% believed that recovered memories were always accurate and that false memories were not possible.

Attributions for non-accuracy/falsity of recovered memories

The content of the therapists' responses was analysed to gain insight into the reasons behind their beliefs. Sixty-one had made sufficiently full comments to code their response to the belief questions. These were equally divided between attributing falsity to particular kinds of therapists and therapeutic practice (n=30), and to the clients themselves (n=31). Ten of these respondents made comments to the effect that it was the interaction between a vulnerable client and a certain kind of therapist that produced false memories. The majority of the therapists who focused on the clients' role in producing false memories felt that this could happen with very disturbed psychotic clients or those with a borderline personality disorder. One therapist said: "Having met some quite disturbed people, anything's possible, they could say anything". Some discussed the difficulty in distinguishing between fantasy and reality in some patients' accounts; for example, one said: "Some stories are so bizarre and inconsistent ... I'm not sure ... you can't believe all they say." Respondents who attributed false memories to other therapists usually cited risky practices and techniques involving suggestion. For example, one said: "Not with the methods I use, but it would be possible with the methods some people use. I think if it was repeatedly suggested to them under hypnosis that they had had these sorts of experiences, yes." Another said: "The only circumstances in which I could imagine false memories being brought forward would be under conditions when active techniques were being used, which is something I would never do."

Given that this group of therapists all had experience of recovered memory cases, the above comments and the finding that the vast majority held at least some degree of scepticism may appear incompatible with popularly held assumptions. For example, they contradict the assumption that memories recovered in therapy are invariably produced by a particular type of overzealous, misguided or unqualified therapist using 'memory recovery techniques'. But before considering the extent to which these therapists used such techniques it remains to consider the extent to which therapists believed their own clients, and their reasons for doing so.

Therapists' specific beliefs about the accuracy of their own clients' recovered memories

As mentioned above, therapists were questioned in detail on up to three clients they had seen who had recovered memories of trauma. Among the 236 reported cases, 73% involved recovered memories of CSA and 27% were of other trauma not involving CSA. Among other questions, therapists were asked whether the client had reported any corroborating evidence from an outside source, and this was reported in 41% of the cases (Andrews et al., 1999). In 81% of the cases respondents held a marked belief in the accuracy of their client's recovered memory, in 14% there was a moderate belief, in 2% some belief and in a further 2% no belief. It is understandable that a marked belief might be held in cases where the client told the therapist that there was corroborative evidence for the memory. However, lack of corroboration made no difference to the degree of belief held. So why else did therapists believe their clients? Among clients with no corroboration, the most common reasons given were that: the client's emotions/behaviour at recall appeared genuine and would be difficult to fake (38%); the client's account made sense of his or her symptoms (29%); the account was plausible, consistent and/or coherent (18%); the client is truthful (16%); and the client was reluctant and/or dismayed to recall the trauma (12%).

These categories were derived from content analysis of the therapist's reasons in response to an open-ended question. It is of interest therefore that some of these reasons reflect those given by Freud for believing his patients' uncovered memories of sexual trauma a century earlier—namely, the genuineness of the emotions or behaviour at recall, the clients' reluctance or dismay about divulging the memory, and the belief that the memory made sense of the symptoms (Freud, 1896). Nevertheless, it is also important to note that Freud soon changed his opinion about the reality of his patients' accounts, and later wrote that at the time of his first observations he had been unable to distinguish between "falsifications made by hysterics in their memories of childhood and traces of real events" (Freud, 1905, p. 274).

The data are in accord with our original speculation that one of the reasons why therapists with recovered memory cases had a greater belief than those without, in the validity of recovered memories was because of their first-hand experiences with such clients. One reason was perhaps because it was not uncommon for their clients to report corroboration, but another important reason appears to have been their clients' emotions and behaviours at recall. We had questioned respondents about whether their clients' memory recovery involved reliving the trauma, and whether it was accompanied by any emotion. In 83% of relevant cases respondents reported that their clients fully or partially relived the supposed trauma. The most common emotion accompanying memory recovery was fear, reported in 41% of the relevant cases (and in 59% of the cases with full reliving), followed by general distress (24%), guilt (16%), anger (16%), disgust (7%) and sadness (6%). In 9% of the cases, it was reported that the client appeared to be in physical pain (Andrews et al., 2000). Even in the absence of corroboration, the enactment of these behaviours and emotions was a major factor in convincing many of the therapists that their clients' memories were genuine. Some of the therapists' accounts illustrate the extreme reactions observed:

> She was reliving it. Tremendous fear: Cowering, shaking, trembling. Curling up in pain. Blacking out.

> He relived it vividly and felt fearful and angry. He would say things like "get away you bastards". He recounted facts in the sessions and felt terribly frightened.

> She relived the experience, physically and vividly in front me more than once. She gagged and choked, couldn't breathe and was sick. She felt overwhelmed like it was happening again.

THE ROLE OF THERAPEUTIC TECHNIQUES IN THE PRODUCTION OF RECOVERED MEMORIES

The greater belief in the validity of recovered memories among therapists with recovered memory clients may to some extent be explained by their actual experiences with their clients. The majority of these therapists believed that false memories were possible but unlikely, and that recovered memories were usually (but not always) accurate. There is therefore still the question of the extent to which therapists who hold these kinds of attitudes facilitate memory recovery of suspected abuse or other trauma through the use of techniques. Two questionnaire surveys of registered psychologists (Poole et al., 1995; Polusny & Follette, 1996) provide information on a variety of techniques used by their respondents to aid clients' recall. Poole et al. reported that 71% of their respondents used at least one technique "to help clients remember child sexual abuse". Polusny and Follette asked respondents to indicate from a list "memory retrieval techniques you use with adult clients who have no specific memory of childhood sexual abuse but who you strongly suspect were sexually abused". The authors did not report an overall rate, but the most common technique was "journal and letter writing", endorsed by 60% of the respondents. These findings beg further questions, such as the extent to which memories recovered in therapy are the direct result of using specific techniques. In a detailed critique of Poole et al.'s (1995) survey, Olio (1996) argued that their item on techniques was not sufficiently specific to differentiate techniques used with clients who had never forgotten the abuse they reported from those who had forgotten the abuse. Olio also argued that Poole et al. speculated beyond their data in their conclusions that memory recovery in therapy is 'caused' by the use of certain techniques. There is also no evidence, with the possible exception of hypnosis, that as aids to memory the techniques listed by Poole et al. and Polusny and Follette are necessarily risky to use (see Table 9.2 for a list of such techniques). Furthermore, the description of some techniques was rather vague (e.g. 'instructions to remember'). We hoped to shed further light on these issues in our in-depth study by investigating the extent to which memory recovery techniques were used by therapists with clients who appear to have forgotten all or much of what is subsequently recalled, as well as clarification on the stage at which they are used (i.e. before or after memory recovery).

The overall use of possibly 'risky' techniques

In our interview study of therapists with recovered memory clients, we included questions about techniques that have been implicated as 'risky'

Table 9.2: Therapeutic techniques used to aid recall in the client cases

First memory recovered:	In therapy with respondent (n=166)		Before therapy with respondent (n=67)
Technique used:	Before recall (%)	Only after recall (%)	After recall (%)
Hypnosis	8	1	3
Age regression	10	1	5
Dream interpretation	3	2	3
Guided imagery	7	6	6
Use of family photos	5	4	3
Relaxation	7	3	6
Instructions to remember	10	7	13
Interpreting physical symptoms	10	8	9
Writing/artwork	4	2	5
Other techniques	5	3	5
Overall use of techniques	30	14	34

Reprinted from Andrews et al. (1999), with permission.

(Lindsay & Read, 1994) (see Table 9.2). Respondents were asked whether they had used any from the list with the client in question to help him or her to remember past experiences. Where the respondent indicated having used a specific technique, but for purposes other than to aid memory recovery, this was noted. In addition, if the clients' first reported memory was recovered in therapy with the respondent, they were asked if the technique was used before or after it had been recovered. Overall, in 67% of the 233 client cases for which there was information, at least one of the listed techniques had been used for some purpose either before or after the first reported memory was recovered. This proportion decreased to 42% where techniques were considered only when they were used specifically to help the client remember past experiences, with a further decrease to 21.5% when only techniques to aid recall before the first memory was recovered were considered. The use of memory recovery techniques before the first recovered memory dropped further to 16% when only memories recovered from total amnesia (as opposed to partial amnesia) were considered.[1]

The use of techniques to aid recall

Including only techniques used to aid recall, Table 9.2 lists the different types and the proportions of client cases with whom the technique had been used, either *before*, or *only after* reported memory recovery (whether from total or partial amnesia). Clients who were reported to have recovered their first memory in therapy with the respondent were distinguished from clients who were reported to have recovered their first memory prior to therapy with the respondent. Among clients who had recovered their first memory in the context of therapy with the respondent, at least one technique to aid recall had been used before the first memory had been recovered in just under a third. In a further 14% such a technique had been used after but not before the first memory was recovered. At least one technique to aid recall was also used with just over a third of the clients who had already recovered their first memory prior to therapy with the respondents. Among clients recovering their first memory in therapy with the respondent, techniques to aid recall were no more likely to have been used where memories involved CSA than where memories only involved other trauma; rates were 28% CSA, 19% both CSA and other trauma, 42% child maltreatment, and 39% other trauma, $\chi^2(3, N=165)=4.5, p>0.05$.

---

[1] In the interview study a recovered memory was defined as the recovery of a traumatic event (whether real or illusory) where there was no previous conscious memory (i.e. from total amnesia), or recovery of a significant new piece of information about a partially remembered trauma (i.e. from partial amnesia).

Techniques used for other purposes

A further question raised by these results concerns whether particular techniques are more or less likely to be used for purposes other than to aid recall. Clients with whom respondents had only used techniques for other purposes before their memory recovery (n=40) were compared with clients with whom techniques to aid recall were used before memory recovery (n=50). Table 9.3 shows that hypnosis was significantly more likely to be used to aid recall, and relaxation was significantly more likely to be used for other purposes. By definition, neither age regression nor instructions to remember were used for purposes other than to aid recall. Examination of the respondents' accounts indicated that, in general, techniques used for other purposes were used to alleviate current symptoms, and explore current feelings and behaviours. In the cases where hypnosis was reported to have been used for other purposes, it was used in one to treat a phobia, and in two for relaxation. Where relaxation was used for other purposes, it was used to alleviate anxiety and other emotional symptoms.

Techniques and corroboration

Clients with whom techniques had been used before first reported memory recovery were no less likely to have found corroborating evidence, according to the respondents, than clients with whom no techniques had been used before memory recovery. Rates of corroboration were 38% for clients with whom at least one technique was used to aid recall, 45% for clients with at least one technique used for other reasons,

Table 9.3: Techniques used with clients before first memory recovery to aid recall and for other purposes

	Clients with whom techniques were used:				
	To aid recall (N=50)		Only for other purposes (N=40)		$\chi^2(1)$
	(%)	(N)	(%)	(N)	
Hypnosis	28	(14)	8	(3)	4.83*
Working with dreams	10	(5)	25	(10)	2.73
Guided imagery	22	(11)	15	(6)	0.30
Use of family photos	16	(8)	5	(2)	1.64
Working with physical symptoms	31	(16)	25	(10)	0.19
Relaxation	22	(11)	48	(19)	5.69*
Writing/artwork	14	(7)	15	(6)	0.03

*$p<0.05$

and 43% for clients with whom no techniques were used, $\chi^2(2, N=231)=0.49$, $p>0.05$. The result did not change when those who had not recovered their first memory in the context of therapy with the respondent were excluded from the analysis.

Techniques and beliefs

Finally we looked to see whether therapists who reported having used a technique to aid recall prior to memory recovery with at least one client they had described, differed in their beliefs from those who had not. They were, if anything, marginally more likely than those who had not used such techniques to believe recovered memories were possible: not possible, unlikely and likely were endorsed by 6%, 80% and 14% respectively compared to 22%, 70% and 9% of the other therapists, $\chi^2(2)=4.7$, $p<0.10$. In response to questions about the accuracy of recovered memories, 22%, 70% and 8% believed they were sometimes, usually or always accurate, compared to 31%, 59% and 10% of the other therapists, $\chi^2(2)=1.19$, $p>0.10$.

DISCUSSION OF TECHNIQUES

It is noteworthy that, contrary to popular assumption, most (78%) of the clients' initial recovered memories either preceded therapy or preceded the use of memory recovery techniques used by the respondents. Techniques seemed to be used more to help the clients to elaborate the memories than to facilitate their initial recovery. This unexpectedly low rate of using techniques for the initial recovery of memories (22%) does not appear to be explained by cultural differences if account is taken of Poole et al.'s (1995) survey. The British therapists who took part in that study (all BPS members) were as likely as their American counterparts to indicate that they had used at least one technique to aid recall of CSA, with an overall rate of 71%. Similarly, in two-thirds of the client cases in the present study at least one technique had been used for some purpose at some time. The lower estimate of 22% (16% where there was prior total amnesia) was arrived at after taking account of the stage at which it had been used (before or after first memory recovery), and the respondents' intentions when using it. The stage at which techniques were used was not considered in detail in the previous questionnaire surveys, and Poole et al. (1995) did not specifically exclude their use with clients who had never forgotten or had only partially forgotten abuse.

Furthermore, the majority of memory recovery techniques implicated by some theorists as 'risky' (e.g. Lindsay & Read, 1994; Loftus, 1993) are commonly used for reasons other than memory retrieval. It is possible that some respondents in previous questionnaire surveys may have been checking techniques that they had used, but not specifically for memory recovery purposes. Indeed, Polusny and Follette (1996) mentioned this as a possibility in the context of their own survey. There is a danger that variability in the interpretation of paper and pencil survey items may lead to unreliable estimates of particular practices, beliefs and experiences in this relatively new and contentious area (Olio, 1996; Pope, 1997). The in-depth interview is of value in this regard as such complexities can be teased out and queries clarified.

OVERALL CONCLUSIONS

The evidence from our investigations has provided insight into what may underlie therapists' beliefs about recovered memories, and helped elucidate previous survey findings of a 'tension' between the beliefs and practices of qualified therapists (e.g. Poole et al., 1995). While not, in general, holding very conservative beliefs, careful interview assessment revealed that even among respondents who reported having seen clients with recovered memories, only very small proportions believed that recovered memories were always accurate and that false memories were not possible. Furthermore, rather than propelling 'risky' practices, their beliefs about the validity of recovered memories appeared more likely to have been a consequence of their actual experiences with clients with recovered memories.

While certain techniques had been used with around two-thirds of clients who had recovered memories, only in the minority were they used with the intention of retrieving memories, and even then they were usually used after the first memory had been recovered or with clients who already had a partial memory of the trauma. In this sample of qualified therapists, there did not appear to be any tension between beliefs and practices because, in the main, techniques appeared to have been used in appropriate and cautious ways. Although we cannot rule out that some therapists may have used techniques incautiously, the evidence was that the majority did not. Furthermore, therapists did not appear to be in transition in the sense that the enthusiastic use of techniques was giving way to more cautious beliefs—firstly, because techniques were not necessarily being used with clients in incautious ways and, secondly, because there was no evidence to suggest that their beliefs had changed.

Whereas cognitive psychologists and other non-clinical commentators have focused exclusively on external influences—particularly the use of 'memory recovery techniques' in the production of false memories (e.g. Loftus, 1993; Lindsay & Read, 1995) — in the light of their clinical knowledge and experience, our respondents were equally likely to implicate the clients themselves. Some therapists in the study commented about the difficulty that some clients have in distinguishing fantasy from reality. It is ironic in this regard that Freud has been implicated in some quarters as the originator of the so-called recovered memory movement (e.g. Crews, 1997). Since, with the exception of a short-lived episode near the beginning of his career, Freud's concerns were with uncovering the unconscious repression of uncomfortable libidinal and destructive feelings rather than with uncovering memories of actual traumatic experiences. According to traditional psychoanalytic theory the client's reports of sexual trauma should be treated as fantasy; that is, the projection of repressed desires onto others.

Such ideas may seem extreme within the context of current knowledge about the reality of childhood sexual abuse, and growing evidence of corroboration for at least a proportion of recovered memories (e.g. Cheit, 1998; Feldman-Summers & Pope, 1994; Herman & Harvey, 1997; Schooler, Bendiksen & Ambadar, 1997). But given the likelihood that both false and genuine recovered memories for trauma are possible — cognitive mechanisms exist to explain both (Brewin & Andrews, 1998; Freyd, 1996) — a clinical explanation for false memories involving fantasy might be just as plausible and useful as cognitive explanations involving external suggestion. The evidence presented suggests that the beliefs and practices of qualified therapists, rather than being misguided, are for the most part based on clinical knowledge and experience. To further understanding in the highly contentious area of recovered memory, recent glimmerings of a bridge between clinicians and cognitive researchers need further encouragement (Lindsay & Briere, 1997). In this area of inquiry it is likely that clinicians and researchers can benefit from each others' expertise.

REFERENCES

Andrews, B., Brewin, C. R., Ochera, J., Morton, J., Bekerian, D. A., Davies, G. M. & Mollon, P. (1999). The characteristics, context and consequences of memory recovery among adults in therapy. *British Journal of Psychiatry*, **175**, 141–146.

Andrews, B., Brewin, C. R., Ochera, J., Morton, J., Bekerian, D. A., Davies, G. M. & Mollon, P. (2000). The timing, triggers and qualities of recovered memories in therapy. *British Journal of Clinical Psychology*, **39**, 11–26.

Andrews, B., Morton, J., Bekerian, D. A., Brewin, C. R., Davies, G. M. & Mollon, P. (1995). The recovery of memories in clinical practice: Experiences and beliefs of British Psychological Society Practitioners. *The Psychologist: Bulletin of the British Psychological Society*, **8** (5), 209–214.

Brewin, C. R. & Andrews, B. (1998). Recovered memories of trauma: Phenomenology and cognitive mechanisms. *Clinical Psychology Review*, **18**, 949–970.

Cheit, R. E. (1998). Consider this, skeptics of recovered memory. *Ethics and Behavior*, **8**, 141–160.

Crews, F. et al. (1997). *The Memory Wars: Freud's Legacy in Dispute*, London: Granta.

Elliott, D. (1997). Traumatic events: Prevalence and delayed recall in the general population. *Journal of Consulting and Clinical Psychology*, **65**, 811–820.

Feldman-Summers, S. & Pope, K. S. (1994). The experience of 'forgetting' childhood abuse: A national survey of psychologists. *Journal of Consulting and Clinical Psychology*, **62**, 636–639.

Freud, S. (1896). The aetiology of hysteria. In J. Strachey (Ed. and trans.) *The Standard Edition of the Complete Psychological Works of Sigmund Freud* (Vol.3, pp.191–221). London: Hogarth Press.

Freud, S. (1905). My views on the part played by sexuality in the aetiology of neuroses. In J. Strachey (Ed. and trans.) *The Standard Edition of the Complete Psychological Works of Sigmund Freud* (Vol.7, pp.270–279). London: Hogarth Press.

Freyd, J. J. (1996). *Betrayal Trauma: The Logic of Forgetting Childhood Abuse*. Cambridge, Mass.: Harvard University Press.

Herman, J. L. & Harvey, M. R. (1997). Adult memories of childhood trauma: A naturalistic clinical study. *Journal of Traumatic Stress*, **10**, 557–571.

Lindsay, D. S. & Briere, J. (1997). The controversy regarding recovered memories of childhood sexual abuse: Pitfalls, bridges and future directions. *Journal of Interpersonal Violence*, **12**, 631–647.

Lindsay, D. S. & Read, J. D. (1994). Psychotherapy and memories of childhood sexual abuse: a cognitive perspective. *Applied Cognitive Psychology*, **8**, 281–338.

Lindsay, D. S. & Read, J. D. (1995). "Memory work" and recovered memories of childhood sexual abuse: Scientific evidence and public, professional and personal issues. *Psychology, Public Policy and the Law*, **1**, 846–908.

Loftus, E. F. (1993). The reality of repressed memories. *American Psychologist*, **48**, 518–537

Olio, K. (1996). Are 25% of clinicians using potentially risky therapeutic practices? A review of the logic and methodology of the Poole, Lindsay et al. study. *Journal of Psychiatry and Law*, **24**, 277–298.

Palm, K. M. & Gibson, P (1998). Recovered memories of childhood sexual abuse: clinicians' practices and beliefs. *Professional Psychology, Research and Practice*, **29**, 257–261.

Polusny, M. & Follette, V. (1996). Remembering childhood sexual abuse: A national survey of psychologists' clinical practices, beliefs, and personal experiences. *Professional Psychology: Research and Practice*, **27**, 41–52.

Poole, D. A., Lindsay, D. S., Memon, A. & Bull, R. (1995). Psychotherapy and the recovery of memories of childhood sexual abuse: U.S. and British practitioners' opinions practices and experiences. *Journal of Consulting and Clinical Psychology*, **63**, 426–437.

Pope, K. (1997). Science as a careful questioning: Are claims of a false memory syndrome epidemic based on empirical evidence? *American Psychologist*, **52**, 997–1006.

Schooler, J. W., Bendiksen, M. & Ambadar, Z. (1997). Taking the middle line: Can we accommodate both fabricated memories and recovered memories of sexual abuse? In M.Conway (Ed.), *False and Recovered Memories*. Oxford: Oxford University Press.

Terr, L. (1994). *Unchained Memories: True Stories of Traumatic Memories, Lost and Found*. New York: Basic Books.

10

ESTABLISHING PRACTICE-BASED GUIDELINES FOR THERAPISTS

Noelle Robertson

This is no case of petty right or wrong
That politicians or philosophers
Can judge
EDWARD THOMAS

The dispassionate observer, entering the debate on the status and legitimacy of recovered memories for the first time, must be reminded of a war zone. Positions taken are entrenched, diplomacy has often all but ceased, and dialogue has been abandoned in favour of intemperate language and unreasoned propaganda. At times it would appear that each side wants to amass sufficient theoretical, empirical or anecdotal resource to muster the final push, break from the trenches and rout the opposition. Sadly, what is likely to be scythed down should such a conflict continue is the very reflective practice that researchers and practitioners need to maintain: both to develop the debate and ensure that optimal information and psychotherapeutic practice is available to patients and professionals alike. Trench warfare, it should be remembered, blights a landscape leaving little to flourish or blossom.

Recovered Memories: Seeking the Middle Ground. Edited by Graham M. Davies and Tim Dalgleish. © 2001 John Wiley & Sons Ltd.

For some time, and eloquently described by Courtois (1996), political and ideological issues have prevailed in the debate on recovered memories. Advocates on both sides of the divide (crudely, an applied cognitivist/clinical splitting) have overstated their positions with consequences both offensive and defensive. Offensive, in that practitioners in both research and clinical domains have felt their expertise to be denigrated or ignored. Defensive in that each side believes in its own truths more absolutely and ceases to listen. This has particular dangers if trying to ensure a dialogue between the psychologist as researcher and clinician. Cape and Parry (2000), for example, suggest that despite the common principles underpinning psychological therapies, diversity is the norm—both in theoretical orientation and delivery of therapy. Because practitioners may have very different professional origins and training, shared schemas to interpret and incorporate new research and ways of working may be scarce. Practitioners will also be fairly tribal—understandably valuing their own tried and tested techniques. What is needed therefore with such a variety of paradigm and practice is not further fruitless polarisation. To progress knowledge and practice surrounding recovered memories, we should be aiming for a shared appreciation of clinical process and evidence-base that develops consensus. One means of achieving this is to develop tools to shape that process. This chapter will introduce and discuss the role of one such tool—clinical guidelines.

It would be churlish at the outset of this chapter to fail to acknowledge the considerable work already undertaken to establish the status of recovered memories by organisations such as the American Psychological Association and the British Psychological Society. Both of these national bodies have devoted extensive resource and diverse professional expertise to the review of current scientific studies. From the collected evidence, they have sought to make generic recommendations for practice. From a predominantly clinical perspective, the need for evolving guidance on standards of care has been articulated by Brown (1995) and Courtois (1997). Both stress that standards should be driven by a combination of opinion and rigorously assessed literature tempered by regulatory and ethical concerns. All practitioners in this area of enquiry should be amenable to a developing information base and strive to ensure that their practice is guided by such.

CLINICAL GUIDELINES: THE CONTEXT

Clinical guidelines, also known as clinical practice guidelines, or less frequently "protocols of care", have developed within a wider context of quality improvement in public services, most notably health care. Over the last two decades or so, government agencies and professional bodies have sought, as never before, to enhance the skills base of professionals, often motivated by visible inadequacies (the changes in professional practice following the case of Harold Shipman is a classic example, see Whittle & Ritchie, 2000). This process has been further accelerated by easier access to information that might have relevance for clinical practice. Since a substantial amount of the available information may have limited relevance or validity, the philosophy of evidence-based health care has evolved. Rosenberg and Donald (1995) define this as the "process of turning clinical problems into questions and then systematically locating, appraising and using contemporary research findings as the basis for clinical decisions".

Systematising the provision of new (research) information, in the hope that this will translate into improved quality of patient care, has as yet not been wholly successful. Reviews of the effectiveness of strategies to develop professional practice (embracing novel, effective behaviours and dispensing with well-established, but ineffective behaviours) has revealed some surprises. Traditionally valued means of imparting information or developing new skills, such as the conference circuit or workshops, are relatively unsuccessful in promoting change (Davis, Thomson, Oxman & Haynes, 1995). A growing body of research is demonstrating the limitations of simple information transfer (Greco & Eisenberg, 1993). There is increasing recognition that professionals' acquisition of knowledge does not necessarily foster either attitude or behaviour change and has caused a re-evaluation of how such change should be stimulated and maintained. Feedback on clinician performance, structured educational events and knowledge dissemination through expert and peer influence may improve quality (Grol, 1992). Increasingly, recourse to clinical guidelines has been sought as a principal way forward.

WHAT ARE CLINICAL GUIDELINES?

Of all tools employed to improve quality of care, guidelines are most explicitly rooted in and shaped by research evidence. Guidelines themselves are not new. Statements defining levels of adequate care or best practice were first articulated in the times of the ancient Greeks. As presently defined, guidelines uniquely offer the opportunity to integrate current, critically appraised comments with clinical expertise to produce recommendations of use to practitioner, researcher and client. In so doing they may reduce uncertainties surrounding the management of clients' problems and enhance the rate by which research findings are incorporated into routine practice (Woolf, 1992).

Field and Lohr's (1992) definition seem to encompass the essence and intent of guidelines as "systematically developed statements to assist practitioner and patient decisions about appropriate health care for specific clinical circumstances".

Guidelines thus embody three key elements: support for decision making in a set of clinical circumstances, a systematic approach to their construction, and a focus on specific clinical problems or entities.

The notion of a supportive function is important in an era of health care often perceived to offer "cook book" medicine. Guidelines were originally conceived of to fulfil an educative function, embodied in the idiom "tools not rules". In some managed care environments, guidelines have been perceived as a punitive means of exercising control or have fermented anxieties about their use in litigation. It is therefore important to reiterate that the use of a guideline is discretionary, not obligatory. There are plentiful examples of unused or discarded guidelines, which have failed the test of usefulness. Guideline statements should be flexibly applied depending on the circumstances faced by the clinician. While clinicians might fear that their autonomy will be reduced, guidelines should not be unduly prescriptive and some variation in practice is perfectly acceptable, provided it can be justified.

The supportive function of guidelines is sometimes forgotten as other reasons for their use have become more prominent—inappropriate variation in clinical practice or, especially, cost containment. It is increasingly evident that there are substantial variations in clinical care (at times potentiating adverse reactions for clients; Yapko, 1994) and that there may be efficiency gains in an organisation if guidelines are implemented. However, this should not diminish the potential of guidelines to deliver evidence and evidence-based recommendations in a palatable and usable way to busy clinicians.

WHAT ARE THE PRINCIPLES OF GUIDELINE DEVELOPMENT?

Many authors who discuss guidelines (Eccles et al., 1996; Shekelle & Schriger, 1996) stress that for validity to be assured, development should be undertaken in a rigorous and systematic way. Most commonly this comprises a number of phases: establishing which clinical decisions will be addressed by the guidelines (setting criteria for inclusion of evidence); convening and running a guideline development group; systematically reviewing evidence; summarising conclusions; and translating into recommendations. Finally, the guidelines will need to be subjected to external review by those with clinical expertise and potential users, to ensure that the review is complete. Importantly, and neglected to date in statements on recovered memories, professionals competent in guideline development method should be included in this process.

WHICH CLINICAL DECISIONS OR TOPICS NEED GUIDELINES?

A number of pertinent questions need to be asked in defining a subject worthy of guideline development relating to cost, variations in practice, potential for improvement, likelihood of consensus and of benefiting patients (Thomson, Lavender & Madhok, 1995). Without a clear specification of the guidelines' remit, there are significant pitfalls -specifically spiralling costs, if the scope is too large.

Convening and running a development group

Shekelle, Woolf, Eccles and Grimshaw (1999) offer constructive advice regarding constituent membership and process of a guideline development group. They suggest an over-arching project management team responsible for the identification and interpretation of evidence, convening the panel and producing the guidelines. They also suggest additional groups who can provide recommendations on the collected evidence or its absence. Consideration should be given to the participants in the development group. This will be discussed more fully with regard to consensus methods, but should not be ignored even where the evidence-base is more extensive.

Reviewing the evidence

Psychological therapies often have a limited evidence base (and guidelines may rely more heavily on consensus) in comparison to the medical arena, where guidelines first gained their impetus. However, the principles of identification and assessment remain important. They comprise exhaustive collection of all available evidence; assessment of how relevant evidence is to the topic under review and potential sources of bias; and the extraction and summarising of research findings. Shekelle et al. (1999) suggest that a preliminary check should be made to establish whether a systematic review has been undertaken (the Cochrane library is an essential source). If none exists, then searches of relevant specified databases should follow. Experts in the group who can detect significant omissions should examine articles identified by this process. Once studies are identified they need to be appraised for their relevance to the guideline remit and assessed for susceptibility to bias. There are a number of classification schemes which attempt to grade proneness to bias—often known as "the strength of evidence"—particularly referring to study design, with the randomised controlled trial as the gold standard. To this author's knowledge, no such formal grading system has ever been attempted for the recovered memories literature. Shekelle et al. (1999) cite one such classification scheme:

Ia   Evidence from a meta-analysis of randomised controlled trials (RCTs)
Ib   Evidence from at least one RCT
IIa Evidence from at least one controlled study without randomisation
IIb Evidence from at least one other type of quasi-experimental study
III Evidence from non-experimental descriptive studies (such as comparative, correlational or case-control studies)
IV   Evidence from expert committee reports or opinions or clinical experience of respected authorities, or both.

This demonstrably appraises evidence on methodological grounds and does not assess the quality of the studies. Assessment of quality should also be included, because of the recent findings that treatment benefit may be overestimated in poorer quality trials (Moher et al., 1998). Whatever scheme is ultimately used, the grading criteria should be explicit enough to allow the guideline user to understand the weight of recommendation made (Breen & Feder, 1999). This final stage of translating assessed evidence into recommendations is likely to be the most contentious part of guideline development. It is here that additional subgroups, preferably multi-professional, can come into their own, to offer expert opinion and to consider what practical obstacles may be faced by the guideline user if recommendations are to be implemented. This final stage should be as transparent as those that precede it since interpretation of evidence, being subjective, is most likely to raise accusations of bias.

THE CONTRIBUTION OF CONSENSUS TO GUIDELINE DEVELOPMENT

The very need for consensus stems from a lack of consensus.
SKRABANEK (1990)

Studies on the utility of guidelines stress priority should be given to the development of guidelines where routine care is variable or deviates from best practice (Effective Health Care, 1994). This clearly has relevance to the management of recovered memories and sequalae of trauma. Priority should also be given to guideline development where an evidence base is readily available. This is undoubtedly more difficult with regard to psychotherapeutic practice where evidence review will inevitably yield thin pickings. In general this is the result of a lack of substantive empirical work, particularly for some therapies. Evidence in the published domain tends to promote brief, manualised therapies at the expense of larger, less-structured ones. Furthermore, there exists a lively debate as to whether psychological therapies are amenable to the assessment methodologies advocated for other clinical phenomena (Firth-Cozens, 1997).

Within the field of recovered memories, where the very status remains contested, obviously no such agreed and accessible evidence base exists. Guidance published to date (American Psychological Association, 1998; British Psychological Society 1995; Frankland & Cohen, 1999) amply demonstrate that only preliminary steps have so far been taken. What is absent is not merely the shared evidence, but an agreed linguistic and conceptual framework. With such a state of affairs, it seems imperative to consider how valid and useful recommendations can be achieved by other means. It is here that the consensus process comes into its own, indicated where contradictory evidence or an evidence vacuum prevails.

Some would argue that if rigorous scientific evidence does not exist, then no recommendations for practice should be made. Woolf, Di Guiseppe, Atkins & Kamerow (1996) have persuasively contested this, demonstrating that clinical practice will continue, irrespective of the availability of evidence. Practitioners will resort to habit and anecdote without clear evidence, and while they may offer good enough care, they may equally place their clients at risk. Woolf et al. describe their own experience of a preventative task force in the US and press for systematic production of recommendations even when there is limited or equivocal evidence. At the very least, a statement of current status focuses the psychology community on the research that needs to be done to answer extent empirical questions (see Davies, this volume, for an example).

The development of consensus within and for psychological practice is likely to be fraught. Cape and Parry (2000) point out that psychological therapy has largely autonomous status. It is often underpinned by private practice and from training onwards there is a focus on individual differences and interventions tailored to suit individual client needs. All these factors may militate against consensus development.

Accepting that such difficulties may be encountered, are there means by which valid consensus statements can be achieved? McIntosh (1999) outlines five issues that need to be considered in this process: group membership; reaching agreement; presentation of evidence; formal consensus building methods; and achieving consensus. Transparency, as referred to in the context of evidence-based guidelines, is particularly important since bias may emerge through the group process.

Group membership is obviously key, since the individuals comprising the group will determine selection, analysis and application of a knowledge base in the guideline's production. At the outset the values and judgements of participants should be explicitly articulated. Overt criteria should dictate the selection of the group with thought given to the expertise offered and personal and professional interests being served. Consideration should also be given to a pre-existing familiarity of group members, possible relationships in other contexts (antagonistic or synergistic) and means of overcoming potential hostilities. Again, to this author's knowledge, no such formal procedures were used for selecting members of the BPS and APA working parties on recovered memories, beyond ensuring that both clinical and cognitive specialists were represented. Where areas of debate, such as legitimacy of recovered memories, span international boundaries, consideration should be given to cultural factors that may impinge on the consensus process and ultimately limit generalisability (Kleinjen & Bonsel, 1998).

Reaching agreement

McIntosh points out that unanimous agreement seldom occurs in all recommendations inherent in a guideline—that there may be partial agreement in some areas but complete agreement in others. To overcome such variability she suggests that the level of necessary agreement, and the domains to which it applies, should be established as the process unfolds.

Presentation of evidence

Developing consensus statements requires that opinion and evidence are seamlessly merged. Unfortunately the decision making involved in this process can be skewed, if inadequate thought is given to how evidence is conveyed to group members (Gigone & Hastie, 1997). A staged, transparent process is needed to enhance the accuracy of the decision-making process, to obviate errors and ensure completeness.

Methods of building consensus

The introductory nature of this chapter precludes detailed examination of formal consensus-finding methods. However, Murphy et al. (1998) have most recently reviewed the emerging literature on such techniques. In essence, guideline development has used four major methods. Firstly, there is the use of *consensus development conferences*. These are most frequently used in North America, and bring panel members together for a two-day period where they may be publicly presented with written and oral summaries of research evidence, with panel members then retiring privately, yet collectively, to consider and produce recommendations. Something of this procedure seems to have been attempted by the APA working party on recovered memories, but with mixed results. Secondly, there is the *Delphi technique*. Unlike consensus conferences, this method does not require panel members to meet, but instead may employ successive voting rounds by post. An iterative process (of questionnaires or group discussion) continues until maximum convergence of views occurs (Jones & Hunter, 1995). The third method is the *nominal group technique*. This again requires facilitated face-to-face contact by someone with domain-based expertise or credibility with the consensus group. Ideas are elicited from panel members in a systematically structured way before being considered and ranked. The final ranking forms the basis of the consensus achieved. Finally, there is the *RAND appropriateness method*. This method is gaining credibility on both sides of the Atlantic and employs arguably the most effective elements of those previously mentioned. It is commended for its emphasis on rigorous, explicit process, which is fully documented. Given that the evidence pertaining to recovered memories is still in a germinal stage, it is this final technique that may be the most fruitful way forward.

Achieving consensus

This final element in consensus development is often overlooked, not unreasonably in circumstances where group members' views converge. However, should general agreement have been reached, but the wording of a recommendation prove a stumbling block, provision should be made for further methods (informal or more structured) to minimise dissent.

In developing guidelines in the area of recovered memories, consensus may hold promise. The dearth of immediately applicable research to clinical settings will mean that, for the foreseeable future, opinion (articulated by means of consensus) building may coalesce with a growing research base to inform practice. However, it is paramount that the way in which consensus is produced is seen to be transparent and honest about potential sources of bias in order that the recommendations are adapted.

IMPLEMENTING GUIDELINES: WHAT BRIDGES THE EVIDENCE–PRACTICE GAP?

> *Guidelines are not self-implementing.*
> (GROL, 1992)

Given the extensive time and resources that can be devoted to the production of guidelines, it is essential that adequate thought is given to their use. Sadly the history of guideline development is littered with examples of massive expenditure only for guidelines to sit gathering dust on a shelf (Kanouse, Kallich & Kahan, 1995). Development strategies have undoubtedly received more attention than implementation. If guidelines are to achieve their full potential, however, planning for implementation (i.e. ensuring that recommendations are complied with) needs prioritisation early in the development process. An obvious strategy is to ensure the brevity and readability of recommendations. Weighty tomes make excellent doorstops but less effective guidelines. Grilli and Lomas (1994) found that compliance with recommendations was reduced for more complex guidelines. To ensure that practitioners and patients use guidelines, a summary of recommendations in shortened format is desirable. Commonly this is achieved with perhaps a desktop version, supplemented with a volume containing all the evidence on which the recommendations are based. One criticism of the original BPS report on recovered memories was that the published guidelines were not backed up by such a systematic review of the literature (Weiskrantz, 1995).

Implementation success can crudely be examined by reference to two factors and their interaction—the characteristics of the guideline dissemination and implementation process, and the beliefs and attitudes of practitioners and the culture in which they practise (often defined as barriers or obstacles to change).

Early forays into guideline development naively assumed that simply by alerting practitioners to a guideline's existence it would be read, assimilated and practice modified accordingly. A review of 19 studies of passive dissemination of consensus-based recommendations for aspects of medical care concluded that behaviour change rarely occurred (Lomas, 1991) and this somewhat naive approach has rapidly been abandoned in medicine. Dissemination is now viewed as likely only to raise awareness, but while necessary as a precursor to change, is not sufficient to ensure it. It is noteworthy that this method has been favoured for guidelines on recovered memories in therapy and the impact of such guidelines on process remains to be established.

More concerted efforts have been directed at a wider variety of implementation strategies. These are broadly the use of reminders, for example: marking files for relevant patients; audit and feedback on clinical performance; the use of local opinion leaders to exert peer pressure; dissemination of educational materials and educational outreach (face-to-face discussion between the practitioner and a person credible to that practitioner supported by educational materials). While the latter has shown promise in changing prescribing behaviour in North America, it is still being trialled in UK and European settings. Of the other strategies, reminders are generally effective across a range of behaviours and the other interventions show rather mixed beneficial effects (Effective Health Care, 1999; Bero et al., 1998). As Oxman stated in 1994, "there is no magic bullet", and while most strategies are effective in implementing guidelines in some circumstances, there is no universal panacea that can bridge the evidence–practice divide. The use prompts and reminders in a therapeutic context is another area where no significant research has been undertaken.

The variable effectiveness of strategies has prompted an examination of potential users in addition to the guidelines themselves. Since practitioners are so resistant to the messages delivered in guidelines, reasons have been sought for their non-compliance. Some researchers have advocated greater awareness and analysis of the barriers to change that might stand in the way of guideline adoption (Robertson, Baker & Hearnshaw, 1996). They have also emphasised that resistance to change of this kind is not necessarily a bad thing, but reflects changes within the status quo and fear of the consequences of change. Certainly obstacles to improving quality of care have been identified in a number of aspects of medical care and nursing (Grol & Wensing, 1995; Closs & Cheater, 1996). Goss and Rowland (2000) suggest a conservatism too in the psychological therapies, where a lack of commitment to, and understanding of, the need for evidence-based health care is a key barrier.

However reasonable barriers may be, if guidelines are ultimately to succeed in their objectives, the reasons for resistance need to be elicited and thought given to how they may be addressed. Most attempts to classify barriers propose examination of individual practitioner beliefs and attitudes, the immediate support system surrounding the practitioner and the cultural values and pressures brought to bear by the organisation in which the practitioner works. Social psychological perspectives are useful in this regard. Again, a similar analysis could and should be conducted in relation to guidelines for recovered memories elicited in therapy.

Successful implementation of guideline initiatives for recovered memories may also need to consider how evidence-based care can be more fully embraced, by both practitioners and researchers. This will require mutual respect of different paradigms by researcher and clinician. This will not simply mean that practitioners will need to develop expertise in critical appraisal and research skills. They will need time, resource and organisational support to prioritise research activity and contribute more fully to the evidence base. Researchers, for their part, must consider how their methodological preferences can be broadened to represent the full complexities of therapeutic practice since, to date, traditional experimental methodologies have not adequately addressed the process of therapeutic change (Bergin & Garfield, 1994).

GUIDELINES: THE FUTURE

This chapter has sought to describe the origins and status of clinical guidelines in informing and shaping the behaviour of clinician and researchers working in the field of recovered memories. Guidelines are but one tool by which professionals can improve the quality of their work in this arena. Despite their undeniable weaknesses (and, if inadequately prepared, their potential costliness), systematically developed guidelines can make more accessible and usable the findings of experimental research and ensure that these are efficiently incorporated into clinical practice. At the same time they can flag up the difficulties of application in real-world clinical practice. Given their potential, it is incumbent on professionals debating the research and management of recovered memories to develop effective skills in guidelines usage. Some familiarity with the principles of guideline development and implementation, as practised in the wider sphere of medicine, should enable researchers and clinicians to use them with increasing sophistication and improve the quality of care received by a vulnerable client group.

REFERENCES

American Psychological Association (1998). Final report of the American Psychological Association working group on investigation of memories of childhood abuse. Washington, DC: Author. (*Psychology, Public Policy and Law, 4*, 579–726.)

Brown, D. (1995). Pseudomemories: The standard of science and the standard of care treatment. *American Journal of Clinical Hypnosis, 37*,1–24.

Bergin, A. E. & Garfield, S. L. (1994). Overview, trends and future issues. In A. E. Bergin & S. L. Garfield (Eds), *Handbook of Psychotherapy and Behaviour Change*. New York: Wiley.

Bero, L. A., Grilli, R., Grimshaw, J. M. et al. (1998). Closing the gap between research and practice: An overview of systematic reviews of interventions to promote the implementation of research findings. *British Medical Journal, 317*, 465–468.

Breen, A. & Feder, G. (1999). Where does the evidence come from? In A. Hutchinson & R. Baker (Eds), *Making Use of Guidelines in Clinical Practice*. Oxford: Radcliffe Medical Press.

British Psychological Society (1995). *Recovered Memories: The Report of the Working Party of the British Psychological Society*. Leicester: Author.

Cape, J. & Parry, G. (2000). Clinical practice guidelines development in evidence-based psychotherapy. In N. Rowland & S. Goss (Eds), *Evidence-Based Counselling and Psychological Therapies: Research and Applications*. London: Routledge.

Closs, J. & Cheater, F. M. (1996). Audit or research—what is the difference? *Journal of Clinical Nursing, 5*, 249–256.

Courtois, C. A. (1996). Informed clinical practice and the delayed memory controversy. In K. Pezdek & W. P. Banks (Eds), *The Recovered Memory/False Memory Debate*. San Diego: Academic Press.

Courtois, C. A. (1997). Delayed memories of child sexual abuse: Critique of the controversy and clinical guidelines. In M. A. Conway (Ed.), *Recovered Memories and False Memories*. Oxford: Oxford University Press.

Davies, G. M., Morton, J., Mollon, P. & Robertson, N. (1998). Recovered memories in theory and practice. *Psychology, Public Policy and Law*, **4**, (4), 1079–1091.

Davis, D. A., Thomson, M. A., Oxman, A. D. & Haynes R. B. (1995). Changing physician performance. A systematic review of the effect of continuing education strategies. *Journal of the American Medical Association*, **274**, 700–705.

Eccles, M. P., Clapp, Z., Grimshaw, J. et al. (1996). Developing valid guidelines: Methodological and procedural issues from the North of England evidence based guideline development project. *Quality in Health Care*, **5**, 44–50.

Effective Health Care (1994). Implementing clinical guidelines. Can guidelines be used to improve clinical practice? *Bulletin No. 8*. Leeds: University of Leeds.

Effective Health Care (1999). Getting evidence into practice. *Bulletin No. 9*. York: University of York.

Field, M. J. & Lohr, K. N. (1992). *Guidelines for Clinical Practice: From Development to Use*. Washington, DC: National Academy Press.

Firth-Cozens, J. (1997). Health promotion: Changing behaviour towards evidence-based health care. *Quality in Health Care*, **6**, 205–211.

Frankland, A. & Cohen, L. (1999). Draft guidelines for psychologists working with clients in contexts in which issues relating to recovered memories may arise. *The Psychologist*, **12**, 82–83.

Gigone, D. & Hastie, R. (1997). Proper analysis of the accuracy of group judgements. *Psychological Bulletin*, **121**,149–167.

Goss, S. & Rowland, N. (2000). Getting research into practice. In N. Rowland & S. Goss (Eds), *Evidence-Based Counselling and Psychological Therapies: Research and Applications*. London: Routledge.

Greco, P. J. & Eisenberg, J. M. (1993). Changing physicians practices. *New England Journal of Medicine*, **329**, 1271–1273.

Grilli, R. & Lomas, J. (1994). Evaluating the message: The relationship between compliance rate and the subject of a practice guideline. *Medical Care*, **32**, 202–213.

Grol, R. (1992). Implementing guidelines in general practice care. *Quality in Health Care*, **1**, 184–191.

Grol, R. & Wensing, M. (1995). Implementation of quality assurance and medical audit; general practitioners perceived obstacles and requirements. *British Journal of General Practice*, **46**, 115–119.

Jones, J. & Hunter, H. (1995). Consensus methods for medical and health services research. *British Medical Journal*, **311**, 376–380.

Kanouse, D., Kallich, J. D. & Kahan, J. P. (1995). Dissemination of effectiveness and outcomes research. *Health Policy*, **34**, 167–192.

Kleinjen, J. & Bonsel, G. (1998). Guidelines and quality of clinical services in the new NHS. *British Medical Journal*, **316**, 299–300.

Lomas, J. (1991). Words without action? The production, dissemination and impact of consensus recommendations. *Annual Review of Public Health*, **12**, 41–65.

McIntosh, A. (1999). Guidance: What role should consensus play in guideline development? In A. Hutchinson & R. Baker (Eds), *Making Use of Guidelines in Clinical Practice*. Oxford: Radcliffe Medical Press.

Moher, D., Jones, A., Cook, J., Jada, A. R., Moher, M. & Tugwell, P. (1998). Does quality of reports of randomised trials affect estimates of intervention efficacy reported in meta-analyses? *Lancet*, **352**, 609–613.

Murphy, M. K. et al. (1998). Consensus development methods and their use in clinical guideline development. *Health Technology Assessment*, **2**, 3.

Oxman, A. D., Thomson, M. A., Davis, D. A. & Haynes, R. B. (1995). No magic bullets: Systematic review of 102 trials of interventions to improve professional practice. *Canadian Medical Association Journal*, **153**, 1423–1431.

Robertson, N., Baker, R. & Hearnshaw, H. (1996). Changing the clinical behaviour of doctors: A psychological perspective. *Quality in Health Care*, **5**, 51–54.

Rosenberg, W. & Donald, D. (1995) Evidence based medicine: An approach to clinical problem solving. *British Medical Journal*, **310**, 1122–1126.

Shekelle, P. G. & Schriger, D. L. (1996). Evaluating the use of the appropriateness of method in the agency for health care policy and research clinical guideline development process. *Health Services Research*, **31**, 453–468.

Shekelle, P. G., Woolf, S. H., Eccles, M. & Grimshaw, J. (1999). Developing guidelines. *British Medical Journal*, **318**, 593–596.

Skrabanek, P. (1990). Nonsensus consensus. *Lancet*, **335**, 1446–1447.

Thomson, R., Lavender, M. & Madhok, R. (1995). How to ensure that guidelines are effective. *British Medical Journal*, **311**, 237–242.

Weiskrantz, L. (1995). Comments on the report of the working party of the British Psychological Society on "Recovered Memories". *The Therapist*, **2**, 4.

Whittle, B. & Ritchie, J. (2000). *Prescription for Murder: The True Story of Harold Shipman*. London: Warner.

Woolf, S.H. (1992). Practice guidelines—a new reality in medicine. II: Methods of developing guidelines. *Archives of Internal Medicine*, **152**, 946–952.

Woolf, S. H., DiGuiseppi, C. G., Atkins, D. & Kamerow, D. B. (1996). Developing evidence-based clinical practice guidelines: Lessons learned by the US Preventative Services Task Force. *Annual Review of Public Health*, **17**, 511–538.

Yapko, M. (1994). *Suggestions of Abuse: True and False Memories of Childhood Sexual Training*. New York: Simon & Schuster:

11

PSYCHOGENIC AMNESIAS: FUNCTIONAL MEMORY LOSS

Michael Kopelman and John Morton

INTRODUCTION

Our intention is to report on a case of functional amnesia and examine a range of accounts of functional amnesia in the framework of a particular model of event memory, Headed Records (Morton, Hammersley & Bekerian, 1985; Morton & Bekerian, 1986; Morton, 1990; Abeles & Morton, 1999; Barreau & Morton, in press; Newcombe & Siegal, 1996; Smith, Morton & Oakley, in press; Wilkinson, 1998a, 1998b). In addition, we will draw some parallels between the properties of functional amnesia and those of recovered and false memory.

HEADED RECORDS

The Headed Records model of memory, in common with many other models, proposes that memory is made up of individual *Records* each corresponding to an event. Both Tulving's encoding specificity principle (Tulving, 1983) and the principle of state-dependent learning were essential foundation blocks for the model, and were implemented in it through the operation of *Headings*, attached to each record, within which the modality of

Recovered Memories: Seeking the Middle Ground. Edited by Graham M. Davies and Tim Dalgleish. © 2001 John Wiley & Sons Ltd.

stimuli are preserved, and where contextual cues are encoded. Encoding specificity is actually not so much a theory as a hypothesis about behaviour, predicting that more will be recalled when the conditions of testing match the conditions of recall. The hypothesis is neutral as to why this happens or what mechanisms are employed. Tulving (1983) puts forward the concept of "synergistic ecphory" as an explanatory principle. Headed Records uses "headings" in the same way. This would include state information.

The information used in retrieval is termed the *Description* (Norman & Bobrow, 1979) and is formed from both internal and external information sources. For the successful retrieval of a particular record, the attached heading must be matched to some extent by the description. If a description fails to match a heading, or if the retrieved record does not contain the information which is sought, then the process recycles using a modified description. Well-worked-out examples of this cyclical process have been provided by Williams and Hollan (1981).

Within the model there are two categories of record distinguished by the type of information in their headings. They are called *primary records* and *secondary records*. Primary records are the result of normal activity in the interpretation of the perceptual world. As a result, the internal and external contexts at the time of the record's creation become incorporated into the heading. Examples of internal context are mood and current goal, and examples of external contexts are location and companions. This contextual information, due to its presence in the heading, plays an important role in retrieval of the record. If the same contextual information is present at the time of retrieval, it will form part of the description used in the search process. The more overlap there is between heading and description, the more likely it is that there will be a successful match, and the more likely that the target record will be retrieved. An experimental way of determining the components of headings is through a comparison of the relative effectiveness of variables on recognition memory compared with recall. It has been established that recall, unlike recognition memory, is sensitive to state variables, such as emotion, as well as being sensitive to the reinstatement of the original environmental context (Bower, 1981; Eich, 1980; Godden & Baddeley, 1975, 1980). This indicates that such variables are to be found in headings. (See Morton et al., 1985, for a more detailed account.) Primary records contrast with secondary records which result from the retrieval of a primary record during reminiscence or as part of a narrative. The secondary record will thus tend to have verbal rather than perceptual information in its heading.

The basic architecture of the model is shown in Figure 11.1. The central device is the interpreter buffer, into which is passed (partially processed) information from the environment. Memory records are also retrieved into the interpreter buffer in order to guide the process of interpreting the environment. The interpreter processes the contents of the interpreter buffer according to some principles which are fixed and other principles which comprise the current *Task Specification*. The task specification can be seen as a list of current processing goals. When the current task-demands require the retrieval of further information, the process of retrieval is initiated by the interpreter which prompts the formulation of a new description (see Morton et al., 1985, for a discussion of this process). Use of the new description leads to the retrieval of a record which might include the required information. If the current task specification still cannot be satisfied, the cyclical retrieval process continues as indicated above.

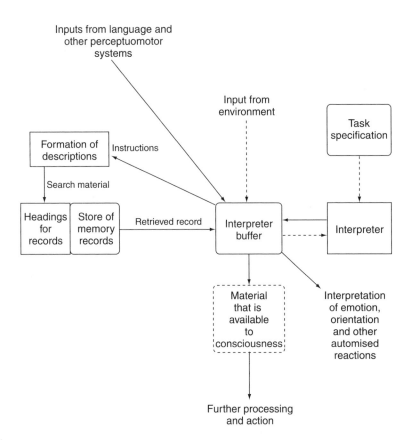

Figure 11.1:   A partial sketch of the system of retrieval of event records. Event records are retrieved into the *interpreter buffer* which also receives information from the environment. The contents of the *interpreter buffer* are interpreted and modified by the *interpreter*, whose operation is partially controlled by a set of goals in the *task specification*. Included in this control is whether or not particular information is made available to consciousness.

It should be noted that some other models of event memory equate *retrieval* with *consciousness*. However, it should also be noted that these models mostly equate *retrieval* with *response*. Accordingly, we should explicitly stress that by the term *retrieval* we mean retrieval into the interpreter buffer. In some other models this might be equivalent to what is called *access*, though use of all these terms is variable. Material in the buffer is not automatically available to consciousness, and the operation of the interpreter buffer is not equivalent to the operation of consciousness. While we do not intend here to define consciousness, what we need to do, in the context of functional amnesia, is to indicate something of the scope of consciousness. We have indicated in Figure 11.1 that information in the interpreter buffer can be made available to consciousness.[1] Whether or not this would be the case for any particular piece of information in the interpreter buffer would depend on the current task specification. For example, if you were asked for the address of your best friend, there would be an entry in the task specification to that end. As long as that goal was dominant, the material in the interpreter buffer would be screened such that only the address or information deemed relevant to the determination of the address would be available to consciousness. There are other outputs from the interpreter buffer which have not been well specified. These include the automatic processing of emotional material which would not be under the control of the task specification.

Smith et al. (in press) have recently used the Headed Records model to analyse alternative explanations for post-hypnotic amnesia. They point out that within the model there are three basic mechanisms by which an attempted retrieval of a record to consciousness may be unsuccessful. Firstly, the description may contain insufficient information to match the heading, leading to retrieval failure. If post-hypnotic amnesia reflects an inability to retrieve dissociated memories (Hilgard, 1977; Kihlstrom, 1978), the Headed Records model would account for the failure in terms of critical mismatch of the information in the description with that in the heading (cf. Morton, 1991). This could be because the task description includes goals which preclude the efficient formulation of an appropriate description. These goals would be formulated as a result of the interaction between the subject and the experimenter. In effect, the task specification would contain the information which controlled the dissociation between records that could be retrieved and those that could not. Thus, if the post-hypnotic suggestion was that the subject would not be able to recall a particular word list, a goal could be

---

[1] Indeed, within the present form of the model, the only information that can be made accessible to consciousness is autobiographical information plus other, related, information within the interpreter buffer.

set up in the task specification which operated to prevent certain elements from being formulated in the description.

A second sequence whereby post-hypnotic suggestion could lead to failure of retrieval would be if hypnosis represents a *state*. In that case, information pertaining to that state would be contained within the heading. As with other states such as mood (Bower, 1981; Teasdale, 1983; Teasdale & Fogarty, 1979; Lloyd & Lishman, 1975), alcohol (Goodwin, Powell, Bremer, Hoine & Stern, 1969) and location (Godden & Baddeley, 1975), access to records will be improved when the relevant state information is also in the description. Note, however, that such state-dependency effects are never all-or-nothing.

A third possible account of post-hypnotic amnesia in the Headed Records model hinges on the specification in the model that retrieved records are evaluated in the interpreter buffer, prior to their reaching conscious awareness, with respect to their relevance to current task specifications. If the information in the record is not congruent with the higher order goals of the recalling individual, as listed in the task specification, the record will not reach awareness. Equally, as already discussed, if a record does contain the required information, the associated irrelevant information will usually be screened out in a similar way. In relation to hypnosis, within a socio-cognitive theory, the task evaluation mechanisms (task specification plus the operation of the interpreter) would screen out from conscious awareness those records which were incongruent with the goal of maintaining a particular self-presentation, induced by the situation. The self-presentation is that of someone who is hypnotised, and the goal would be to maintain that self-presentation by not being able to recall the material in question. Smith et al. (in press) have shown that the subject's behaviour depends, in effect, on their theory of cognitive functioning. Thus, subjects who are given a set of words to free associate should produce the same responses the next time they have to do this task and should respond faster. In fact, this depends on the priming of perceptuo-motor structures rather than on event memory. However, for the non-psychologist this distinction has rarely been made, and the typical behaviour of hypnotised subjects who have been asked to forget the first set of associations is to avoid the previous response, even if it was a common one. In consequence, their response times are much greater than on the first trial. This can only be explained if there is a post-retrieval block on responding. It is generally accepted that at least some of these subjects are not behaving in this way deliberately (Spanos, Radtke & Dubreuil, 1982; Bertrand, Spanos & Radtke, 1990).

It can be seen that the Headed Records framework is neutral with respect to the major alternative accounts of hypnotic amnesia but allows them all to be formulated in a way which makes reference to other cognitive phenomena.

FUGUE STATES

Many aspects of functional or psychogenic amnesia bear interesting resemblances to what has been described in organic brain disease. There may be islands or fragments of preserved memory within an amnesic gap. For example, Schacter, Wang, Tulving and Freedman (1982) described a young man, who slipped into a fugue state following his grandfather's funeral, and who recalled a cluster of details from a short period during that year which he described (after recovery) as having been the happiest of his life. The subject may often adopt a detached attitude to these memory fragments, describing them as "strange and unfamiliar" (Coriat, 1907). In many cases, semantic knowledge remains intact (e.g. foreign languages, and the names of streets, towns, and famous people; Kanzer, 1939; Schacter et al., 1982). In other cases, there is some impairment of semantic memory, although other aspects of semantic knowledge are largely spared (Coriat, 1907; Abeles & Schilder, 1935; Kanzer, 1939), and this also seems to be the case in at least some cases of so-called "isolated retrograde amnesia" (Stracciari, Ghidoni, Guarino, Poletti & Pazzaglia, 1994; De Renzi, Lucchelli, Muggia & Spinnler, 1995). Performance at verbal learning tests has been reported as unaffected (Abeles & Schilder, 1935; Kopelman, Christensen, Puffett & Stanhope, 1994a), but in other cases it has been mildly impaired (Schacter et al., 1982), or more severely impaired (Gudjonsson & Taylor, 1985). It can also be compromised by concomitant brain disorder (Kopelman, Green, Guinan, Lewis & Stanhope, 1994b). Memory for skills is often preserved (e.g. Coriat, 1907), consistent with evidence demonstrating preserved procedural memory in organic amnesia. Sometimes, memory retrieval may be facilitated by chance cues in the environment (e.g. Abeles & Schilder, 1935; Schacter et al., 1982; Kopelman, 1995), but deliberate cueing is often unsuccessful (Coriat, 1907; Kanzer, 1939) and the results of interview under sodium amylobarbitone are very variable.

Some recent publications have elucidated the nature of this form of amnesia in more detail. As already mentioned, Schacter et al. (1982) described a young man who developed a "fugue" episode (functional retrograde amnesia) after attending the funeral of his grandfather, to whom he had been very close. Relative to his performance after recovery, there was a mild impairment of anterograde memory as indicated on the memory quotient from the 1945 Wechsler Memory Scale. On the Crovitz test (Crovitz & Schiffman, 1974), the median age of retrieved autobiographical memories to cue words was very brief, relative to both healthy controls and his own subsequent (post-recovery) performance. However, a "constrained" cueing procedure revealed some preserved 'islets' of autobiographical memory from a time period that the subject later described (on recovery) as one of the happiest of his life.

Kopelman et al. (1994a) reported a reversed temporal gradient in a patient, AT, with psychogenic amnesia. This patient showed a severe impairment for early time periods and pronounced recency effect, both on measures of autobiographical memory and public events. On the latter task, this performance could not be attributed to the patient simply remembering things since the onset of her amnesia, because the most recent items had occurred six years before the onset. The pattern was very similar to that described in patients with "focal retrograde amnesia". In addition, the patient failed to show word-completion priming for the names of people and places preceding the onset of her amnesia, whereas she showed normal word-completion for the names of people and places that she had known only since the onset of her disorder. Despite the latter finding, there was some clinical evidence that she could show familiarity with (recognise) or 'know' items from her past that she could not explicitly recollect. O'Connell (1960) reported statements in offenders claiming amnesia for their offence which are consistent with the notion that there are varying levels of awareness in such psychologically based forms of amnesia. Some offenders, who did not claim amnesia, described the memory of their offence as being allowed to "drift into the background ... like putting something into ... a safe and locking it away". Subjects reporting amnesia described having "buried everything about (the) case" and feeling that recollection would be "so (horrifying) that I just can't remember anything" or that "there is something in my mind it seems to be forming a picture and then ... my mind hurts ... (and) it gets all jumbled up again".

Campodonico and Rediess (1996) explored this issue in more detail using measures of semantic knowledge in another patient who was reported to have "profound psychogenic retrograde amnesia". On a measure of indirect remote memory, their patient, LJ, showed more rapid learning in associating the names of famous people to their faces, relative to novel faces and names, despite having been unable to name the famous faces at baseline. She also learned the occupations of famous people better than she did those for novel items. The authors interpreted these findings as evidence for preserved "implicit" remote semantic knowledge, despite impaired "explicit" recall for the same material.

Markowitsch, Fink, Thöne, Kessler and Heiss (1997) reported a 37-year-old man, NN, who appeared to experience a "fugue" episode lasting five days when out bicycling, and who then had a persistent loss of autobiographical memory, lasting eight months or more. Like the Kopelman et al. (1994a) patient, NN showed a 'reverse' temporal gradient on measures of autobiographical incident recall and personal semantic memory, although he appeared normal in recalling famous faces and events. Kritchevsky, Zouzounis and Squire (1997) also obtained a pronounced recency effect on an autobiographical memory measure (the Crovitz test) in nine patients with 'functional retrograde amnesia'.

Markowitsch et al. (1997) carried out a ^{15}O-PET scan, in which their patient was required to listen to sentences containing information about his past, either preceding or following the fugue episode. The authors found reduced right hemisphere activation relative to healthy controls who performed a similar task. Costello, Fletcher, Dolan, Frith and Shallice (1998) also carried out a PET activation study in a similar patient. Their subject was a man in his forties who, following a left superior dorsalateral prefrontal haemorrhage, developed a dense retrograde amnesia for the 19 years preceding the stroke. The authors considered that "a purely organic account of the condition does not seem very plausible". During their PET study, the subject attempted to recall events from family snapshots in one of three conditions — events for which he was amnesic but at which he had been present, events from the amnesic period but at which he was not present, and events outside the amnesic period. In the "amnesic-present" condition, activation was increased in the precuneus, but diminished in both the right posterior ventro-lateral frontal cortex and a region close to the site of haemorrhage. This finding of reduced right ventro-lateral frontal activation is broadly consistent with Markowitsch et al.'s (1997) finding of diminished right hemisphere activation.

Case description

Patient HP was a 40-year-old man who came to the Accident and Emergency Department of a central London hospital complaining of feeling "unwell, exhausted, with sore feet and loss of memory". He had "come round" on a park bench. He did not know who he was, and he could not remember anything about himself. It was early summer, and his hands and face appeared sunburnt. He was wearing a clean shirt.

HP asked a passer-by where the nearest hospital or police station was, and he was directed to the Accident and Emergency Department. On arrival, he appeared confused about his age, name, and where he was. He could not remember any details about himself. He complained of exhaustion and said that it felt as if he had been walking for weeks. He had blisters on his feet. Later, he said that he thought that he was from the north of the country. While still in the Accident and Emergency Department, a casualty officer had called out his first name (referring to somebody else), and HP recognised this, after which his surname "popped" into his head as if he were performing a word-completion task.

HP was transferred to a medical ward for exclusion of any underlying brain disease. Local police stations were contacted, and his brother and sister soon arrived, as HP had already been reported to the police as a missing person.

On their arrival, HP did not appear to recognise either of them at first, nor could he remember his wife's or children's names.

From his relatives, we learned that HP had disappeared some eight days earlier. He had been separated from his wife during the previous six weeks, because she had commenced an affair. There had been an altercation between them the night before his disappearance and, on the morning of his disappearance, a lawyer had told HP that his wife was trying to block access to their children. In addition, there had been difficulties at work. HP had to move from a previously well paid job to another employment, and then to a third job, in different parts of the country and at progressively lower rates of pay. HP lived approximately 200 miles from London, and had evidently travelled this distance during his fugue episode.

There was a past history of two or three episodes of "blackout" lasting a few minutes each, which had occurred some years earlier and were investigated in another general hospital. A current EEG showed a few brief bursts of sharpened theta and faster components over both hemispheres with a left mid-temporal preponderance, particularly during and after hyperventilation. A CT brain scan was normal.

HP appeared rather drawn, tense and anxious, perplexed but only mildly depressed. Over the ensuing four weeks, HP's memory steadily improved, although he continued to have great difficulty retrieving memories which involved his wife or his workplace, particularly for events or incidents during the previous two to three years. He had an 'islet' of memory of visiting London a few months earlier, together with his wife, but he could not remember any details or describe any emotional response to this. However, he knew that he had been immensely distressed that his marriage had broken up and that, during the period of separation, he had not been seeing his children. During his four-week admission, an interview was conducted after administration of sodium amylobarbitone: this appeared to help HP to recover at least some memories, although there was still not total recollection. At the end of his period of hospital admission, HP spent a weekend leave staying with a friend. During this visit, he met some other old friends, and he reported that he was "aware" of them from his past, although he could not remember much about them. Because of this, he felt anxious and distressed, and he burst into tears at one point. HP's memories appeared to return in a patchy fashion from the most remote towards the recent, and some retrieved memories appeared to have been cued from things that HP read in the newspapers or heard on television. He emphasised that, as memories returned, no emotions appeared to be "attached" to them. On occasion, he would ask in a rhetorical fashion "Do I really want to remember what I have forgotten?" At the time of his discharge, HP remained totally amnesic for the period of one week, in which he had disappeared, and his memory appeared somewhat 'clouded' for a period of five or six months before that.

HP was seen regularly in the outpatient clinic during the following seven months. During that period, further details returned. HP listed for us cues which had triggered memory retrieval. These included photographs, television programmes, talking with friends, talking with his children, going to familiar places, going out walking or running, bus and billboard advertisements, newspapers, meeting people, and going shopping. He commented that "Things can often be unrelated but will seem to trip thoughts, and often sometime later, something will be seen, said or done, that will build with other things and bring (memories) back." For example, an advertisement for swimming pools was said to have triggered a memory for a mosaic of a small animal, which HP could not place. Gradually, he started to recall details about his employment, and the fact that his original firm had been taken over leading to his being made redundant. He also started to recall details of the difficulties that had occurred in his relationship with his wife, since she had had a "breakdown" some time earlier. In particular, he recalled how he had been depressed during the period of enforced separation, in which he had had to live in a rented flat a little distance away from the family home. After six months, HP obtained a job and, when last seen seven months after his fugue episode, HP appeared much more settled and relaxed. He stopped attending the clinic after this.

At his penultimate visit, HP described the period of his disappearance, for which he was still amnesic, in these terms: "It's like a locked box locked away and I don't really want to open it." HP had been back to previously familiar places to see if he could cue his memory for the missing period, but he had been unsuccessful in this. He had discovered that he had not drawn any money from his bank during the period of his disappearance and, from his wife, he had learned that he had apparently taken with him only the clothes that he was dressed in, including the shirt that he was wearing when he arrived in hospital. The mystery of how this shirt was clean when he first appeared at the hospital, despite his having been missing for seven days and not having any luggage with him, was never resolved.

COGNITIVE TESTING

Cognitive assessment was carried out at intervals during the six months following HP's admission to hospital.

The NART-R reading test (Nelson & Willison, 1991) gave an estimated premorbid IQ of 102. Compared with this, the WAIS-R (Wechsler, 1981) gave a full-scale IQ of 91 (Verbal 92; Performance 92). On the Logical Memory test (Wechsler, 1987) for immediate recall, HP scored 30 out of 50 (75th percentile) and for delayed recall 23 out of 50 (56th percentile). On the Recognition Memory Test (Warrington, 1984) for words, HP scored 49 out of 50 (92nd percentile) and for faces 46 out of 50 (75th percentile). On the Doors and People (Baddeley, Emslie & Nimmo-Smith, 1994), HP performed consistently well, and his overall scaled memory score was 12 (75th percentile). In brief, HP performed satisfactorily or well on all these tasks. At the time that these tests were carried out, he scored 11 on the Beck Depression Inventory and 13 on the Beck Anxiety Inventory (Beck & Steer, 1993), indicating only mild levels of depression and anxiety. Moreover, HP "passed" two tests of simulation — Coin-in-hand (Kapur, 1994) and Modified Rey (Kapur, personal communication) — i.e. he did not give any evidence of simulation.

On a measure of recall for famous news events from the 1960s, 1970s and 1980s (Kopelman, Stanhope & Kingsley, 1999), HP scored 55%, 65% and 85% for each decade respectively, and on the recognition memory equivalent of this test, he scored 60%, 100% and 100% for each decade respectively — all of which are "normal" scores. HP was first tested on the Autobiographical Memory Interview (AMI; Kopelman, Wilson & Baddeley, 1990) seven days after his hospital admission (14 days after his original disappearance). By this time, his scores for childhood personal semantic facts (21) and autobiographical incidents (7) were normal. Likewise, his scores for early adult facts (17) and incidents (8) were also normal. However, his score for recent facts (16) was "definitely abnormal" and for recent incidents (6) was "borderline", consistent with HP's continuing complaint of impaired memory for several months preceding his disappearance. When re-tested six months later, HP's score for recent facts (18) had improved to "borderline", but his incidents score (6) remained unchanged.

We also administered the Crovitz test of autobiographical retrieval (Crovitz & Schiffman, 1974) on two occasions, the first being two weeks after HP's hospital admission, and the second nearly five months later. This was performed in a manner analogous to that used by Schacter et al. (1982) in an "unconstrained" condition to a "fugue" patient before and after recovery from his amnesia as well as to a healthy control. There were 24 cue words, consisting of 8 object words, 8 action words and 8 affect words, randomly distributed among one another. HP was requested to describe an episode, relating to each cue word, and to date and place each memory as well as he could. Scoring was on a 3-point scale, according to the descriptive richness and specificity in time and place of each memory (Baddeley & Wilson, 1986). Reaction times were also recorded.

Figure 11.2 shows that, on the first occasion of testing, HP's scores were worse for affect and action words than for object words. Moreover, Table 11.1 shows that his response latencies were slowest for affect words, intermediate for action words and fastest for object words. On

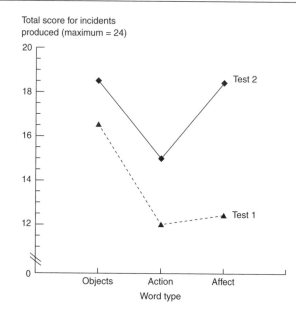

Figure 11.2:   Scores on Crovitz test two weeks after hospital admission and five months later.

the other hand, comparison with Schacter et al.'s (1982) data (Table 11.1), indicates that HP's latency for affect words was much closer to Schacter's control than to his patient, even during the latter's recovery phase. Five months later, HP's scores for affect words had substantially improved, and were now identical with his scores for object words (Figure 11.2).

In summary, HP performed well at measures of anterograde memory. He also scored highly on a test of remote news events. During the weeks and months following his fugue episode, he showed impairment in the recall of recent autobiographical facts and incidents (AMI), consistent with his clinical complaint of clouded memory for the months preceding the onset of his amnesia. In the retrieval of autobiographical memories to

Table 11.1:   Reaction times (median in seconds) at Test 1

	Objects	Actions	Affect
HP	5.0	9.0	12.0
PN (during amnesia)*	18.8	22.5	35.6
PN (post amnesia)*	7.2	6.2	22.9
Control (mean)	6.9	10.4	11.8

* From Schacter et al. (1982).

cue-words (Crovitz test), he showed an initial impairment in his response to affect words, which improved over the ensuing five months, although his impairment was never as severe as that described by Schacter et al. (1982) in their patient, PN, during and immediately following an episode of fugue.

DISCUSSION

In discussing this case, we shall consider somewhat separately the period of the fugue itself, for which no memories returned (as is characteristic in this disorder), and the preceding period of several months, for which memories were patchy and "clouded". Presumably the memories from this latter period were originally normal, and they have returned, albeit with reduced affect.

During the period of the fugue itself, it is conceivable that HP was in such an abnormal mental state and cognitive processing was so altered that either no event records were laid down at all or, at least, encoding was severely compromised. Kopelman (1987, p. 439) commented:

> What mechanisms underlie psychogenic amnesia? One possibility is that many instances of psychogenic amnesia may result from faulty encoding of information at initial input and that deficits in retrieval may arise in consequence of this. In support of this view, it should be noted that psychogenic amnesia commonly occurs in states of abnormal mood or extreme arousal, in which normal cognitive processing might well be compromised. Fugues arise in the context of depressed mood and severe stress; amnesia for offences in situations of extreme emotional arousal, severe intoxication, or florid psychosis; and memory disorder in depression in association with impaired attention and motivation. This view, emphasising a disturbance in memory 'acquisition', suggests that the impairment in psychogenic amnesia mimics that in organic amnesia — of which there is so often an earlier history.

As an alternative to such problems of encoding, it is possible that, with HP, memory records were laid down, but the headings were structured in such a way that normal methods of memory search — i.e. the usual content of the descriptions in the theory expounded above — could not access these records (Morton, 1991). The latter case could be thought of as an extreme example of encoding specificity (Tulving & Thomson, 1973). One aspect of this encoding specificity may be state-dependency: memories encoded following the intense personal crisis, which always precedes the fugue episode, are impossible to retrieve when the subject has returned to a more normal and relaxed state. In addition, there may be a further retrieval component to the memory loss, as indicated in the discussion of post-hypnotic suggestion above. HP's description that it felt as if his memories were "locked away" in a box resembles the statements quoted by O'Connell (1960) from amnesic offenders and, indeed, from other fugue patients we have seen. Such statements suggest that some kind of memory record exists, however compromised, but, after evaluation in the interpreter buffer, is prevented from reaching conscious awareness in the manner postulated above in our account of post-hypnotic amnesia.

Those memories for the period of several months preceding the fugue which were initially lost returned in a progression from the more remote to the more recent, sometimes in response to cues and sometimes as associations to other memories or thoughts — as evident in HP's remark that "something will be seen, said or done, that will build with other things and bring (memories) back". This phenomenon is somewhat analogous to recovery from head injury. It is also subject to the same range of interpretation as the effects of post-hypnotic amnesia. In post-hypnotic amnesia and in the present instance, a resident entry in the task specification is postulated to the effect that certain information is not to be allowed into consciousness. In principle, there are two possible consequences of this.

1. A failure to create descriptions involving that information. In the case of HP, this would mean not formulating descriptions characteristic of the prohibited period in his life. As a result of this, there would be reduced access to the relevant records. In principle, however, it would still be possible in some cases to address the records by content rather than by period. Note that it would not be possible within the current Headed Records framework to directly inhibit *en bloc* all the records from the critical period. Retrieval inhibition has to occur through the descriptions.

2. There is retrieval of the relevant record, but nothing is let out of the interpreter buffer into consciousness. In this case, there might be affective consequences of the retrieval of emotional incidents, since the control of the processing by the task specification only extends to the propositional content of the information in the interpreter buffer.

While the original setting-up of the task description might have been deliberate, it is no more necessary within this framework to think of psychogenic amnesia in terms of conscious faking than it than it would be for the case of post-hypnotic amnesia.

It should be noted that most of us, at one time or another, try to forget something. Our success usually lies only in not thinking about the event in question. If we are reminded about it, however, we would recall it. HP, like other fugue cases, was very difficult to remind by deliberate (as opposed to incidental) cueing. Here, again, we find a similarity to people who have forgotten information under post-hypnotic instruction. There have been experiments in which subjects have viewed video recordings of hypnotic procedures involving themselves in an attempt to breach their amnesia: in these studies, approximately half of the highly hypnotisable subjects continue to show a degree of recognition failure even after viewing the videos (Coe & Sluis, 1989; McConkey & Sheehan, 1981). However, it is only the highly susceptible hypnotic subjects who exhibit this phenomenon. We have to consider what distinguishes HP and other fugue patients from other people who have gone through personal crises without developing amnesia. One factor may be the extreme emotion of the personal crisis, perhaps in combination with pre-existing depression, which resulted in the rule-like block on material of a particular kind passing from the interpreter buffer into conscious processing.

COMPARISON OF PSYCHOGENIC AMNESIA AND RECOVERED MEMORIES

In previous reviews of the literature, it has been suggested that fugue episodes occur following a severe and extreme precipitating stress, usually in the context of a depressed mood and often suicidal ideas, and there is frequently a past history of a transient organic amnesia (Kopelman, 1987, 1995, 1997). In HP's case, a marital crisis was the immediate precipitant to fugue, as in earlier examples (Abeles & Schilder, 1935; Kopelman et al., 1994a). HP was also extremely distressed and depressed by the marital separation, his wife's affair and, in particular, by the enforced separation from his children. Furthermore, he had had a past history of transient blackouts, lasting a few minutes, which were investigated at another hospital, and which might have been epileptic: a current EEG did show some abnormalities, which could have been consistent with this. A past history of transient organic memory loss may act as a 'learning experience' predisposing to the later development of fugue in times of crisis (Kopelman, 1987, 1995, 1997): this presumably works by resetting the threshold for change within the components (task specification, interpreter buffer, formation of descriptions) of the model sketched in Figure 11.1.

By analogy, child sexual abuse is certainly an extreme stress, and it is very commonly associated with various forms of affective disturbance both at the time (Browne & Hamilton, 1997) and subsequently (Mullen, Martin, Anderson, Romans & Herbison, 1993; Romans, Martin, Anderson, O'Shea & Mullen, 1995; Briere, 1997). Others have documented the evidence that highly emotional or traumatic experiences can enhance memory storage transiently but in a fragmented form, in which 'free floating' memory fragments are poorly located in temporal and spatial context: such memory fragments would be especially vulnerable both to forgetting and to distortions and augmentations such that, if memory were reinstated, it might be partial, incomplete, or contain inaccuracies (Shimamura, 1997). Somewhat similarly, Schacter (1996; Schacter, Norman & Koutstaal, 1997) has argued that, in some subjects, memories for abuse are never completely forgotten, but they are retained in a vague, unelaborated form, because they have seldom or never been rehearsed. Such memories would be vulnerable to the normal processes of decay and interference, as well as conscious avoidance or suppression. Appropriate cueing might result in re-retrieval of these memories, although the 'weak trace' might also make them vulnerable to distortion. The specific nature of memory recovery in such circumstances has been studied by Andrews et al. (2000).

As we have already pointed out, child sexual abuse is an extreme stress. We would also suppose that repeated abuse would create an increasing level of stress. In addition, it is supposed by some authors that high levels of stress early in life can lead to substantive changes in brain anatomy and physiology (Bremner, Krystal, Southwick & Charney, 1995; Stein, Koverola, Hanna, Torchia & McClarty, 1997). If this were accepted, we could point to these two similarities — stress and putative brain dysfunction — between the pre-conditions for memory loss in functional amnesia and in the recovered memory situation. At the moment, however, we have no firm evidence to link the nature or location of the brain dysfunction in the two cases.

Recovered memories and functional amnesia have in common that they often operate as much for recognition as for recall. This is established formally in the case of functional amnesics who sometimes even fail to recognise their wives and children. As far as we are aware, no experiments have been carried out on the recognition memory of people who are in the amnesic state prior to recovering memories of childhood sexual abuse. However, they subsequently report that, during the amnesia, they had not been reminded of the abuse in the presence of the alleged abuser or other cues.

Functional amnesia and RM amnesia have in common the extreme variability of the recovery process. Functional amnesia can be reversed by a single event. For example, in the case reported by Schacter et al. (1982), where the amnesia was caused by the death of a grandparent, the amnesia started to reverse after the patient saw a funeral scene on television. In other cases the amnesia seems to have reversed without there being any particular cue which triggered the reversal. Recovered memories show a similar variability. They have been reported as being triggered by single events, such as seeing a baby or a small child, but also have been reported as having emerged slowly, without any triggering event and without any suggestion from friend, family or therapist.

There are some differences between recovered memories and functional amnesia. For example, RM amnesia tends to be restricted to the abusive events and is not in general extended to other events of the same period (but see Parks & Balon, 1995). This lack of generalisation also occurs in amnesia for offences and in memory loss in PTSD, but in fugue states, subjects are amnesic for all aspects of a particular time period. A second example of differences between the two states is that functional amnesia, in the initial stages, tends to be extremely dense. RM amnesia is much more variable, some people recovering memories reporting a dense amnesia and others reporting that they always knew that a particular person had abused them but could not remember any details, or being able to recall some instances of abuse but not others (Andrews et al., 1999; Andrews et al., 2000).

FALSE MEMORIES

For an example of a false memory, we can quote from Gudjonsson (1997, p. 4):

> A typical case involves a well-educated female in her thirties who has attended therapy for some psychological problem, such as depression or an eating disorder. During therapy the patient reveals that she was sexually abused by her father many years previously, but the memory for the abuse was "repressed" until it was "recovered" during the therapy.

As far as we are aware, there are no cases of proven false memory which have arisen without the participation of some kind of therapist, support group or other influence. The closest one can get to this outside CSA is the area of false confessions. There are numerous documented examples of innocent persons confessing to crimes they could not have conceivably committed, sometimes accompanied by otherwise convincing detail (Gudjonsson, 1992; Gudjonsson, Kopelman & McKeith, 1999). Is there a parallel here with "false memories"? The answer seems to be if there is any parallel, it is a very imperfect one.

According to Gudjonsson (1992), many confessions are coerced — that is, the individuals are encouraged to make confessions through threats or inducements offered by the interrogator; they make a confession in order to try to escape from the situation they find themselves in. There is no suggestion that they actually believe themselves guilty of the crime to which they confess. Perhaps a closer parallel is the voluntary confession: suspects on occasion will come to believe that they must have committed a crime despite their initial denials. Such voluntary confessions are frequently the result of a long period of interrogation when accusations are repeatedly put to a suspect that he or she is guilty. There may also be a contribution from source memory deficits (the individual not knowing whether a "memory" has been generated by what he has read or been told), and people who are depressed or have low self-esteem seem to be excited by the sense of importance an interrogation gives them and are particularly vulnerable to making false confessions (Gudjonsson, 1992; Gudjonsson et al., 1999). Such individuals may confess under the belief that they must have been responsible, even though they were unaware of the event.[2]

However, even with voluntary confessions the analogy with "false memory" is very inexact. Both groups will show belief in their stories and display often quite convincing details. Both may arise from prolonged interviewing in which certain themes are repeated over and over again. Moreover, false confessions are often abandoned in the face of contradictory evidence — Carole Richardson rapidly came to the conclusion that the events she had described could not have happened — or may be held for longer but with fluctuating levels of conviction (Gudjonsson et al., 1999) whereas "false memories" are persistent and, with the exception of a few "retractors", survive repeated denials by others of the reality of the events victims describe.

RECOVERED MEMORIES

The accounts that are available in the literature for the amnesia and subsequent recovery of memories are limited by the theoretical frameworks employed. Two terms predominate: "dissociation" and "repression". However, there is no consistent usage in the literature of the two terms and, indeed, some authors regard them as interchangeable (e.g. Erdelyi, 1990). The reason for this confusion is that the retrieval of a memory

---

[2] An example, of this was Carole Richardson's 'confession' of involvement in the Guildford bombings where she eventually concluded she must have been present but so far under the influence of drink and drugs as not to recollect the event clearly. Another case was AE who spent 25 years in prison following a false confession, triggered in part by inappropriate use of sodium amytal as " truth drug" (Gudjonsson et al., 1999).

record is conceptualised as a unitary process with just two states: either you retrieve or you do not retrieve. As an example of authors who do make a distinction between two terms, we can quote from Brewin and Andrews (1998, p. 965):

> *Ordinarily, autobiographical memories are more or less accessible to being retrieved into "working memory", a short-term, limited-capacity store in which memories can be readily rehearsed and edited. A memory that has been repressed may be thought of as being subject to active inhibitory processes that work to prevent it from entering working memory ... In contrast, retrieval of a dissociated memory will reflect the mental state present at encoding and the fact that there has been little integration of the traumatic experience with ordinary autobiographical memory. Dissociated states, whether consisting of flash backs, depersonalisation, de-realisation, out-of-body experiences, absences, or more complex alternative personality states, may be conceptualised as modular, informationally encapsulated processes that are spontaneously triggered by internal or external stimuli. Retrieval is therefore likely to be accompanied by changes in consciousness that disrupt working memory and will not guarantee the possibility of interaction with the rest of the autobiographical memory system. In these respects the retrieval of dissociated memory has many of the characteristics of an informationally encapsulated, modular process being run off.*

We are largely in agreement with these authors in the way they distinguish between repression and dissociation. Within the Headed Records framework we would want to elaborate their account along the lines that we have already used in offering different possible accounts of functional amnesia. We would first want to specify how the "active inhibitory processes" might be implemented. For us, the inhibitory processes would operate through the task specification (see Figure 11.1). This is a list of instructions or goals which controls the operation of the interpreter. The interpreter is the set of computational processes which operate on the contents of the interpreter buffer. There are two ways in which the task specification can produce effects which could be characterised by the term *repression*. The first of these would involve restricting the search process. In the introduction to this chapter we outlined how in the Headed Records framework, following Norman and Bobrow (1979), the process of searching for an autobiographical memory record starts with the creation of a "description". The description is the material, that is used during the search process and, for retrieval to be successful, the description must match, to some criterion, the heading of the relevant record. The heading includes information concerning time, place, mood, and the protagonists.

It would be possible, then, for the task specification to include instructions to the effect that the description should not include kinds of information which characterised headings of a particular set of memories. These restrictions would apply equally to both deliberate and automatic memory retrieval and mean that the particular set of memories would never be addressed and, therefore, could not be retrieved.

The second way in which the task specification can have the effect of repression depends upon our characterisation of the interpreter buffer. As we have already pointed out, in most other theories, all autobiographical material which has been retrieved is available for conscious processing. Within the framework we are presenting this is not the case, and whether or not particular material within the interpreter buffer is allowed into consciousness is under the control of the interpreter. In turn, the interpreter follows the instructions laid down in the task specification.[3] We have already discussed post-hypnotic amnesia in these terms, proposing that the effect of the hypnotic suggestion that a particular episode should be forgotten is to lay down a task specification such that no information relevant to that particular episode is allowed through to consciousness. One possible account of HP is similar. It requires no extra theoretical apparatus to extend the principle to autobiographical memories of childhood sexual abuse.

The account we give of dissociation is very different and is, more or less, an implementation, within the Headed Records framework, of the account given by Brewin and Andrews. Of course, this account may not be the equivalent of what some authors mean when they use the term *dissociation* but, as we have already remarked, there is no universal agreement about the use of these terms. What makes sense for us is to contrast dissociation and repression. Dissociation, then, is a problem of addressing which is not a function of the operation of the interpreter and task specification. Rather, we would use the term to refer to the operation of perfectly normal context sensitive processes. We have already outlined how recall is sensitive to location, mood and other contextual variables. The operation of dissociation within childhood sexual abuse would be similar. During the abusive episodes, the specificity of location, protagonist and, especially, the emotions engendered by the abuse, would constitute a unique context for the memory record. Within the framework we

---

[3] Note that we are not trying to *explain* consciousness in terms of the interpreter. Our use of the interpreter and the task specification is a step we take on the road to de-mystifying consciousness. We believe that whether or not autobiographical material is available to consciousness is sometimes subject to control processes. In time we will have to both specify these control processes in more detail, and propose an anatomical substrate. In Figure 11.1, the boxes labelled Task specification and Interpreter are place markers for these future steps.

use, this context would be within the heading, though this is merely the way we implement a universally accepted principle of autobiographical memory retrieval.

We should note, in passing, a further possibility in relation to memory records of traumatic experience. This is the idea that, in traumatic circumstances, encoding is impaired. This could mean that only certain details (perhaps idiosyncratic) might be encoded, or that the record of the event might be fragmented, with the component parts (such as sight, sound and smell) being disconnected. The result of this would be that the memory record, even if it were accessed, would be impoverished or even uninterpretable. If the encoding impoverishment were extended to the heading, the result may be that the record would remain inaccessible in any circumstances.

The usual account of false memories is that memory records are laid down including information from outside sources together with some information from previous autobiographical records. These outside sources could include other people's experiences or the suggestions of an authority figure such as a therapist who has a particularly strong theory about the origins of an ongoing problem such as depression or eating disorder. If this record is going to be retrieved and interpreted as though it were a true autobiographical record, then it is essential that the original source information be missing. In the absence of any detailed theory concerning the nature of source information it would not seem profitable to speculate on this further. However, loss of source information in everyday memory seems to be sufficiently common for it to be an acceptable explanatory principle in the case of false memories.

The equivalent to this in the case of functional memory loss is paradoxical. Some people with functional amnesia claim not to remember their wives or children. However, they (usually) accept the personal histories that are given to them even though they have no initial feeling of familiarity with these histories. A closer analogy might be with confabulation states, where patients either fabricate or incorporate from outside whole events which they then accept as true autobiographical records (Burgess & Shallice, 1996).

In summary, we have shown that psychological forms of memory loss, as occur in fugue episodes, can be accounted for within psychological theories such as Headed Records. While we cannot say whether any particular case of "recovered memory" for child sexual abuse is true, partially accurate, distorted, or false, the same psychological mechanisms can be postulated to account for these phenomena as we have discussed in considering our case of "fugue". No special theory within mainstream cognitive psychology is required to account for 'functional memory loss' or for subsequent re-retrieval.

REFERENCES

Abeles, M. & Schilder, P. (1935). Psychogenic loss of personal identity. *Archives of Neurology and Psychiatry*, **34**, 587–604.

Abeles, P. & Morton, J. (1999). Avoiding misinformation: reinstating target modality. The *Quarterly Journal of Experimental Psychology*, **52a**, 581–592.

Andrews, B., Brewin, C. R., Ochera, J., Morton, J., Bekerian, D. A., Davies, G. M. & Mollon, P. (1999). Characteristics, context and consequences of memory recovery among adults in therapy. *British Journal of Psychiatry*, **174**, 141–146.

Andrews, B., Brewin, C. R., Ochera, J., Morton, J., Bekerian, D. A., Davies, G. M. & Mollon, P. (2000). The timing, triggers and qualities of recovered memories in therapy. *British Journal of Clinical Psychology*, **39**, 11–26.

Baddeley, A., Emslie, H. & Nimmo-Smith, I. (1994). *Doors and People: A Test of Visual and Verbal Recall and Recognition*. Bury St Edmunds: Thames Valley Test Co.,

Baddeley, A. D. & Wilson, B. (1986). Amnesia, autobiographical memory, and confabulation. In D. C. Rubin (Ed.), *Autobiographical Memory*. Cambridge: Cambridge University Press.

Barreau, S. & Morton, J. (in press). Recalling one's own past beliefs: Headed Records applied to children. *Cognition*.

Beck, A. T. & Steer, R. A. (1993). *Beck Anxiety Inventory*. St Antonia: The Psychological Corporation: Harcourt, Brace & Co:.

Bertrand, L. D., Spanos, N. P. & Radtke, L. H. (1990). Contextual effects on priming during hypnotic amnesia. *Journal of Research in Personality*, **24**, 271–290.

Bower, G. H. (1981). Mood and memory. *American Psychologist*, **36**, 129–138.

Bremner, J. D., Krystal, J. H., Southwick S. M. & Charney, D.S. (1995). Functional neuroanatomical correlates of the effects of stress on memory. *Journal of Traumatic Stress*, **8**, 527–553.

Brewin, C. R. & Andrews, B. (1998). Recovered memories of trauma: phenomenology and cognitive mechanisms. *Clinical Psychology Review*, **18**, 949–970.

Briere, J. (1997). In integrated approach to treating adults abused as children with specific reference to self-reported recovered memories. In. J. D. Read & D. S. Lindsay (Eds), *Recollections of Trauma: Scientific Research and Clinical Practice* (pp. 25–41). New York and London: Plenum Press.

Browne, K. D. & Hamilton, C. E. (1997). The repeat and revictimisation of children: possible influences on recollections for trauma. In. J. D. Read & D. S. Lindsay (Eds), *Recollections of Trauma: Scientific Research and Clinical Practice* (pp. 425–433). New York and London: Plenum Press.

Burgess, P. W. & Shallice, T. (1996). Confabulation and the control of recollection. *Memory*, **4**, 359–411.

Campodonico, J. R. & Rediess, S. (1996). Dissociation of implicit and explicit knowledge in a case of psychogenic retrograde amnesia. *Journal of the International Neuropsychological Society*, **2**, 146–158.

Coe, K. M. & Sluis, A. S. E. (1989). Increasing contextual pressure to breach posthypnotic amnesia. *Journal of Personality and Social Psychology*, **57**, 885–894.

Coriat, I. H. (1907). The Lowell case of amnesia. *Journal of Abnormal Psychology*, **2**, 93–111.

Costello, A., Fletcher, P. C., Dolan, R. J., Frith, C. D. & Shallice, T. (1998). The origins of forgetting in a case of isolated retrograde amnesia following a haemorrhage: Evidence from functional imaging. *Neurocase*, **4**, 437–446.

Crovitz, H. F. & Schiffman, H. (1974). Frequency of episodic memories as a function of their age. *Bulletin of the Psychonomics Society*, **4**, 517–518.

De Renzi, E., Lucchelli, F., Muggia, S. & Spinnler, H. (1995). Persistent retrograde amnesia following a minor trauma. *Cortex*, **31**, 531–542.

Eich, J. E. (1980). The cue-dependent nature of state-dependent retrieval. *Memory and Cognition*, **8**, 157–173.

Erdelyi, M. H. (1990). Repression, reconstruction, and defense: History and integration of the psychoanalytic and experimental frameworks. In J. L. Singer (Ed.), *Repression and Dissociation*. Chicago: University of Chicago Press.

Godden, D. R. & Baddeley, A. D. (1975). Context-dependent memory in two natural environments: On land and underwater. *British Journal of Psychology*, **66**, 325–331.

Godden, D. R. & Baddeley, A. D. (1980). When does context influence recognition memory? *British Journal of Psychology*, **71**, 99–104.

Goodwin, D. W., Powell, B., Bremer, D., Hoine, H. & Stern, J. (1969). Alcohol and recall: State dependent effects in man. *Science*, **163**, 1358.

Gudjonsson, G. H. (1992). *The Psychology of Interrogations, Confessions and Testimony*. Chichester: Wiley

Gudjonsson, G. H. (1997). Accusations by adults of childhood sexual abuse: A survey of the Members of the British False Memory Society (BFMS). *Applied Cognitive Psychology*, **11**, 3–18.

Gudjonsson, G. H., Kopelman, M. D. & MacKeith, J. A. C. (1999). Unreliable admissions to homicide: A case of misdiagnosis of amnesia and misuse of abreaction. *British Journal of Psychiatry*, **174**, 455–459.

Gudjonsson, G. H. & Taylor, P. J. (1985). Cognitive deficit in a case of retrograde amnesia. *British Journal of Psychiatry*, **147**, 715–718.

Hilgard, E. R. (1977). *Divided Consciousness: Multiple Controls in Human Thought and Action*. New York: Wiley.

Kanzer, M. (1939). Amnesia: A statistical study. *American Journal of Psychiatry*, **96**, 711–716.

Kapur, N. (1994). The coin-in-the-hand test: A new "bed-side" test for the detection of malingering in patients with suspected memory disorder [letter]. *Journal of Neurology, Neurosurgery and Psychiatry*, **57**, 385–386.

Kapur, N. (unpublished). Modified Rey test. Presented at the Memory Disorders Video workshop, Friday 30 August 1996.

Kihlstrom, J. F. (1978). Context and cognition in posthypnotic amnesia. *International Journal of Clinical and Experimental Hypnosis*, **26**, 246–267.

Kopelman, M. D. (1987). Amnesia: Organic and psychogenic. *British Journal of Psychiatry*, **150**, 428–442.

Kopelman, M. D. (1995). The assessment of psychogenic amnesia. In A. Baddeley, B. Wilson, & F. Watts (Eds), *Handbook of Memory Disorders* (pp. 427–448). Chichester: Wiley.

Kopelman, M. D. (1997). Anomalies of autobiographical memory: Retrograde amnesia, confabulation, delusional memory, psychogenic amnesia, and false memories. In J. D. Read & D. S. Lindsay (Eds), *Recollections of Trauma: Scientific Research and Clinical Practice* (pp. 273–297). New York and London: Plenum Press.

Kopelman, M. D., Christensen, H., Puffett, A. & Stanhope, N. (1994a). The Great Escape: A neuropsychological study of psychogenic amnesia. *Neuropsychologia*, **32**, 675–691.

Kopelman, M. D., Green, R. E. A., Guinan, E. M., Lewis, P. D. R. & Stanhope, N. (1994b). The case of the amnesic intelligence officer. *Psychological Medicine*, **24**, 1037–1045.

Kopelman, M. D., Stanhope, N. & Kingsley, D. (1999). Retrograde amnesia in patients with diencephalic temporal lobe or frontal lesions. *Neuropsychologia*, 37, 939–958.

Kopelman, M. D., Wilson, B. A. B., Baddeley, A. D. (1990). *The Autobiographical Memory Interview*. Bury St Edumunds: Thames Valley Test Company.

Kritchevsky, M., Zouzounis, J. & Squire, L. R. (1997). Transient global amnesia and functional retrograde amnesia: Contrasting examples of episodic memory loss. *Philosophical Transactions of the Royal Society of London B*, **352**, 1747–1754.

Lloyd, G. C. & Lishman, W. A. (1975). Effect of depression on the speed of recall of pleasant and unpleasant experience. *Psychological Medicine*, **5**, 173–180.

Markowitsch, H. J., Fink, G. R., Thöne, A., Kessler, J. & Heiss, W-D. (1997). A PET study of persistent psychogenic amnesia covering the whole life span. *Cognitive Neuropsychiatry*, **2**, 135–158.

McConkey, K. M. & Sheehan, P. W. (1981). The impact of videotape playback of hypnotic events on posthypnotic amnesia. *Journal of Abnormal Psychology*, **90**, 46–54.

Morton, J. (1990). The development of event memory. *The Psychologist*, **3**, 3–10.

Morton, J. (1991). Cognitive pathologies of memory: a headed records analysis. In W. Kessen, A. Ortony & F. Craik (Eds), *Memories, Thoughts and Emotions: Essays in Honor of George Mandler* (pp. 199–210). New Jersey: Erlbaum.

Morton, J. & Bekerian, D. A. (1986). Three ways of looking at memory. *Advances in Cognitive Sciences I* (pp.43–71). Chichester: Ellis Horwood.

Morton, J., Hammersley, R. H. & Bekerian, D. A. (1985). Headed Records: A model for memory and its failures. *Cognition*, **20**, 1–23.

Mullen, P. E., Martin, J. L., Anderson, J. C., Romans, S. E. & Herbison, G. P. (1993). Childhood sexual abuse and mental health in adult life. *British Journal of Psychiatry*, **163**, 721–732.

Nelson, H. & Willison, J. (1991). *The National Adult Reading Test* (2nd edition). Windsor: NFER-Nelson.

Newcombe, P. A. & Siegal, M. (1996). Where to look first for suggestibility in young children. *Cognition*, **59**, 337–356.

Norman, D. A. & Bobrow, D. G. (1979). Descriptions: An intermediate stage in memory retrieval. *Cognitive Psychology*, **11**, 107–123.

O'Connell, B. A. (1960). Amnesia and homicide. *British Journal of Delinquency*, **10**, 262–276.

Parks, E. D. & Balon, R. (1995). Autobiographical memory for childhood events: Patterns of recall in psychiatric patients with a history of alleged trauma. *Psychiatry*, **58**, 199–208.

Romans, S. E., Martin, J. L., Anderson, J. C., O'Shea, M. L. & Mullen, P. E. (1995). Factors that mediate between child sexual abuse and adult psychological outcome. *Psychological Medicine*, **25**, 127–142.

Schacter, D. L. (1996). *Searching for Memory: the Brain, the Mind and the Past*. New York: Harper Collins.

Schacter, D. L., Norman, K. A. & Koutstaal, W. (1997). The recovered memories debate: A cognitive neuroscience perspective. In M. A. Conway (Ed.), *Recovered Memories and False Memories*. New York: Oxford University Press, Inc.

Schacter, D. L., Wang, P. L., Tulving, E. & Freedman, M. (1982). Functional retrograde amnesia: A quantitative case study. *Neuropsychologia*, **20**, 523–532.

Shimamura, A. P. (1997). Neuropsychological factors associated with memory recollection: What can science tell us about reinstated memories? In J. D. Read, & D. S. Lindsay (Eds), *Recollections of Trauma: Scientific Research and Clinical Practice*. New York and London: Plenum Press.

Smith, C. H., Morton, J. & Oakley, D. (2001). An investigation of the state-dependency of recall following a hypnotic amnesia suggestion. *Manuscript submitted for publication.*

Spanos, N. P., Radtke, L. H. & Dubreuil, D. L. (1982). Episodic and semantic memory in posthypnotic amnesia: A reevaluation. *Journal of Personality and Social Psychology,* **43**, 565–573.

Stein, M. B., Koverola, C, Hanna, C., Torchia, M. G. & McClarty, B. (1997). Hippocampal volume in women victimized by childhood sexual abuse. *Psychological Medicine,* **27**, 951–959.

Stracciari, A., Ghidoni, E., Guarino, M., Poletti, M. & Pazzaglia, P. (1994). Post-traumatic retrograde amnesia with selective impairment of autobiographic memory. *Cortex,* **30**, 459–468.

Teasdale, J. D. (1983). Affect and accessibility. *Philosophical Transactions of the Royal Society of London B,* **302**, 403–412.

Teasdale, J. D. & Fogarty S. J. (1979). Differential effects of induced mood on retrieval of pleasant and unpleasant events from episodic memory. *Journal of Abnormal Psychology,* **88**, 248–257.

Tulving, E. (1983). Ecphoric processes in episodic memory. *Philosophical Transactions of the Royal Society of London B,* **302**, 361–371.

Tulving, E. & Thomson, D. M. (1973). Encoding specificity and retrieval processes in episodic memory. *Psychological Review,* **80**, 353–373.

Warrington, E. K. (1984). *The Recognition Memory Test.* Windsor: NFER-Nelson.

Wechsler, D. (1981). *Wechsler Adult Intelligence Scale — Revised.* London and New York: Psychological Corporation.

Wechsler, D. (1987). *Logical Memory Test.* New York: The Psychological Corporation; Harcourt, Brace, Jovanovitch, Inc.

Wilkinson, J. (1998a). Context effects in children's memory. In: M. M. Gruneberg, P. E. Morris & R. N. Sykes (Eds), *Practical Aspects of Memory Current Research and Issues: Volume I* (pp. 107–111). Chichester: Wiley.

Wilkinson, J. (1998b). *Preschoolers Event Memory: Methods for Facilitating Recall.* PhD Thesis, University College, London.

Williams, M. D. & Hollan, J. D. (1981). The process of retrieval from very long term memory. *Cognitive Science,* **5**, 87–119.

PART IV

CONCLUDING COMMENTS

12

MEMORIES OF ABUSE AND ALIEN ABDUCTION: CLOSE ENCOUNTERS OF THE THERAPEUTIC KIND

M. J. Power

> Those who remember the past are masters of the future.
> CHINESE PROVERB

INTRODUCTION

One of the perhaps more intriguing aspects of the whole literature on false memory has to be the reports of alien abduction. If these increasing numbers of claims are to be believed, then it is estimated that several thousand Americans are *each day* taken aboard fleets of spaceships hovering somewhere over the mid-West of the USA where lengthy medical examinations are carried out by groups of intergalactic physicians. The abducted individuals are then returned back to their humdrum lives and only manage to recall these abduction episodes using memory recovery techniques such as hypnosis. In their studies of these phenomena, Newman and Baumeister (1998) observed that about 80% of abductions occur in the USA, with virtually none being reported in Asia and Africa. (It is possible to be facetious at this point and ask why would *intelligent* life forms from

Recovered Memories: Seeking the Middle Ground. Edited by Graham M. Davies and Tim Dalgleish. © 2001 John Wiley & Sons Ltd.

other planets only be interested in middle-aged guys in campervans in some unknown part of the US mid-West?) Newman and Baumeister have also noted an increasing trend towards reported sexual interference from the alien abductors. If we can assume that there is no such fleet of extraterrestrial, NASA, or Hollywood spacecraft, these reports of alien abduction are surely proof that individuals can recover "memories" of events that have never occurred. They are proof that suggestible individuals, when placed under the influence of credible experts such as therapists, are vulnerable to the recovery of false memories. The question of false memory becomes, therefore, not *whether* but *how* and *when*.

The other side of the argument about false memory is whether or not a memory can be forgotten for a long period of time and then subsequently recovered. In contrast to the case of alien abduction (for which, at least as yet, I can offer no personal recollections), the following example is of a personal memory of an event that occurred when I was 8 years old and which I did not recall until 38 years later at the age of 46:

My family had recently moved to the city of Birmingham and my mother, my sister, and I had gone to visit some relatives some distance away by bus. As we returned that night, a very heavy fog descended, so that when we got off the bus we became completely disoriented. We were lost in an open park area and unable to find our way out. We were lost for some considerable time wandering around in this cold and anxious state before we spotted some lights from a building and were then able to go and ask for directions.

The trigger or cue that led to this recollection was seeing a TV programme listed in a newspaper about a famous London fog of 1952 in which many thousands of individuals died. The newspaper summary of the TV programme led to the complete recovery of the memory, together with a sense of certainty that I had not recollected this memory previously. In addition, the memory recovery was accompanied by a re-experiencing of the considerable anxiety with which the original experience had been associated. The memory has now been corroborated by my mother who was present at the event, but obviously the additional recollection that this memory has never previously been remembered can only be trusted to my belief that this is the case. The fact is, and this could be put to an empirical test, that most individuals probably have long-forgotten memories that, once cued, they would estimate not to have recalled for some considerable time. So why, therefore, is there such a debate about this issue? The question is whether or not *traumatic* events (i.e. events that would be judged by most as difficult if not impossible to forget because of their nature) can in fact be forgotten. In addition, the question is whether special intrapsychic mechanisms such as "repression" need to be mooted to account for such forgetting or whether such forgetting can be accounted for by the characteristics of remembering and forgetting about which everyone would agree.

In the remainder of this chapter, therefore, a framework will be presented in which the many extreme views that have been presented on the recovered memory debate can be drawn together. In doing so, the many excellent earlier chapters in this volume will be drawn upon heavily together with a sprinkling of material from elsewhere.

A FRAMEWORK FOR EXAMINING RECOVERED MEMORY

The preliminary framework for examining the issues around recovered memories is presented in Table 12.1. This table is adapted from one in which we have previously considered some of the conditions under which individuals' accuracy on judgement and reasoning tasks varies

Table 12.1:   Four categories of the status of "Memories" generated by a consideration of Truth Value (True or False) and Memory Status (Remembered or Forgotten/Subsequently Recovered).

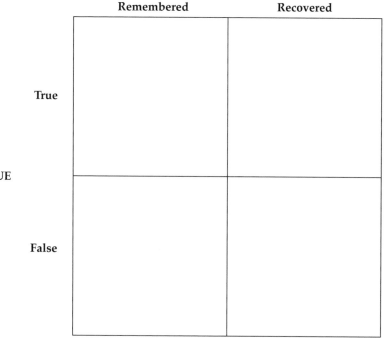

according to the truth value of the information (i.e. True or False), the valence of the information (i.e. Positive or Negative) and the mood state of the individual (e.g. Normal or Depressed) (see Power, 1991; Power & Dalgleish, 1997; cf. Nash, 1998). On reasoning and judgement tasks there is evidence that depressed individuals may be more accurate in accepting True Negatives and rejecting False Positives, whereas normal non-depressed individuals may be more accurate at rejecting False Negatives and accepting True Positives. The application of this framework to recovered memory as shown in Table 12.1 suggests that each of the equivalent four categories needs to be considered, that is, True Remembered, True Recovered, False Remembered, and False Recovered. By summarising information about each of these four categories, useful illustrations can be provided about the operation of memory under different conditions.

1. *True Remembered memories*

This is the majority category that most people associate with memory. Memory is widely assumed to be an accurate and veridical process, a longstanding tradition that included Freud among its proponents (e.g. Freud, 1900). Perhaps Freud's influence may be one reason why Loftus and Loftus (1980) obtained the astonishing finding that over 80% of therapists when surveyed stated that they believed all memories to be permanently recorded in the brain.

The tradition in memory research that stems from the work of Bartlett (1932) presents a contrasting view of the process of memory. Bartlett studied memory for complex prose passages such as the famous "War of the Ghosts" story over extended periods of time, even to the extent of reputedly jumping off his bicycle in the middle of Cambridge years after the initial study and asking former participants to recall the text. Memory research in this tradition has demonstrated that memory can be surprisingly accurate over long periods of time, but in addition the process of retrieval is often a *reconstructive process* rather than simple retrieval. Such a process is evident in Morton's Headed Records model (see Kopelman & Morton, Chapter 11) in which a series of retrieval "Descriptions" may be used in attempts to retrieve appropriate records related to an event.

In this context of discussing True Memories, it is worthwhile flagging up some of the distinctions that have been made between different types of memory and examining the issue of Truth Value in relation to them. For example, Magner and Parkinson (see Chapter 4) refer to the useful distinction between semantic memory, procedural memory, and autobiographical memory. Semantic memory is the long-term memory for knowledge, properties of language, and so on. Although it is normally thought of as true or accurate, general knowledge is verifiable and therefore can easily be shown to be false. For example, a belief that Sydney is the capital of Australia, that the Earth is flat, or that all birds can fly, are all patently false but any one of them could be held with conviction.

Procedural memory is the memory involved in *knowing how* and is best seen in the learning of skilled actions. Again, it may initially seem odd to categorise procedural memory as True or False, but individuals frequently learn incorrect sequences of action that then have to be re-learned, or sequences of action that have to be changed because they are no longer applicable. The moral is that, even for semantic and procedural types of memory, it is necessary to distinguish between True and False memories; our memories for facts and procedures can simply be wrong.

The third category in this grouping is of autobiographical memory. In contrast to semantic and procedural memory there is often no external test possible of the Truth Value of such memories, and even apparent corroboration by others can, depending on the context, sometimes be doubted. Although individuals rarely doubt their own autobiographical memories because of the vividness and persuasiveness with which they can be recollected, there are famous documented cases in which supposedly accurate recollections have subsequently been disproved (see below). Even in the case of so-called "flashbulb" memories (Brown & Kulik, 1977), in which dramatic events are meant to be specially encoded, there is now evidence that these memories are also not necessarily accurate despite being reported with great conviction by the individual (e.g. Neisser & Harsch, 1992). One experimental analogue of such effects has been found in the "eyewitness testimony" work of Elizabeth Loftus and others (e.g. Loftus & Zanni, 1975), in which misleading post-event questioning can lead to the incorporation of false information into the memory for the event, again a finding that will be further discussed below. The point to remember in relation to theoretical models of autobiographical memory such as the recent proposal by Conway and Pleydell-Pearce (2000), is that autobiographical memories are viewed as reconstructions that draw on knowledge structures but which also incorporate other current aspects of the self such as goals and mood state.

One final distinction that must be made in this section that is of particular relevance to autobiographical memory is a distinction that roughly covers types of memory referred to as implicit memory, classical conditioning, conditioned emotional responses, and so on (see, e.g., Ohman, 1999; and Chapter 8 by Bekerian and O'Neill). The following example from a patient of mine provides a clinical illustration of this category.

Bill was initially referred with problems in social situations, which he avoided, especially if there was a risk of having to eat or drink, because of a fear of choking. He had had this fear as long as he could recall, but had no idea of when or how it had started. After some time in therapy however he found out from his mother that at about the age of 3 he had eaten poisonous berries from his garden and had been rushed to hospital where he had been stomach-pumped. The original experience of having the stomach pump inserted then returned as a memory, but the fear of choking had been with him from that early experience on.

Now it might be arguable that this example is of a recovered memory of an early traumatic experience. However, it is included here because the conditioned reaction was never forgotten but continued to affect the patient's life even though the original traumatic event itself was forgotten. That is, the continued effect of the trauma showed that the experience was not inhibited at an automatic level, but continued to exert an influence over Bill for many years. Later in the chapter we will briefly consider the types of model that would be needed to account for this complexity of effects in memory and emotion.

2. True Recovered memories

The category that we have labelled "True Recovered" memories refers to memories that, although present in some form or other, may remain inaccessible for long periods of time. This category is of course one of the most controversial of the four categories and is one on which (some) clinicians and experimentalists have been sharply divided (see Chapter 1 by Dalgleish & Morant; Chapter 3 by Skinner; Chapter 5 by Lindsay & Read; and Chapter 6 by Shobe & Schooler).

There is one sense in which the category is completely non-controversial and in which the failure to recall the memory simply refers to *passive inhibitory* processes (Power & Dalgleish, 1997). In relation to memory, such passive inhibitory processes refer to normal processes related to memory and forgetting, such as trace decay, interference, retrieval failures, and so on. In the personal example presented earlier of being lost in the fog, therefore, there would be no need to propose anything other than normal processes to explain the absence of recall over a long period of time; it was simply a memory awaiting the appropriate trigger or context-related cues that, when they finally arrived, led to the recovery of the original memory. The problem with such long-lost autobiographical memories, as Davies summarises (see Chapter 7), is how might it be possible to distinguish true from false autobiographical memories. This section will be considered in more detail in the next sections on false memories.

The controversial version of the category of True Recovered memories refers of course to the possibility of *active inhibitory* processes in memory. The best-known claims draw on Freud's (e.g. 1915) proposals for repression and infantile amnesia, but other dramatic examples relate to Janet's (e.g. 1889) accounts of *dissociative* rather than repressed states, seen for example in psychogenic amnesia and fugue states (see Kopelman & Morton, Chapter 11). The reaction to Freud's proposal for repressed memories have included extreme responses such as Holmes's (1990) outright rejection of the possibility on the grounds that repression has never been demonstrated in the laboratory. Fortunately, psychology is, for ethical reasons, limited in what can be done to subjects in laboratories and, just as in the case of neurological disorders, brain injury, etc. it is essential to draw on single case studies that reflect "experiments of nature". More recent longitudinal studies of children who have experienced childhood sexual abuse (e.g. Widom, 1997; Williams, 1995) have provided support for the possibility of repressed memories of sexual abuse. For example, Williams (1995) reported that from a group of children whose abuse had been corroborated a substantial proportion did not report the abuse when followed up many years later. In addition, there have now been demonstrations that a proportion of individuals possess a so-called repressive coping style (operationally defined as high scores on social desirability and low self-reported levels of anxiety; see, e.g., Weinberger, Schwartz & Davidson, 1979). These individuals have been shown to have poor recall of early negative memories (Myers & Brewin, 1994) together with poor recall of negative items on the Directed Forgetting Task (Myers, Brewin & Power, 1998).

The Directed Forgetting Task (e.g. Bjork, 1989) may in fact provide a useful experimental analogue for the type of active inhibitory processes that are key to this category of memory and, thereby, address some of the concerns raised by Holmes (1990) in his rejection of repression as a useful concept. In this task, the subject is typically presented with a list of words to be learned, but half-way through is informed that the words so far have been for practice only and should therefore be forgotten. However, after the presentation of the second half items, the subject is asked to recall *all* of the items presented, including those in the to-be-forgotten (TBF) list. In his summary published in 1989, Bjork summarised studies that showed that the most likely explanation for the fate of the TBF items was that they were actively inhibited and therefore retrieval failure occurred although the items were endorsed correctly on a recognition test. As stated above, we have shown that this effect is especially strong for individuals with a repressive coping style who "forget" more of the TBF negative items (Myers et al., 1998). We have also shown that currently depressed individuals show the opposite pattern and recall *more* of the TBF negative than positive items, a finding that suggests an active facilitatory rather than inhibitory process operating with negative material in depression (Power, Dalgleish, Claudio, Tata & Kentish, 2000).

One comment that must be made about the Directed Forgetting Task is that it might not simply be a clever laboratory demonstration of active inhibitory processes in memory, but it could also provide a possible mechanism for the "forgetting" of childhood sexual abuse. Shobe and Schooler (Chapter 6) point out that *self*-directed forgetting may occur for painful experiences, but it is also well known from studies of the survivors of sexual abuse that the perpetrators frequently attempt to persuade their child victims either to keep their "special secret" or threaten them in order to prevent them talking to anyone else. In other words, perpetrators often instruct their victims to forget their abuse experiences. Such instructions are therefore powerful naturalistic examples of the Directed Forgetting effect which would explain how the memory is actively inhibited but later triggered following the presentation of strong context-related cues. This possibility has largely gone unremarked, but certainly warrants further exploration.

A second comment concerns a related type of forgetting that of so-called *retrieval-induced forgetting* (e.g. Anderson & Spellman, 1995; Macrae & MacLeod, 1999). Whereas directed forgetting is often explicit and intentional, retrieval-induced forgetting is typically automatic and unintentional. The phenomenon refers to the fact that the retrieval of practised items can lead to the inhibition of unpractised but related items. In terms of the perception of self and others, therefore, Macrae and MacLeod (1999) have demonstrated that recall of practised trait adjectives about one individual may lead to the inhibition of unpractised trait adjectives about the same individual. In relation to abuse, therefore, the possibility would be that the victim's recollection of positive information about an abuser such as a parent might lead to the automatic inhibition of abuse-related negative information about the same individual. This possibility does of course await further laboratory and clinical testing, but the paradigm highlights the role of automatic inhibitory processes in everyday memory and cognition.

Finally in this section mention must be made of state dependent learning, the importance of which was highlighted in Chapter 11 by Kopelman and Morton. The classic example of this effect is that of the alcoholic who can only remember where the drink is hidden when drunk. Despite the concept having a somewhat chequered history (e.g. Bower, 1992), its relevance for the forgetting and remembering of events is of paramount importance. Perhaps the most dramatic contrasts between conscious states occur in the switches between different emotions; thus, there is clear evidence of mood state dependent effects on learning and recall (e.g. Dalgleish & Watts, 1990). The relevance to the "forgetting" of memories of abuse is clear in that very powerful emotional states are characteristic of such abuse, including extreme dissociative experiences in the more severe cases (e.g. Lynn & Rhue, 1994). One of the characteristics of abnormal emotional development is that one or more basic emotions may not be integrated as part of the developing self (Power & Dalgleish, 1997). The exclusion of certain emotions can occur for a variety of intrapsychic, interpersonal, and cultural reasons (e.g. men in Western cultures not traditionally being supposed to experience or express "weak" emotions such as fear and sadness), but we have proposed that stronger state dependent effects should be found where such excluded or modularised emotions have developed.

In summary, therefore, there are a number of potential mechanisms by which memories may apparently be forgotten over long periods of time, mechanisms that operate through active inhibitory processes. The mechanisms involved in directed forgetting, repression, dissociation and mood-state dependent effects demonstrate, both in the clinic and in the laboratory, that such active inhibitory processes occur. They do not, however, guarantee that any such memory that has been forgotten and then remembered is necessarily true, as will be shown in the next two sections.

3. False Remembered memories

One of the early examples of this category is probably represented in Freud's (1899) proposal for the existence of "screen memories". Freud argued that these memories were invariably wrong, at least if not in their entirety, in some of the detail. He proposed that their function was literally to screen the individual against some earlier repressed memory to which the screen memory was linked in a meaningful way. One of the interesting pieces of evidence that Freud adduced in support of this proposal was the observation that many childhood memories occur as if one were observing oneself. My own personal earliest memory is of seeing myself being pushed in my pram and of my mother having problems with the handle (the memory presumably screens something of an "attachment" problem!). However, Freud's argument was that I could not have observed myself in the pram in the way that is encoded in the memory; such self-perception is impossible so therefore the memory must be false in at least some respects.

An even more dramatic example of a false memory comes from Jean Piaget (see Ross, 1991, for an interesting discussion of Piaget's account). Piaget reported an early visual memory again of being in his pram, but of his nanny fighting off an attacker in a would-be kidnap attempt. Many years later the nanny confessed that she had invented the whole story, so Piaget's vivid "memory" turned out to be false and presumably constructed on the basis of the nanny's account and his parents subsequent re-telling of the story.

In order to understand how false memories such as these can occur, we must again consider the evidence from both the clinic and the laboratory. The clinic gives access to those unfortunate experiments of nature, while the laboratory allows us to explore some of the proposed mechanisms in a small-scale fashion, akin to modelling the "Big Bang" theory of the Universe in a test-tube! The question, therefore, for this category of memory is: How can memories be constructed without there ever being any substantive period of forgetting? There are a number of phenomena that will be mentioned briefly, including work on eye-witness testimony, memory illusions, and reality monitoring failures.

A considerable body of work has stemmed from the work of Elizabeth Loftus (e.g. Loftus & Zanni, 1975) demonstrating that post-event questioning about incidents can lead the individual to incorporate information from the question into the memory for the incident. For example, a question such as "What colour was the car that was parked on the left?" presupposes that there was a car parked on the left; in a range of eyewitness testimony studies subjects have been found to be prone to the incorporation of such information into their memories for the events.

A second relevant area of laboratory research involves the study of "memory illusions". In a similar fashion to the demonstration of perceptual illusions, researchers such as Roediger and McDermott (1995) have found that with a word list containing associates of the word "sleep", subjects will report with considerable confidence that the word "sleep" appeared in the list even though it was never presented. Similar effects can be found with more complex prose. For example, Brewer (1974) found that for sentences such as "The angry rioter threw a rock at the window" subsequent recall often included the inference that the rock broke the window *more often* than the original sentence itself was recalled.

A third area of relevant research from the laboratory concerns the area of reality monitoring (e.g. Johnson & Raye, 1981; see Davies, Chapter 7 this volume). One of the crucial factors in deciding on the truth or accuracy of a memory is the decision about whether the experience was generated from an internal source (e.g. through imagination, dreams, etc.) or from an external source (e.g. the event actually happened). Johnson and her colleagues have shown that there are a number of influences on source monitoring including the fact that the more different types of cues that are recalled (e.g. smell, sound, visual characteristics), the more likely the memory is to be attributed to an external source. The implications for false memories (both of the "remembered" and the "recovered" varieties) are very clear; that is, there are circumstances in which individuals are likely to attribute imagined events to external reality.

Finally in this section, it might also be added that the increased number of hours that children and adults spend exposed to TV, film and video now provides a constant source of external imagined events that some individuals may be prone to recall as if they were personal memories. Given that there is evidence that imagined events can be subsequently recalled as if they had occurred (see Loftus, 1998, for a summary), there must also now be scope for exploring the impact of the increased use of these media on the occurrence of false memories. Interestingly, the work on imaginary memories suggests that individuals who score high on measures of dissociative experiences are more likely to remember previously imagined events as if they were real events (see Loftus, 1998).

4. False Recovered memories

The most controversial category of all in recent years has been that of False Recovered memories, that is, memories that are believed to be true by the individual and are recalled as having been actively inhibited over some period of time, but which are eventually shown to be false (see Gudjonsson, Chapter 2, and Andrews, Chapter 9). The recent controversy surrounding this category has been the claims and counter-claims surrounding the issues of child sexual abuse and the possibility that certain techniques, such as memory recovery techniques used in some types of therapies, may lead to "memory implantation". These controversies have focused around some of the high-profile legal cases, particularly in the USA, and the formation of False Memory Societies such as the British society that was surveyed by Gudjonsson (Chapter 2).

The results from Gudjonsson's survey of the British False Memory Society characterise some of the key issues. First, many of the recovered memories involve alleged sexual abuse that occurred before the age of 5 years and in some cases as young as in the first year of life. Second, the majority of these memories were claimed to have been forgotten and only later recovered. Third, the majority of the recovered memories were recovered during therapy. The question then becomes: Is it possible that a false memory can either be actively inhibited or experienced as if it had been actively inhibited, then subsequently "recovered" by the individual? There are a number of sources of evidence that have been flagged up already, together with one or two additional sources that will be summarised next.

Several of the areas of research already reviewed have implications for the possibility of recovery of false memories. These areas include the reality monitoring, eyewitness testimony, directed forgetting, and memory illusions literatures, all of which are relevant to the possibility of false memory production. The memory illusion, reality monitoring, and eyewitness testimony literatures now show some of the conditions under which partial or complete false memories can be produced, including recent demonstrations of the implantation of memories that subjects believe are recovered childhood memories. For example, Loftus and her colleagues (e.g. Loftus & Pickrell, 1995; Loftus, 1998) have shown how false memories can be implanted in some individuals for imagined childhood events such as being "lost in a shopping mall" or "getting a finger caught in a mousetrap". These studies show that even under laboratory conditions it is possible to create false memories and a belief that they have been recovered after a long period of time.

A further area that is worth mentioning is that of *déjà vu* and other related experiences (e.g. *déjà entendu, déjà raconté,* etc.), an area that was noted by Lindsay and Read (Chapter 5). These experiences provide interesting examples of what will be classified here as Recovered False memories. The reason for this classification is that the *déjà vu* experience, as Ross (1991) proposed "is not a valid memory at all but only a misplaced emotional experience posing as a memory" (p. 198). That is, the individual believes that there is a memory triggered by the current situation, a false memory that is accompanied by a feeling of strangeness similar to that of the re-experiencing of a recovered memory. Such experiences are rarely researched these days except as symptoms of organic pathology, but they also reveal aspects of the working of memory.

The final piece in the jigsaw of the current false memory controversy has to concern the role of a powerful and significant other, such as a therapist, in the production of "recovered" false memories. This effect, in parallel to the "Directed Forgetting" effect mentioned earlier, might appropriately be labelled "Directed Remembering". The work summarised in the chapters by Gudjonsson (Chapter 2), Shobe and Schooler (Chapter 6), and Magner and Parkinson (Chapter 4) provides a clear picture of many of the factors involved. For example, in their careful analyses of cases of recovered memories, Shobe and Schooler have shown that the false memories are typically "planted" at one or more early points in therapy and then subsequently "recovered" at later points. Although this typically occurs in individual therapy work with therapists using memory recovery procedures such as hypnosis, they have found that it can also occur with group therapy sessions, through reading material on Multiple Personality Disorder (Dissociative Identity Disorder in recent DSM-IV parlance), through the use of medication regimes, and so on. Shobe and Schooler suggest from their case analyses that a period of 2–12 months is needed from the initial suggestions to the eventual "recall" of the false memories in therapy. Such studies demonstrate dramatically the plasticity of memory and its reconstructive nature; they demonstrate too that it is often the most vulnerable individuals who are prone to the implantation of such false memories when in a dependent relationship.

Nevertheless, the laboratory studies show that there are conditions under which we can all believe in what are actually false memories.

FINAL COMMENTS AND CONCLUSIONS

The framework provided in this chapter has a number of implications for models of memory. There is insufficient space to explore these implications fully, but some brief comments are warranted. The traditional view of memory has been to consider *multi-store models* such as the classic Atkinson and Shiffrin (1968) model. Atkinson and Shiffrin proposed that there were three major types of memory store that consisted of sensory stores, the short-term store, and the long-term store. This model and related ones have proven of considerable value over the last 40 years in memory research, but the examples summarised in this chapter alone show, for example, that the proposal that there is a unitary long-term store is seriously inaccurate. The types of memory and other evidence considered earlier would seem to require in addition to *multi-store* models, the need for incorporation with the more recent *multi-level* models as well. For example, Johnson's (e.g. Johnson & Multhaup, 1992) Multiple Entry Modular Memory System (MEM) approach is one such model, which would provide a far more complex approach to the long-term store that might begin to account for some of the phenomena considered. Although not specifically designed to account for memory, our own Schematic Model, Propositional, Analogical, and Associative Representation Systems (SPAARS) approach provides additional explanatory power, in particular, in relation to the role of modular systems, the role of mood and emotion, and the role of inhibitory and facilitatory processes in these complex systems (Power & Dalgleish, 1997). Such multi-level models readily deal with issues such as conflicting information stored at different levels, the role of state dependent memories (especially in relation to strong emotions and dissociation), and the fact that traumatic events can lead to multiple unintegrated memories in different systems.

In summary, the combination of work from the clinic and from the laboratory has begun to provide a clearer picture of the complexity of memory. Memory is not simply the retrieval of facts from a permanent store, but, especially in the case of autobiographical memory, involves the reconstruction of information that includes current goals, mood-state and context. There is evidence that everybody is, in one way or another, right about the controversies that have surrounded memory in the last couple of decades. Memories can be forgotten and then recovered, but memories can also be false. Although further development of the discourse credibility analysis techniques highlighted by Davies (Chapter 7) may go some way to resolving whether or not a memory is likely to be true or false, there are many individual cases which will not be decidable one way or another "beyond a reasonable doubt". Perhaps we should leave the last word to Ambrose Bierce whose definition in *The Devil's Dictionary* astutely sums up the situation:

"*Recollect*, v. To recall with additions something not previously known."

REFERENCES

Anderson, M. C. & Spellman, B. A. (1995). On the status of inhibitory mechanisms in cognition — memory retrieval as a model case. *Psychological Review*, **102**, 68–100.

Atkinson, R. C. & Shiffrin, R. M. (1968). Human memory: A proposed system and its control processes. In K. W. Spence & J. T. Spence (Eds), *The Psychology of Learning and Motivation* (Vol. 2). New York: Academic Press.

Bartlett, F. C. (1932). *Remembering*. Cambridge: Cambridge University Press.

Bjork, R. A. (1989). Retrieval inhibition as an adaptive mechanism in human memory. In H. L. Roediger III & F. L. M. Craik (Eds), *Varieties of Memory and Consciousness: Essays in Memory of Endel Tulving*. Hillsdale, NJ: Lawrence Erlbaum Associates.

Bower, G. H. (1992). How might emotions affect learning? In S. A. Christianson (Ed.), *The Handbook of Emotion and Memory: Research and Theory*. Hillsdale, NJ: Lawrence Erlbaum Associates.

Brewer, W. F. (1974). There is no convincing evidence for operant or classical conditioning in adult humans. In W. B. Weimer & D. S. Palermo (Eds), *Cognition and the Symbolic Processes*. Hillsdale, NJ: Lawrence Erlbaum Associates.

Brown, R. & Kulik, J. (1977). Flashbulb memories. *Cognition*, **5**, 73–99.

Conway, M. A. & Pleydell-Pearce, C. W. (2000). The construction of autobiographical memories in the self-memory system. *Psychological Review*, **107**, 261-288.

Dalgleish, T. & Watts, F. N. (1990). Biases of attention and memory in disorders of anxiety and depression. *Clinical Psychology Review*, **10**, 589–604.

Freud, S. (1899). Screen memories. In J. Strachey (Ed.), *Standard Edition of the Complete Psychological Works of Sigmund Freud* (Vol. 3). London: Hogarth Press (pub. 1973).

Freud, S. (1900). *The Interpretation of Dreams* (Pelican Freud Library, Vol. 11). Harmondsworth, UK: Penguin (pub. 1976).

Freud, S. (1915). The unconscious. In J. Strachey (Ed.), *Standard Edition of the Complete Psychological Works of Sigmund Freud* (Vol. 14). London: Hogarth Press (pub. 1973).

Holmes, D. S. (1990). The evidence for repression: An examination of sixty years of research. In J. L. Singer (Ed.), *Repression and Dissociation*. Chicago: University of Chicago Press.

Janet, P. (1889). *L'Automatisme Psychologique: Essai de Psychologie Mentale sur les Formes Inferieures de l'Activite Mentale*. Paris: Alcan.

Johnson, M. K. & Multhaup, K. S. (1992). Emotion and MEM. In S. A. Christianson (Ed.), *The Handbook of Emotion and Memory: Research and Theory*. Hillsdale, NJ: Erlbaum.

Johnson, M. K. & Raye, C. L. (1981). Reality monitoring. *Psychological Review*, **88**, 67–85.

Loftus, E. F. (1998). Imaginary memories. In M. A. Conway, S. E. Gathercole & C. Cornoldi (Eds), *Theories of Memory* (Vol. II). Hove: Psychology Press.

Loftus, E. F. & Loftus, G. R. (1980). On the permanence of stored information in the brain. *American Psychologist*, **35**, 409–420.

Loftus, E. F. & Pickrell, J. L. (1995). The formation of false memories. *Psychiatric Annals*, **25**, 720–724.

Loftus, E. F. & Zanni, G. (1975). Eyewitness testimony: The influence of the wording of a question. *Bulletin of the Psychonomic Society*, **5**, 86–88.

Lynn, S. J. & Rhue, J. W. (Eds) (1994). *Dissociation: Clinical and Theoretical Perspectives*. New York: Guilford Press.

Macrae, C. N. & MacLeod, M. D. (1999). On recollections lost: When practice makes imperfect. *Journal of Personality and Social Psychology*, **77**, 463–473.

Myers, L. B. & Brewin, C. R. (1994). Recall of early experience and the repressive coping style. *Journal of Abnormal Psychology*, **103**, 288–292.

Myers, L. B., Brewin, C. R. & Power, M. J. (1998). Repressive coping and the directed forgetting of emotional material. *Journal of Abnormal Psychology*, **107**, 141–148.

Nash, M. R. (1998). Psychotherapy and reports of early sexual trauma: A conceptual framework for understanding memory errors. In S. J. Lynn & K. M. McConkey (Eds), *Truth in Memory*. New York: Guilford Press.

Neisser, U. & Harsch, N. (1992). Phantom flashbulbs: False recollections of hearing the news about Challenger. In E. Winograd & U. Neisser (Eds), *Affect and Accuracy in Recall: Studies of "Flashbulb Memories"*. Cambridge: Cambridge University Press.

Newman, L. S. & Baumeister, R. F. (1998). Abducted by aliens: Spurious memories of interplanetary masochism. In S. J. Lynn & K. M. McConkey (Eds), *Truth in Memory*. New York: Guilford Press.

Ohman, A. (1999). Distinguishing unconscious from conscious emotional processes: Methodological considerations and theoretical implications. In T. Dalgleish & M. J. Power (Eds), *Handbook of Cognition and Emotion*. Chichester: Wiley.

Power, M. J. (1991). Cognitive science and behavioural psychotherapy: Where behaviour was, there shall cognition be? *Behavioural Psychotherapy*, **19**, 20–41.

Power, M. J. & Dalgleish, T. (1997). *Cognition and Emotion: From Order to Disorder*. Hove: Psychology Press.

Power, M. J., Dalgleish, T., Claudio, V., Tata, P. & Kentish, J. (2000). The directed forgetting task: Application to emotionally valent material. *Journal of Affective Disorders*, **57**, 147–157.

Roediger, H. L. & McDermott, K. B. (1995). Creating false memories: Remembering words not presented in lists. *Journal of Experimental Psychology: Learning, Memory, and Cognition*, **21**, 803–814.

Ross, B. M. (1991). *Remembering the Personal Past: Descriptions of Autobiographical Memory*. New York: Oxford University Press.

Weinberger, D. A., Schwartz, G. E. & Davidson. R. J. (1979). Low-anxious, high anxious and repressive coping styles: Psychometric patterns and behavioural responses to stress. *Journal of Abnormal Psychology*, **88**, 369–380.

Widom, C. S. (1997). Accuracy of adult recollections of early childhood abuse. In J. D. Read & L. S. Lindsay (Eds), *Recollections of Trauma: Scientific Research and Clinical Practice*. New York: Plenum.

Williams, L. M. (1995). Recall of childhood trauma: A prospective study of women's memories of child sexual abuse. *Journal of Consulting and Clinical Psychology*, **62**, 1167–1176.

AUTHOR INDEX

SUBJECT INDEX